D1286276

Springer Series on
REHABILITATION

Editor: Thomas E. Backer, Ph.D.
Human Interaction Research Institute, Los Angeles

Advisory Board:

Carolyn L. Vash, Ph.D., Elizabeth L. Pan, Ph.D., Donald E. Galvin, Ph.D.,
Ray L. Jones, Ph.D., James F. Garrett, Ph.D., Patricia G. Forsythe,
and Henry Viscardi, Jr.

Myron G. Eisenberg, Ph.D. is the Coordinator of Psychosocial Rehabilitation on the Spinal Cord Injury Service, Veterans Administration Medical Center, Cleveland, Ohio, Clinical Assistant Professor of Psychology, Case Western Reserve University, and Adjunct Associate Professor of Psychology, Kent State University. He is a National Sex and Disability Task Force member and a U.S. Contact Person for the International Clearing House Concerning Social and Sexual Intercourse for Disabled Persons, an organization co-sponsored by The Rehabilitation International Social Commission and the Swedish Central Committee for Rehabilitation. Dr. Eisenberg has published widely in the area of rehabilitation and serves as Consulting Editor for the *Journal of Sex and Disability* (Human Sciences Press). He has received numerous awards in recognition of his work. Dr. Eisenberg currently serves as President to the American Psychological Association's Division of Rehabilitation Psychology.

Cynthia Griggins is a doctoral student in Clinical Psychology at Case Western Reserve University and a graduate of the Gestalt Institute, Cleveland, Ohio. She has had extensive work experience in the areas of medical psychology and rehabilitation, and is currently employed at the Free Medical Clinic of Greater Cleveland.

Richard J. Duval is a psychologist in private practice in Cleveland, Ohio. Previously, he worked on the Spinal Cord Injury Service at the Cleveland Veterans Administration Medical Center as well as on the Comprehensive Care Unit at Cleveland Metropolitan General Hospital. His present areas of interest include behavioral medicine, the psychophysiology of anxiety and depression, and the development of coping skills training procedures for the physically disabled.

Disabled People as Second-Class Citizens

Myron G. Eisenberg, Ph.D.
Cynthia Griggins
Richard J. Duval
Editors

HU
1553
.D55
1982

Foreword by Max Cleland
Former Administrator, Veterans Administration

Springer Publishing Company
New York

Rinteker Memorial Library
Concordia University Wisconsin
12800 N. Lake Shore Drive
Mequon, WI 53097

Copyright © 1982 by Springer Publishing Company, Inc.

All rights reserved

No part of this publication may be reproduced, stored in a
retrieval system, or transmitted in any form or by any means,
electronic, mechanical, photocopying, recording, or otherwise,
without the prior permission of Springer Publishing Company, Inc.

Springer Publishing Company, Inc.
200 Park Avenue South
New York, New York 10003

82 83 84 85 / 10 9 8 7 6 5 4 3 2 1

Library of Congress Cataloging in Publication Data

Main entry under title:

Disabled people as second-class citizens.

   (Springer series on rehabilitation; 2)
   Includes bibliographical references and indexes.
   1. Handicapped--United States--Addresses, essays,
lectures. 2. Discrimination--United States--Ad-
dresses, essays, lectures. I. Eisenberg, Myron G.
II. Griggins, Cynthia. III. Duval, Richard J.
IV. Series. [DNLM: 1. Rehabilitation--Psychology.
2. Handicapped--Psychology. 3. Prejudice. W1
SP685SF v. 2 / HD 7255 D611]
HV1553.D55   362.4'042'0973   81-13546
ISBN 0-8261-3220-0   AACR2
ISBN 0-8261-3221-9 (pbk.)

Printed in the United States of America

Contents

Foreword

A new minority group is making its presence felt in our society. Certainly not insignificant in numbers, its members represent one in every eleven Americans. They are the disabled who have been relegated to a second-class position. Until recently, they remained cloistered away from the able-bodied public, silently waiting to be liberated from lives of quiet desperation. This role was accepted by most as a proper and legitimate one for people whose battered bodies or minds serve as a vivid reminder of the fragility of the human state. In a society which demands uniformity and worships physical health and beauty, the physically disabled have often been viewed as outcasts from our social and work circles.

Now, partially motivated by other disadvantaged groups who have organized, fought for, and won new personal freedoms for themselves, the physically disabled are no longer satisfied with their second-class status. They are no longer content to accept a social structure which has, by omission or commission, kept them out of the employment market; a society whose buildings and public transportation systems are not accessible, and whose educational systems are not designed to accommodate them.

From this new perspective, successful coping with physical disability necessitates more than merely learning to live with recurring pain and frustration. It means acquiring a whole new life-style in which the disabled actively work to confront and change dominant societal attitudes. *Disabled People as Second-Class Citizens* focuses on these various forms of discrimination experienced by the physically disabled as they attempt to reintegrate themselves into society. The text attempts not only to sensitize the reader to these issues but also to suggest new and creative solutions for remediating them. It does not attempt to produce compromises from divergent viewpoints or conflicting data. Its purpose is to raise major issues that the investigators see emerging in the field of physical disability and rehabilitation. Useful as a resource to practitioners in rehabilitation settings, the text is also of value to disabled individuals who themselves are demanding information from which they can develop creative and effective strategies to deal with discriminatory practices. This book is designed to assist the disabled to overcome widespread discrimination, enabling them to develop more rewarding and satisfying life-styles.

A new social revolution is at hand, one in which another minority group, the disabled, is seeking its full rights as citizens. The public is becoming increasingly aware of their needs as reflected through the passage of the Rehabilitation Act. In the American tradition of accommodating such groups, I am confident their struggle will be won. It is hoped *Disabled People as Second-Class Citizens* will also aid them in their quest.

Max Cleland
Former Administrator
Veterans Administration

Acknowledgments

Sincere appreciation is extended to Elaine White for the care shown in typing the many revisions of this manuscript. The editors also wish to acknowledge the assistance provided by Barbara Hampton, who prepared the final typed version of this work.

Contributors

RUSSELL BRUCH, M.A. is the Director of Life/Career Development, Davis, California. He is the former Director of the Placement Center at the University of California at Davis. Mr. Bruch is a colleague of Richard Bolles, the author of *What Color Is Your Parachute?* (Ten Speed Press, 1981), a manual for life and career planning which has been on the best seller list for approximately six years. Although Mr. Bruch has not worked specifically with the disabled, he is an authority on vocational counseling, and salient issues in this area are similar for both the disabled and able-bodied.

LILLY BRUCK, Ph.D. is the former Director of Consumer Education of New York City's Department of Consumer Affairs. Her book, *Access: The Guide to a Better Life for Disabled Americans* (Random House, 1978), has been nationally acclaimed as a primer in its field. Currently Dr. Bruck is a consumer advocate and broadcaster on "In Touch," New York's Radio Information Service for the Visually and Physically Handicapped. She contributes a weekly commentary on consumer affairs for disabled consumers to "Let's Hear It," a program for print-handicapped listeners on National Public Radio, beamed via satellite to radio stations and radio reading services around the USA.

CENTER FOR INDEPENDENT LIVING (CIL) is a nonprofit organization devoted to helping people with disabilities make a successful transition from nursing homes to independent living. CIL has accepted as its primary task changing the environment, removing architectural, communicational, and attitudinal barriers confronting the disabled. To meet this goal, a variety of services have been made available to its clients including attendant referral services, deaf services, a housing department, an independent living skills program, a transportation service, services for the visually impaired, and a job development, training, and education program. A Disability Law Resource Center to deal with the disability rights movement has also been established at the Center.

CAROL CUMMINGS, Ph.D. is Director of Psychological Services at the Centinela Hospital Pain Management Center, Inglewood, California. She has lectured widely on the psychological aspects of chronic pain and is the author of numerous articles on the psychological assessment and treatment of chronic pain.

CHERYL DAVIS is a teacher (University of California, Berkeley, and Harvard), writer, and environmental consultant to architects, planners, and gov-

ernment agencies. Ms. Davis has spina bifida and thus has personal experience of the architectural barriers facing the physically disabled. She has col-
laborated on an Exxon Education Foundation funded project investigating the
use of the handicapped as consultants in architectural design education.

JEROME R. DUNHAM, Ph.D. is an Assistant Professor in the Rehabilitation Department of Seattle University, Seattle, Washington. Except for periods of counseling able-bodied persons, most of his professional career has
been working with the visually impaired. Dr. Dunham has himself been
blind since the age of sixteen. He has served on many rehabilitation-
oriented committees and boards in Washington State, including the Governor's Committee on Employment of the Handicapped, the Washington Coalition of Citizens with Disabilities, the Washington Council of the Blind,
and city, county, and Seattle University Section 504 committees.

JUDITH FALCONER, Ph.D. is a Staff Psychologist at the Veterans Administration Medical Center in Cleveland, Ohio, where she works with hemodialysis and kidney transplant patients and with patients undergoing total lar-
yngectomies. Her interests include the use of hypnosis and auto-hypnosis
with the chronically disabled, psychosocial development in the congenitally
deaf, and compliance with medical regimens.

BETTY GOLDIAMOND, Ph.D. has expertise in a variety of areas, including
sociology, labor relations, psychology, and gerontology. She has taught at
Southern Illinois University and at Roosevelt University and has also been
employed as a Research Associate at the University of Chicago. In addition,
she has worked as a labor organizer. Dr. Goldiamond's familiarity with problems and discrimination which family members face when disability strikes
are well known to her from both personal experience and as a volunteer at
the Rehabilitation Institute of Chicago.

JOHN S. HICKS, Ed.D. is the Coordinator of the Graduate Programs in
Special Education and an Associate Professor in the Division of Psychology
and Educational Services at Fordham University, New York City. Prior to
assuming a position at Fordham, Dr. Hicks was associated with the school
and rehabilitation center of United Cerebral Palsy of Queens as a part-time
research coordinator. He has published in the area of language disorders in
emotionally handicapped children and programs for main-streaming the handicapped. In addition, he directed a series of research projects examining
the adjustment of parents of preschool handicapped children and the effects
of the disabling condition on the family unit.

ELLIOTT A. KRAUSE, Ph.D. is Professor of Sociology at Northeastern University, Boston, Massachusetts. He is the author of *The Sociology of Occupations* (Little, Brown, 1971), and *Power and Illness* (Elsevier, 1977), a book
which investigates the political sociology of health and medical care sys-

tems. He has served as a consultant to local, state, and federal agencies, including the Office of Economic Opportunity and the Office of the Secretary of Health, Education and Welfare.

LEONARD KRIEGEL, Ph.D. is a Professor of English at the City College of New York. He has been both a Guggenheim and Rockefeller Fellow, has lectured throughout the United States and Europe, and has authored five books, the most recent of which is titled *On Men and Manhood* (Hawthorn, 1979). The theme of many of his texts reflect his personal experience with and societal reactions to disability.

RAYMOND LIFCHEZ, M.A. is a practicing architect and an Associate Professor at the University of California at Berkeley. Since 1974, in practice, teaching, and research, he has focused on psychosocial issues of environmental access for vulnerable populations, including children, the physically disabled, the frail elderly, and the socially and economically disadvantaged. Mr. Lifchez has served as an architect and consultant on barrier-free design in private industry, technical consultant to the California Department of Vocational Rehabilitation, member of the University of California Chancellor's Committee on Environmental Access for the Handicapped, and consultant to the American Association for the Advancement of Science's Project on the Handicapped.

SCOTT MANLEY, Ed.D. is the Assistant Hospital Director at the Craig Hospital, Rocky Mountain Regional Spinal Cord Injury Center, Englewood, Colorado. Dr. Manley has published in the area of rehabilitation and is actively involved in acquainting the professional community with the vocational needs and potential of the spinal cord injured.

ALEXIS M. NEHEMKIS, Ph.D. is currently a member of the psychology staff of the Veterans Administration Medical Center, Long Beach, California, where she serves as a consultant to the Medical Service. She is also a member of the clinical faculty of the Department of Psychology at the University of Southern California. Dr. Nehemkis was formerly affiliated with the Los Angeles Suicide Prevention Center and has served as a behavioral consultant to the Los Angeles County Medical Examiner-Coroner's office. She has published in the areas of suicide, indirect self-destructive behavior, drugs, chronic pain, and consultation-liaison psychology.

MARY D. ROMANO, M.S.W., A.C.S.W. is a Supervisor in the Social Service Department, Presbyterian Hospital, New York City. Mrs. Romano has practiced in acute and rehabilitation hospitals and served as a consultant to consumer and professional organizations concerned with the problems of the ill and physically disabled. She has published numerous articles related to health care service delivery, psychosocial aspects of illness, the management of staff problems, and sexuality and disability.

CONSTANTINA SAFILIOS-ROTHSCHILD, Ph.D. is a Professor of Human Development at The Pennsylvania State University. She has written a text, *The Sociology and Social Psychology of Disability and Rehabilitation* (Random House, 1970), published a number of articles on disabled peoples' social movements and self-definition, and authored articles on the international dimensions of rehabilitation research and policy especially in developing nations. In 1977–78, Dr. Safilios-Rothschild served as a consultant to the World Health Organization in epidemiological research on the disabled in India.

OLIVER C. SCHROEDER, Jr., J.D. is the Albert and Richard Weatherhead Professor of Law and Criminal Justice at the Case Western Reserve University (CWRU) Law School, and Director of the Law and Medicine Center at CWRU. Mr. Schroeder's professional activities include service as a Fellow in the American Bar Foundation and membership on the Committee on Procedures on the Hospitalization and Discharge of the Mentally Disabled. Mr. Schroeder's expertise and interest in the area of forensic medicine and informed consent have resulted in numerous publications and lectures on these topics.

BONNIE SIMS, M.A., is the Home Coordinator at the Craig Hospital, Englewood, Colorado. As a certified rehabilitation counselor, she has also worked for the General Reinsurance Corporation as a Rehabilitation Coordinator, responsible for expediting cases involving catastrophic injuries. A primary goal Ms. Sims established for herself while in this position was to educate primary insurers in the philosophy that early involvement ultimately results in the prudent use of primary funds and savings to the insurance industry.

HENRY SLUCKI, Ph.D., has been a Senior Research Associate in the Medical School at the University of Southern California since 1969. His teaching responsibilities include medical students, interns and residents, members of the hospital staff, and allied health professionals, as well as advanced students in psychology, education, rehabilitation, and social work. Dr. Slucki's focus of research and training is in the experimental analysis of behavior with a special emphasis in its application to rehabilitation and medicine. In addition, he continues to work in the area of behavior modification as it pertains to education and self-management.

Introduction

"Imagine confusing gynecology with the study of women in society, or dermatology with the study of racism."

Absurd, right? However, these words, written by one of the disabled contributors to this text, describe fairly accurately the constricted and myopic thinking that has long characterized not the study of feminism or racism in our society, but the study of disability. As ludicrous as the idea may sound, it nevertheless reflects the perspective that has guided our treatment of disability and the disabled. The study of the blind has been the study of failures in the visual system, or the rehabilitation of the blind via aids such as braille, canes, and dogs. The study of paraplegia has been the study of spinal cord injuries and the use of complex technological gadgetry to compensate for paralyzed limbs. The study of chronic renal failure has been the study of kidneys—real and artificial. And so on. In each case, regardless of the nature of the disability, the study of the disabled has amounted to nothing more than the study of physical malfunctioning—and compensating for it.

Until very recently this paradigm has dominated medical and rehabilitation practice. As with all paradigms, those with power and control promulgated it and in effect set the limits of those fields. With their paradigm they defined what could and could not be studied, which questions could be asked and which could not, what techniques could be used and which could not. The paradigm suggests that that is all there is to disability—physical malfunctioning and compensating for it—and so for many years that is all that was seen in journals, taught in schools, heard in conferences and, worst of all, recognized in treatment centers.

But all along the disabled themselves have known that there was more to disability than a malfunctioning bodily system. They have known that this was not the only, or even the most important, of their problems. They have known that their troubles did not end when they were discharged from the hospital or rehabilitation center, complete with wheelchair and adapted van. Their troubles were, in fact, just beginning, for being disabled, they know, means living in the world as someone "different," "abnormal," "inferior." It means dealing with far-reaching and mind-boggling problems. It means people shying away from you, pitying you, or rejecting you completely. It means trouble finding a job or a decent place to live. It often means living at the poverty level and going on welfare. It means *discrimination*. Being disabled is not just having a bodily defect—it is a complex social-political reality that one lives with day by day, year by year.

The disabled themselves have known this, but they have long tolerated the limited vision of the professionals who ruled the disability field. They bought into the treatment/rehabilitation/sympathy model, apparently believing they had no right to another life-style or that there simply was no way to question it. They accepted the paradigm and the role it prescribed for them—patients, whether in or out of the hospital, and second-class citizens. That is, until recently.

As this book is being written in late 1980, one can see signs everywhere that the disabled are no longer keeping their ideas, their experiences, or their needs as disabled people to themselves. A march on Washington by disabled people. A recent Supreme Court case involving a hearing-impaired woman who sued the college that denied her entrance into a nurses' training program. Lawsuits being brought against public transit systems for being nonaccessible. Books being published about disability and disabled persons. Films being produced such as *Coming Home, The Other Side of the Mountain, The Deerhunter,* and *The Elephant Man,* which feature seriously disabled characters. Two hit Broadway plays about disabled people. And recently, in a small town, mannequins on crutches and in wheelchairs sporting the latest fashions during a disability awareness week. The disabled are emerging as a group, saying, "we are more than 'defectives' to be fixed up and sent home to hide away. This is our reality. Look at it . . . look at us."

One might well ask: why? Why now are the disabled becoming so visible, so vocal, and so discontent? Why are we being called upon as a society to become more "aware"? It is not difficult to understand if one considers a number of social, political, and medical developments that have changed our society over the past 20 years.

First and most basic is the fact that there are simply more disabled people in our society than ever before. If the average person has not become aware of this increase simply by seeing, hearing about, or knowing more disabled individuals among his friends, family, and aquaintances, then he or she has read the statistics available for the first time with the 1970 Census. (Prior to that census, no realistic estimates were available as to the number of disabled persons living in this country.) The statistics indeed were startling to many. One out of every eleven Americans—over 9%—were identified as being disabled. This means that the disabled are no longer isolated, rare cases here and there. They are indeed a minority of considerable size! And with the 1980 census, this minority is expected to be even larger.

Why the huge numbers? And why are the numbers growing? Though the reasons are complex, put simply, we have our advanced technological society to thank for this. As advanced medical procedures continue to save more lives from disease and trauma and enable Americans to live longer, there are simply more scarred and less-than-perfect bodies around. This is the irony with which we must live: As our highly polluted and dangerous environment stresses and batters bodies, we are able to save them—often not able to restore them to their original state of health—but preserve them in some less-than-optimal condition, thereby adding to the ever-growing minority—the disabled. And now, no longer isolated cases, but indeed a minority group, the disabled find each other, especially in large urban centers. They are meeting and beginning to see themselves as a *group*.

The sheer number of disabled is not the only reason for their increased visibility. The type of person who now finds himself or herself disabled is changing the character of this group drastically. Consider the old stereotype of the disabled person: a sickly, perhaps elderly individual, unable to be very active, slowly deteriorating as he or she moves toward death. While never true of all disabled people, this stereotype is becoming increasingly inaccurate as disability strikes younger people who are then treated and given near-average life expectancies—*lifetimes* in wheelchairs or without limbs. Consider for example, a totally new creature—the surviving paraplegic or quadriplegic. Virtually unknown prior to World War II and the discovery of antibiotics, these victims of auto accidents, poliomyelitis, and war injuries have been saved to lead lives in wheelchairs, iron lungs, or beds, sometimes for 50 to 60 years! Who ever before heard of a young, mentally alert and active person, in relatively good health (except for his or her paralysis) confined for life to a wheelchair? Historically, this is a totally new phenomenon. And it is obvious that the kind of lives these individuals will lead, the opportunities they will seek or demand, will not be comparable to those of the weak, elderly, or sickly disabled person, more numerous in the past.

As mentioned above, these more numerous, younger, and more active disabled individuals started finding each other—in hospitals, in institutions, in schools, and in large cities. They talked and shared their experiences and the reality *they* knew—that disability was more than physical. During the 1960s, the era of the free speech movement, civil rights activism, anti-Vietnam war demonstrations, and the beginning of the women's movement, it was becoming more and more common for the dissatisfied and discontented to organize and speak out. It was inevitable that the disabled, too, would emerge from their silence and passivity. Like other minorities they, too, would start to question their role as children, the authority of the establishment, and their second-class status. They were bound to see, as other minorities, that they themselves had skills, that they could take charge of their own lives, and that their oppression was unnecessary, but that organization and activism would be necessary in order to change it. And so they have.

Being the only minority (other than children) who clearly must rely on another group in society (medical/rehabilitation professionals who treat them), the disabled face a special problem. They not only must fact the judgments, stereotypes, and discrimination they encounter within society in general, but they must deal with the "keepers of the paradigm"—the professionals who study them, treat them, write about them, and in many ways, mediate and facilitate their contact with the world. These are the people who often hold the keys, who, at the earliest moments, can help or hinder the disabled individual's struggle with his or her reality. They hold a great deal of power over the disabled individual, and the struggle against old attitudes and roles must begin here.

The purpose of the book is to do just that: begin reaching out to the professional community with the disabled person's message—that being disabled in this society is a complex social/psychological/political reality that breeds extensive and serious problems for the disabled person, far beyond those resulting from the physical impairment itself. Through this text we are trying to establish a new paradigm, a paradigm that says that disability is much more than a physical malfunctioning. This paradigm would imply that we as professionals can no longer naïvely perform operations and fit individuals with prostheses and expect all to be well. We must, if we are truly to understand and deliver proper service to the disabled, recognize the problems they face as a minority, how they fit (or do not fit) into society, *and how they are affected by this.* By way of illustration, need for a new paradigm is implicit in the recent finding that the incidence of decubiti (pressure sores) among discharged para- and quadriplegics is related less to medical factors than to psychological ones. This means that paraplegics develop decubiti perhaps because they have no friends, or cannot get a job, or have poor self-esteem, not because of medical factors.

This text, then, is first for professionals. It is for doctors, nurses, physical and occupational therapists, social workers, psychologists, and all who are involved with the care and treatment of the disabled. It is also for students and teachers in the field of disability and rehabilitation, for those who do research and administer programs— all who define and in turn are defined by the paradigm, those who help shape the lives of the disabled and determine whether they will be first- or second-class citizens.

But this book is not for professionals and students of disability alone, because obviously they are not the only ones who affect the lives of the disabled. It is for those who provide substance to the lives of the disabled after they leave the hospital or rehabilitation center. It is for the mothers and fathers, spouses, lovers, and friends among whom the disabled person lives and seeks intimacy, for they must learn who it is that they are relating to and what internal struggles are being waged in this person who does not hear, cannot walk, or who cannot see. It is for their employers, landlords, attorneys, and legislators. It is for their advocates, teachers, and for all who seek to understand a phenomenon, a movement that is becoming visible and a reality, such as women's groups, the changing structure of the family, and the energy crunch.

And of course, this book is for the disabled themselves. We seek to provide a text in which the disabled can find their own experience validated, articulated, and perhaps analyzed in a way the single individual cannot do in isolation. It is an affirmation that "yes, *this is going on.* Disabled individuals *are* discriminated against in this society and these are the ways!" It also is an attempt to begin to build a literature, which seems vitally necessary to the growth and integrity of any group. The struggle for identity is aided by the expression in words of common experiences, problems, and concerns. The literature of a minority says to the members themselves and to others, "This is who we are. This is what it is like being a member of our group. These are our feelings and our needs." The literature of the disabled as a group is just being born. Of course, biographies, as well as the occasional autobiography, of famous disabled people have been around for some time. But the experience of the average disabled person has not been documented, nor has their common struggle in the midst of a nondisabled society. It is the hope of the editors that the chapters contributed by the able-bodied authors, as well as those by the disabled, will be an accurate reflection of the issues, concerns, and problems facing this minority at this time.

In *Disabled People as Second-Class Citizens* the editors have called upon a number of disabled persons, professionals working with the disabled, and even some specialists outside the field to share their experience and ideas regarding discrimination against

America's newest minority. The result is a collage of sorts—a collection of thoughts, vignettes, facts, opinions—that will expand the reader's view of the disabled, changing it from a one-dimensional, stereotypic vision of the "cripple" to a multi-dimensional and enriched understanding of what it means to be a disabled person in this society.

Because the text is aimed at a wide and varied audience, and because the issues that it seeks to explore also span a wide range, the reader will find that the style of writing and level of complexity of the chapters varies greatly. Some of the chapters, written by professionals and dealing with somewhat technical issues, are written in an objective, sometimes scholarly manner. Other chapters, often those written by disabled individuals about their own experience, are personal statements, highly charged with emotion and written in a subjective and less formal style. The editors have tried as much as possible to preserve the authors' individual styles and allow for the variety of expression necessary to a venture of such breadth as this text.

The text is divided into four parts. The first two parts concentrate on describing the situation facing the disabled person and exploring reasons for the discrimination that is met. The last two parts offer ideas on how such discrimination might best be met and dealt with by individuals and by organized groups. The authors of the six chapters in Part I, "Societal Contributions to Discrimination," identify general attitudes, values, and prejudices present in society that breed discrimination against the disabled. These authors take for granted that such discrimination is no accident but instead grows naturally from certain attitudes and beliefs that are a part of Western industrial society. Our attitudes about sexuality, productivity, conformity, and authority, to mention just a few, all contribute to stereotyping and prejudice. The stigmatization process, first described by Goffman (1963), and even our economic credo, capitalism, help transform these prejudicial attitudes into action. Each of the authors describes a different aspect of these attitudes and their effects upon the disabled as a group, and together they give the reader a perspective and a framework for understanding Part II more fully.

In the second part, the authors focus on the mechanics of discrimination. They analyze the individual institutions of our society—the courts, architecture, transportation systems, employment, the medical system, and the family—and illustrate how discriminatory attitudes are actually put into practice. They show how discrimination has been built into the system, meaning that even if individuals' attitudes toward the disabled become more accepting, we will still have to contend with institutions that practice discrimination daily—

seemingly beyond our control. Even systems that were originally constructed with the intention of *helping* the disabled (e.g., the Social Security system) can in effect harm them, keeping them from gaining employment and utilizing their talents to the fullest, thereby retaining their pride and self-esteem.

In the third and fourth parts of the text the reader's attention is turned to the issue of coping with social, political, and psychological realities described in Parts I and II. In Part III, "Coping with Physical Disability," methods of helping the individual cope with disability and the effects of discrimination are discussed. Psychological treatment, when it takes into account the total picture—social, political and economic—and does not assume that the disabled individual's problems are entirely of his or her own making, can be most helpful. Specifically, the methods being developed by the behavioral therapists seem to hold the greatest promise for treating the psychological problems of disabled people without further adding to the discrimination they already encounter.

In Part IV, "A Call to Action," the authors describe ways in which disabled individuals can combat discrimination by organizing and utilizing their own talents. In securing jobs, housing, and their rights as consumers, the disabled must step out of their old roles as passive and dependent "patients," and become activists for their own cause.

If the change in paradigm that the disabled (and the authors and editors of this text) seek is to come about, it will only be through active and vocal protest by the disabled themselves, and their insistence that there is more to disability than malfunctioning body parts, and more to being disabled than meets the eye.

References

Goffman, E. *Stigma: Notes on the management of spoiled identity.* Englewood Cliffs, N.J.: Prentice-Hall, 1963.

I
Societal Contributions to Discrimination

As the disabled have grown in numbers and surfaced as a new minority group, what has also emerged is the awareness that they are not afforded their full rights as citizens, a situation which has unfortunately been the case with other minorities. Truly, when one realizes that a disabled person cannot live anywhere he wants, that he cannot use most public transportation, that he cannot participate in many public education programs, and that he can expect to encounter difficulty in securing jobs for the sole reason of his disability, one realizes that the disabled are indeed second-class citizens.

Disability brings with it many limitations—physical limitations which can be worked with and worked around, but which limit nonetheless. Over and above these immutable restrictions on mobility, choices, and opportunities, there are other limitations which stem from political, economic, and attitudinal sources that are avoidable and which greatly compound the original problems caused by physical disability. This part is about the realm of societal attitudes, policies, and resistance which turn disabilities into handicaps.

The roots of prejudice have been widely discussed in many texts over the last 40 years. The purpose of this first section is not to discuss prejudice as a phenomenon, but to explore the origins of discriminatory attitudes directed toward the disabled. As an emerging minority, the disabled find they are not being met with open arms by society and its institutions. Although one could blame bureaucratic policies and society's tendency to preserve the status quo (i.e., that society and its benefits have been created for the able-bodied), there are deeply felt personal attitudes which serve to maintain these institutions and keep the disabled isolated and segregated. Eisenberg (Chapter 1) reviews the basic mechanism of prejudice, the stigmatization of the different or deviant group. He discusses how and why the disabled are stigmatized and the moral bases for this process. Hicks (Chapter 2) describes where we stand at this point in time.

*Competence is not the issue nor is ability when we consider accom-
modating the disabled; society has both the competence and the
ability. The questions now are philosophical, and in exploring them
he examines basic American values of the late twentieth century,
from Social Darwinism to the myth of the melting pot. Griggins
(Chapter 3) focuses on what she describes as contradictory or ambivalent feelings that the able-bodied experience toward the disabled
and how these are manifested, especially in the medical community.
Safilios-Rothschild (Chapter 4) discusses the tendency to give second-class citizens of any type only one right—the right to work.
Everything else, the right to live, to have friends, to be entertained
and to have fun, the "nonfunctional" activities, are denied or ignored.
Kriegel (Chapter 5) writes from a personal perspective about the disabled experience and the difficulty encountered while establishing a
unique identity in the eyes of others. He offers this as a metaphor for
the modern American male. Finally, Romano (Chapter 6) discusses
another source of prejudice against the disabled: the tendency to see
them as childlike or neuter—not sexual beings.*

*Although many of the authors make suggestions on ways to
combat these broad prejudicial attitudes, responses to discriminatory attitudes and practices are the subject of Parts III and IV of this
volume.*

1 Disability as Stigma

Myron G. Eisenberg

In his book *The Painted Bird* (1965), Jerzy Kosinski writes of man's fear of those different from himself, "The Other," in his midst. If "The Other" is unlike members of society, he is cast out of the group and destroyed; if he is like them, man intervenes and makes him appear different so that he can then be alienated from the group and destroyed. To man, safety lies in similarity; conformity is good and deviance is evil.

Kosinski's "Other" can easily be extended to include the disabled. In this case, however, one does not have to create a difference to separate them from the group, for their taint is all too obvious. Whether the disability is highly visible or invisible, the disabled is separated from the group by virtue of the nature of his physical needs. If the disability can be readily observed, such as in blindness, deafness, stroke, paraplegia, or amputation, it cannot be hidden; if the disabling condition is invisible, as in the case of diabetes (requiring special diets), cardiac disorders (often necessitating restricted activity), or disabilities requiring the use of special prostheses such as colostomy or urostomy bags, it can be covered up only temporarily and at the cost of much personal anguish and effort.

Many of the handicapped do not realize for some time that they are the objects of ostracism and stigmatization. Disabled children reared in an accepting environment may know intrinsically that they are different but often do not come to an understanding of the significance society places on their "differentness" until they begin school; they must then learn to deal with the ramifications of being visibly different from others. An adult who acquires a disability later in life may continue to feel like the same person he was prior to onset of the disabling condition, but then he comes to learn he is not viewed as such by society, which now greets him with avoidance, derision, guilt, or oversolicitousness.

Goffman (1963) suggests there are three different types of stigma. First, there are bodily stigma—the various physical deformities. Second, there are blemishes of individual character perceived as weak will, domineering or unnatural passions, rigid beliefs, or dishonesty. Finally, there are tribal stigma of race, nationality, or religion which are transmitted through lineage and equally contaminate all members of a family. He continues by stating that "All of these forms of stigma have the same sociological features: an individual possesses a trait which makes him different from normals. He possesses a stigma, an undesired differentness which separates him from the rest of society." A stigma, though, in and of itself, is neither a creditable nor discreditable thing. An attribute that stigmatizes one person can confirm the usualness of another. For example, application for some blue-collar positions may lead the college graduate to withhold or conceal his educational background from the interviewer out of fear that he might be thought of as being overqualified for the job being sought. Other positions, however, may require that candidates have a higher education without which they would be withdrawn from further consideration.

Once the disabled person becomes aware of his stigmatized label, his self-perceptions are affected. Even if he rejects the label, his awareness of the reactions of others will contribute to changing the social interactions of which he is a part. A fundamental question, then, which requires our attention is why able-bodied people stigmatize the physically disabled instead of accepting them as good, if unfortunate, members of the same group?

The Origins, Role, and Importance of the Labeling Process

To assure his survival in a hostile environment, man came to recognize patterns in events around him and to identify which reactions to these events were most useful to him. As man became more adept at controlling his environment through his abstracting abilities, he was able to develop a more complex civilization. At the same time, as threats to his existence continued, he experienced anxiety over them. One means of reducing this anxiety was to classify circumstances, including people, and assign them labels. The process served a variety of purposes for reducing tension: it simplified the environment, helped identify the problem, and eliminated the need to continually examine the reality of the situation or explore it in more depth, making it seem more familiar (Brunner, Goodnow, & Austin, 1967).

Stigmatizing arises as a defense against the anxiety about whether one is responding "correctly" to an unfamiliar situation. It is easy to stigmatize—to assign a label denoting any variance from the group norms, thereby artificially assigning it to a category that does have a recognizable behavioral/emotional response. To accomplish this, an uncommon characteristic is chosen as the most significant feature. This deviant characteristic becomes the focus of attention, and most reactions can then be phrased in terms of that single feature. In structural/functional terms, this allows the clearer identification of those who do not possess this characteristic and those who do, making those who do not feel safer and reinforcing their sense of group identity (Erikson, 1962).

The disabled, then, serve a useful function in society, making "normal" persons feel healthier, brighter, more competent, and secure. Because some disabled persons exact a cost from society, either because of their inability to be self-sufficient or because they are prevented from becoming so as the result of compensation legislation, they are viewed as bad or inferior in some way and hence, deserving of their fate—either directly or as a punishment exacted on someone close to them.

Biblical Contributions to the Stigmatization Process

Just as the Inquisition supplied the stigma theory of witchcraft and psychiatry provided the stigma theory of mental illness, the Bible has in part contributed the moral foundation on which various discriminatory practices have been exercised against those with physical disability and illness. By associating sin and moral transgression with the resultant "just retribution" of disability and illness, our society has found an apparent justification for stigmatizing the disabled.

There are numerous biblical references associating sin with disability. In the Old Testament, for instance, one reads that if God's commandments are transgressed, he will inflict upon them "blindness, the boils of Egypt with ulcers and scurvy, and the itch from which they cannot be healed" (Deuteronomy, 28:20). In the New Testament similar sentiments are expressed. Consider, for example, the statment attributed to Jesus who, upon healing a man, said, "Behold, thou are made whole. *Sin no more* lest a worse thing come unto thee" (John, 5:13). Not only is the concept of individual punishment for sins and immoral behavior found in the Bible, but the concept of the sins of the father being visited upon his children is also firmly rooted in biblical literature.

The concept that disability and illness are divine retribution for sins or transgression against God's laws is embraced by many in our society. Consider, for example, the experience of Marie Killilea (1952), the mother of a cerebral palsied child, who recounts her experience of seeking lodging at a woman's home. When told that the child had cerebral palsy, "the woman's face grew livid and she jumped to her feet. 'Get out of my house' she shouted. 'Only bad, dirty people would have a child like that.' " Further, Kramm (1963), investigating the extent to which this philosophy was held by parents of handicapped children, found that 12 percent of parents of mongoloid children studied saw retardation as resulting from an act of God. Consider this in light of a Gallup poll (1978) which indicates 38 percent of the American people reported that they believed the Bible is the actual word of God and is to be taken literally, 45 percent believed that the Bible is the inspired word of God, and only 13 percent believed that the Bible is a book of fables and legends.

A study conducted by Weinberg and Sebian (1980) shows that the able-bodied feel a moral obligation to help the disabled. The authors conclude that this finding tends to lend support to the conception that the tradition of giving alms to the disabled advocated in biblical literature has led to a patronizing rather than an accepting attitude toward the disabled. Since religion as a force in American life is currently undergoing a period of growth, these findings are particularly meaningful in understanding the extent to which biblical beliefs have influenced our society's moral and philosophical explanations of and justification for disability.

Societal Reactions to the Disabled

The attitudes "normals" have toward a person with a stigma are well documented (e.g., Safilios-Rothschild, 1977). In his definitive work on this subject, Goffman (1963) describes the person with a stigma as someone thought of as being not quite human. On this assumption we practice a variety of discriminations. We construct an ideology to explain the disabled's inferiority; we use stigmatic terms such as "cripple," "moron," and "gimp" in our daily language. We assign a wide range of imperfections to them based on the original one and view them through the lens of the deviant characteristic rather than as a holistic collection of numerous attributes with various degrees of importance at various times and under various conditions (Becker, 1963). At the same time, we often see them as possessing attributes, often of a supernatural nature, such as a "sixth sense" (Goffman, 1963).

For some, there may be a hesitancy about touching or steering the blind, while for others, the perceived failure to see may be generalized into a gestalt of disability so that the individual shouts at the blind as if they were deaf or attempts to lift them as if they were crippled. Those confronting the blind may have a whole range of belief that is anchored in the stereotype. For instance, they may think they are subject to unique judgment, assuming the blinded individual draws on special channels of information unavailable to others. (Gowan, 1957, p. 198)

When the disabled person responds defensively to his situation, we tend to perceive this response as a direct expression of his defect. We can then justify the manner in which we treat him as retribution for something he, his parents, or his tribe has done.

Buying into the Stigmatization Process

What is central in our understanding of the process of stigmatization is that the stigmatized individual tends to hold the same beliefs about self-identity as does the rest of society. The disabled person perceives that although others may claim every human being should be considered worthwhile and equal, in fact they neither accept him, nor are they ready to make contact with him on "equal grounds." At the same time, the disabled individual incorporates society's standards of what "normal" is and, if only for a moment, agrees that he does, indeed, fall short of what he really ought to be. Shame is often experienced as the individual comes to perceive one of his own attributes as being a defiling thing, one he cannot accept as a part of himself and from which he cannot escape. Consider, for example, the confusion and panic experienced by the disabled person upon first examination of his mirrored image following disability.

I didn't want anyone . . . to know how I felt when I saw myself for the first time. But there was no noise, no outcry; I didn't scream with rage when I saw myself. I just felt numb. That person in the mirror couldn't be me. I felt inside like a healthy, ordinary, lucky person—oh, not like the one in the mirror! Yet when I turned my face to the mirror there were my own eyes looking back, hot with shame . . . when I did not cry or make any sound, it became impossible that I should speak of it to anyone, and the confusion and the panic of my discovery were locked inside me then and there, to be faced alone, for a very long time to come. (Hathaway, 1943, p. 157)

Over and over I forgot what I had seen in the mirror. It could not penetrate into the interior of my mind and become an integral part of me. I felt as if it had nothing to do with me; it was only a disguise. But it was not the kind of disguise which is put on voluntarily by the person who wears it, and which is intended to confuse other people as to one's identity. My disguise had been put on me without my consent or knowledge like the ones in fairy tales, and it was I myself who was confused by it, as to my own identity. I looked in the mirror, and was horror-struck because I did not recognize myself. . . . Every one of those encounters was like a blow on the head. They left me dazed and dumb and senseless every time, until slowly and stubbornly my robust persistent illusion of well-being and of personal beauty spread all through me again, and I forgot the irrelevant reality and was all unprepared and vulnerable again. (Hathaway, 1943, pp. 46–47)

The stigmatized person can and often does use the stigma for secondary gains, as an excuse for not being able to compete. However, when what is perceived as being the objective basis of his failings is corrected, problems often surface:

For years the scar, harelip or misshapen nose has been looked on as a handicap, and its importance in the social and emotional adjustment is unconsciously all embracing. It is the "hook" on which the patient has hung all inadequacies, all dissatisfactions, all procrastinations, and all unpleasant duties of social life, and he has come to depend on it not only as a reasonable escape from competition but as a protection from social responsibility.

When one removes this factor by surgical repair, the patient is cast adrift from the more or less acceptable emotional protection it has offered and soon he finds, to his surprise and discomfort, that life is not all smooth sailing even for those with unblemished, "ordinary" faces. He is unprepared to cope with this situation without the support of a "handicap," and he may turn to the less simple, but similar, protection of the behavior patterns of neurasthenia, hysterical conversion, hypochondriasis or the acute anxiety states. (Baker & Smith, 1939, p. 303)

The disabled individual may also view the disability as a blessing in disguise, as a trial through which he has suffered and gained a new understanding of life (Vash, 1978). A mother permanently disabled by polio writes:

But now, far away from the hospital experience, I can evaluate what I have learned. For it wasn't only suffering: it was also learning through suffering. I know my awareness of people has deepened and increased, that those who are close to me can count on me to turn all my mind and heart and attention to their problems. I could not have learned that dashing all over a tennis court. (Henrich & Kriegel, 1961, p. 19)

When disabled and able-bodied meet, an uncomfortable situation often results for both. One response observed among the disabled, that of defensive cowering, can be best understood through the following example:

> When . . . I began to walk out alone in the streets of our town . . . I found then that wherever I had to pass three or four children together on the sidewalk, if I happened to be alone, they would shout at me. . . . Sometimes they even ran after me, shouting and jeering. This was something I didn't know how to face, and it seemed as if I couldn't bear it. . . .
> For a while those encounters in the street filled me with a cold dread of all unknown children. . . .
> One day I suddenly realized that I had become so self-conscious and afraid of all strange children that, like animals, they knew I was afraid, so that even the mildest and most amiable of them were automatically prompted to derision by my own shrinking and dread. (Hathaway, 1943, pp. 155–157)

Just as the disabled may respond to interactions with the able-bodied population with fear, hostility, bravado, or a variety of other kinds of emotional responses, the able-bodied, too, often feel uncomfortable in these interactions:

> Whether the handicap is overtly and tactlessly responded to as such, or as is more commonly the case, no explicit reference is made to it, the underlying condition of heightened, narrowed, awareness causes the interaction to be articulated too exclusively in terms of it. This, as my informants described it, is usually accompanied by one or more of the familiar signs of discomfort and stickiness: the guarded references, the common everyday words suddenly made taboo, the fixed stare elsewhere, the artificial levity, the compulsive loquaciousness, the awkward solemnity. (Davis, 1961, p. 123)

Key Ingredients to Effect Change

Disabled people have in part bought into our society's value system of pronouncing everything young, beautiful, healthy, and vigorous as being "good" and everything at variance to this norm as being "bad." They are, therefore, partially responsible for the current situation in which they find themselves. There are, however, a number of things they can do to help remediate the problem. Certainly they can continue to agitate for additional enforceable legal proscriptions to combat the discrimination they face. Although the Rehabilitation Act of 1973 has provided a foundation on which meaningful progress can be made in the fight for equality, there has been a marked reluctance on the part of both individuals and city, county, state, and, indeed, federal legislators and bureaucrats to live up to the intended spirit of the law. It is not until the disabled insist on strict enforcement of these legal enactments and direct attention to its offenders that the act will, in fact, produce change. It is through civil suits such as that initiated by the Eastern Chapter of the Paralyzed Veterans of America against New York City's Transit Authority, the Manhattan and Bronx Surface Transportation Authority, and the Comptrollers of both the City and State of New York that "justice for all" can be assured (Moakley, 1979). Although this suit focuses on equal access to New York's public transportation system, other legal actions demanding access to educational, vocational, and recreational environments must be and are being instituted.

Another way the disabled can achieve equality is through increased contact with the able-bodied and by providing them with information about disability. A large body of psychological literature (e.g., Anthony, 1972; Gaier, Linkowski, & Jacques, 1968; Semmel & Dickson, 1966; Yuker, Block, & Young, 1966) suggests that attitudinal change can occur with increased contact with the disabled and information about disability. For example, an unpublished study authored by Weinberg and Sebian (1980) indicates that people who show the strongest agreement with biblical beliefs regarding disability come from those who have had the least social interaction with them. This finding holds true for both the able-bodied and the disabled. Thus differences in acceptance of these biblical sentiments is related to how much contact the able-bodied or disabled person has had with disabled people, and his acceptance is not related to whether or not the person is himself disabled. Possibly with increased contact, an informational campaign, and the maintenance of a more highly visible presence, some of the prejudicial feelings many able-bodied members of our society harbor toward the disabled could be ameliorated, as the able-bodied and disabled meet in the marketplace, in the school, in the workplace, and in social-recreational environments. The process through which progress can be made is the subject of this text. Disabled people can, however, accelerate the process by organizing, banding together, and speaking with one voice, rather than continuing to act as special-interest groups interested in effecting only those changes which directly benefit their own highly specialized needs.

Of at least equal importance to increasing the degree of social intercourse between the disabled and able-bodied and to seeking legal remedies to deal with discrimination is that the disabled stop encouraging and participating in their own stigmatization. This essential step along the road to full and real equality must be taken by the disabled themselves. They must establish a healthy self-image. They must come to believe that they can indeed contribute to society as worthwhile, socially competent individuals. No individual can avoid conflicts between the needs and demands of reality and opposing needs within himself. Nor would such a state be desirable, since a reasonable degree of conflict provides the impetus for further development (Eisenberg, 1977). The disabled, however, must be able to integrate the disabling condition into a healthy self-concept. They must learn how to tolerate and deal effectively with conflict and frustration. They must learn to be as independent as possible, develop the capacity for farsighted planning, and be motivated to receive satisfaction from fulfilling the role they play in society. The disabled must develop the skills necessary for vocational self-sufficiency and learn to compete and to co-operate; to assert themselves when necessary and to gain satisfaction from being helpful to others. They must acquire the ability to tolerate anxiety and to remain flexible, trying new responses when old ones fail. In essence, the disabled need to develop a realistic understanding of themselves, of their capabilities and limitations, needs, fears, and sources of conflict. It is only then, after the disabled have come to believe in their own authenticity and value as human beings, that the first major battle against the discrimination they face can be thought of as having been won.

> If I had to choose one group of experiences that finally convinced me of the importance of this problem (of self-image) and that I had to fight my own battles of identification, it would be the incidents that made me realize with my heart that cripples could be identified with characteristics other than their physical handicap. I managed to see that cripples could be comely, charming, ugly, lovely, stupid, brilliant—just like all other people, and I discovered that I was able to hate or love a cripple in spite of his handicap. (Carling, 1962, p. 21)

References and Bibliography

Anthony, W.A. Changing society's attitudes toward the physically disabled. *Rehabilitation Psychology*, 1972, *19*(3), 117–126.
Baker, W. Y., & Smith, L. H. Facial disfigurement and personality. *Journal of American Medical Association*, 1939, *112*, 301–304.

Becker, H. *Outsiders: Studies in the sociology of deviance.* New York: Free Press, 1963.

Brunner, J., Goodnow, J., & Austin, G. *A study of thinking.* New York: Wiley, 1967.

Carling, E. *And yet we are human.* London: Chatto & Windus, 1962.

Davis, F. Deviance disavowal: The management of strained interaction by the visibly handicapped. *Social Problems,* 1961, 9(2), 120–132.

Eisenberg, M. G. *Psychological aspects of disability: A guide for the health care educator.* New York: National League for Nursing, 1977.

Erikson, K. Notes on the sociology of deviance. *Social Problems,* 1962, 9(4), 307–314.

Gaier, E. L., Linkowski, D. G., & Jacques, M. E. Contact as a variable in the perception of disability. *Journal of Social Psychology,* 1968, 74, 117–126.

The Gallup Opinion Index, 1977–78. New York: Random House, 1978.

Goffman, E. *Stigma: Notes on the management of spoiled identity.* Englewood Cliffs, N.J.: Prentice-Hall, 1963.

Gowan, A. G. *The war blind in American social structure.* New York: American Foundation for the Blind, 1957.

Hathaway, K. B. *The little locksmith.* New York: Coward-McCann, 1943.

Henrich, E., & Kriegel, L. (Eds.). *Experiments in survival.* New York: Association for the Aid of Crippled Children, 1961.

Killilea, M. *Karen.* Englewood Cliffs, N.J.: Prentice-Hall, 1952.

Kosinski, J. *The painted bird.* Boston: Houghton Mifflin, 1965.

Kramm, E.R. *Families of Mongoloid children.* Washington, D.C.: U.S. Government Printing Office, 1963.

Moakley, J. And justice for all. *Paraplegia News,* 1979, 32, 36–38.

Semmel, M. I., & Dickson, S. Connative reactions of college students to disability labels. *Exceptional Children,* 1966, 32, 443–450.

Safilios-Rothschild, C. Societal reactions to disability. In J. Stubbins (Ed.), *Social and psychological aspects of disability.* Baltimore: University Park Press, 1977.

Vash, C. Disability as transcendental experience. In M. Eisenberg & J. Falconer (Eds.), *Care and treatment of the spinal cord injured.* Springfield, Illinois: Charles C Thomas, 1978.

Weinberg, N., & Sebian, C. The Bible and disability. Accepted for publication in *Rehabilitation Counseling Bulletin* (March, 1980).

Yuker, H. E., Block, J. R., & Young, J. H. *The measurement of attitudes toward disabled persons: Human resources study No. 7.* Albertson, N.Y.: Human Resources, 1966.

2 Should Every Bus Kneel?

John S. Hicks

To some of us working in the field of exceptional children and adults, November 18, 1979 will be remembered as a significant day. Public Law 94-142 had been signed into law nearly four years earlier and was beginning to produce significant changes in the way the schools in our country treat handicapped children. Another major law, the Rehabilitation Act of 1973, seemed destined to make as much impact on the lives of handicapped adults by forcing public agencies to provide access for the handicapped, and by suggesting many stipulations about the "civil rights" of the handicapped.

What happened on November 18, 1979 was the institutionalization of a backlash against the disabled which many had feared would come forth. It was becoming obvious that providing for the needs of the handicapped was going to be expensive. Unfortunately, the recent federal legislation was passed in a period of economic problems. Inflation coupled with the oil shortage and world unrest suggested that the American economy did not have at its disposal excess funds to pay for the many provisos of that new legislation. Indeed, the handicapped seemed to be crying out for services at a time when national, local, and personal financial resources were sorely strained to meet the ever-increasing cost of living.

And so, the "Eastern liberal press" sounded the first trumpet. The New York Times (which we are led to believe has at least national circulation) ran an editorial on Sunday, March 18, 1979 that called for temperance on the part of the handicapped; it cited recent gains and bemoaned the cost to the public of full implementation of these laws. The title of the editorial was "Must Every Bus Kneel to the Disabled?" It is important to reproduce it in its entirety, so that future claims of misunderstanding or misrepresentation are kept at a minimum.

Do the 30 million Americans afflicted with physical or mental handicaps have a right of access, no matter what the cost, to all publicly sponsored activities? That is now a central question because the price of such access for the disabled promises to become very great.

The handicapped have made vigorous and successful claims on American society in recent years. New laws require schools and colleges to integrate them as much as possible into regular programs. Public buildings must offer easy access. Employers are required to take reasonable steps to allow the disabled to work. One particularly sweeping statute says that no person may be excluded on account of a handicap from any activity that receives federal money.

The fairness and social value of much of this legislation should be obvious. But a vocal segment of the handicapped now hails the broader language, patterned after the 1964 Civil Rights Act, as a declaration of analogous rights to participate in all aspects of American life. These groups want to have removed every barrier that keeps the handicapped somehow apart, at public expense. Plainly, this law needs to be reconsidered with a better understanding of how it will be interpreted and what it will cost.

The costs of rendering the handicapped "equal" have threatened to become especially acute in publicly financed transportation. New rules issued by the Transportation Department require lifts for wheelchairs on buses, room for wheelchairs on railway cars that now cannot handle them, and elevators in many subway and rail stations. Impoverished cities like New York say they cannot afford all this.

The Congressional Budget Office has calculated the nationwide cost at $6.8 billion over the next 30 years. The congressional budgeteers also figure that the modifications would serve no more than 7 percent of the severely disabled, at an estimated cost of $38 per ride. Door-to-door taxi service, by contrast, could serve 26 percent of the same group at a cost possibly less than $8 a ride. That is still expensive, but it dramatizes the problem and even the potential benefit to the handicapped of sensibly weighing alternatives.

Going to incredible expense to remodel trains and buses would be justifiable only if the handicapped, as some insist, have a fundamental legal, even constitutional right, to use public facilities without difficulty. If they are to be classified as a minority that must be compensated for the condition that makes them different, then even a separate-but-better transportation network could be said to violate their rights. Where such a right might be found in the Constitution, or even in logic, is not immediately apparent.

How far would such a right extend? All street signs in Braille? Sign language on every television show? A counselor-guide for each illiterate? Would severe psychosis be a handicap requiring not merely assistance or care but an equalizing remedy?

These objections are too easily misunderstood. Integrating the handicapped into everyday life is a valuable social goal. Vast numbers of them are on welfare when they could be doing productive work—if the barriers to their mobility and opportunities were lowered. The nation is, belatedly, moving in the right direction. For reasons of humanity and sound social policy, it should move faster still. But that hardly justifies making every bus kneel to pick up a few passengers. The handicapped have a right to respect and to reasonable assistance, not to an unlimited claim on public funds in the name of dubious principle. (© 1979 by The New York Times Company. Reprinted by permission.)

Several points in that editorial are critical to the understanding of present discrimination against the handicapped and are also enlightening in describing social policy in this area. To its credit, *The New York Times* does at least admit that the general questions raised apply to a rather substantial group of Americans, 30 million people. That is a sizable minority, even in our 200-million-plus society. The *Times* also alludes to fundamental questions being raised by the 1964 Civil Rights Act, that is, that discrimination is contrary to the civil rights of the handicapped just as it was to the blacks in our country.

The editorial makes reference to the Congressional Budget Office and its calculations that it would cost $6.8 billion over the next 30 years to make certain modifications in the area of transportation. When placed in the perspective of federal expenditures for defense, $125 billion per year, the $240 million per year cost of such modifications seems minuscle! The *Times* goes on, citing that in many cases paying for taxi rides could be cheaper and serve a larger proportion of those disabled workers. As in hundreds of cases prior to this one, the ultimate justification is economic, to get the handicapped off welfare and gainfully employed. Basically, this misses the central issues, that public facilities should be accessible because the handicapped don't want to be chauffered around—they want to be treated as other citizens are treated. The editorial suggests replacing one stigma with another stigma, which is a poor short-term or long-range solution.

The statement that the needs of the disabled " . . . hardly justif[y] making every bus kneel to pick up a few new passengers" represents an attempt to slow down, to limit, to re-think. The article makes reference to "impoverished cities like New York." When national papers like the *Times* print editorials of such a negative nature, one begins to wonder how widespread and pervasive the poverty has become.

Value Systems and Social Policy

It is the premise of this chapter that the fields of special education and rehabilitation are at a point where technical competence alone is not sufficient. Whatever the degree of professional competence, the public is asking other kinds of questions, and the questions are becoming central to the progress of the handicapped in our society. The issues raised in *The New York Times* editorial are philosophical—about the responsibility of the general society to accommodate to the needs of individuals. Questions are raised as to the constitutionality of such requests on the part of the handicapped. Is total access by any citizen a guaranteed right in our society?

Such questions raise the specter of more fundamental problems. Technical competence would not help a disabled worker argue his or her case in front of the editorial board of *The New York Times*. I would assert that several other factors, such as value systems and attitudes, are more relevant to any future progress on the part of the disabled. The remaining parts of this chapter attempt to bring into focus areas which are related to society's attitudes and social policy as they will affect the position of the disabled in the future.

Let me review several important books which I feel have attempted to understand some of the American society's attitudes and values. The first is a book by Hofstadter (1955) which attempts to document the impact of Darwinian theory on social structures and thought in our country. His basic premise was that many of the tenets of Darwinism as a scientific theory of evolution in nature have been applied to the evolution of human societies. In *Social Darwinism in American Thought* he outlines the ideas that have been brought over from the world of science and applied to social progress.

> Darwinism was used to buttress the conservative outlook in two ways. The most popular catchwords of Darwinism, "struggle for existence" and "survival of the fittest," when applied to the life of man in society, suggested that nature would provide that the best competitors in a competitive situation would win, and that this process would lead to continuing improvement. In itself this was not a new idea, as economists could have pointed out, but it did give the force of a natural law to the idea of competitive struggle. Secondly, the idea of development over aeons brought new force to another familiar idea in conservative political theory, the conception that all sound development must be slow and unhurried. Society could be envisaged as an organism (or as an entity something like an organism), which could change only at the glacial pace at which new species are produced in nature. . . .
> But in either case the conclusions to which Darwinism was at first

put were conservative conclusions. They suggested that all attempts to reform social processes were efforts to remedy the irremediable, that they interfered with the wisdom of nature, that they could lead only to degeneration. (Hofstadter, 1955, pp. 6–7)

The implications for the field of the handicapped are clear. Social structures should follow natural laws, and the strongest will survive. The second corollary is that, as in science, social change is very slow and should not be hurried. It is ironic that Darwinism, from the scientific world, should so often be used as a justification for slow and gradual change, especially in this modern world, when scientific change is so rapid.

A second major historical work is Erich Fromm's *Escape from Freedom* (1965). Fromm approaches his analysis from the point of view of a psychoanalyst attempting to interpret certain historical developments. His thesis is that modern man is faced with the problem of technological freedom. For the first time in history, man is freed from the eternal struggle for survival, thanks to the developments of modern industrial technology. Faced with this development, modern man is faced with a psychological dilemma he has not had to face before—that of freedom.

> After centuries of struggles, man succeeded in building an undreamed-of-wealth of material goods; he built democratic societies in parts of the world, and recently was victorious in defending himself against new totalitarian schemes; yet, as the analysis in *Escape from Freedom* attempts to show, modern man still is anxious and tempted to surrender his freedom to dictators of all kinds, or to lose it by transforming himself into a small cog in the machine, well fed, and well clothed, yet not a free man but an automaton. (Fromm, 1965, p. xii)
>
> There can be no doubt that in this last quarter of a century the reasons for man's fear of freedom, for his anxiety and willingness to become an automaton, have not only continued but have greatly increased. . . .
>
> Aside from the nuclear revolution, the cybernetic revolution has developed more rapidly than many could have foreseen twenty-five-years ago. We are entering the second industrial revolution in which not only human physical energy—man's hands and arms as it were—but also his brain and his nervous reactions are being replaced by machines. (Fromm, 1965, pp. xii–xiii)

Fromm's conclusions about the way man will be able to deal with the psychological problem of freedom focus on man's willingness to "escape," by becoming a part of a large corporation, a part of a community, an in-group, a clique which provides an identity. Fromm asserts that individuality produces loneliness and that often freedom is associated with the anxiety of being an individual.

> Man's brain lives in the twentieth century; the heart of most men lives still in the Stone Age. The majority of men have not yet acquired the maturity to be independent, to be rational, to be objective. They need myths and idols to endure the fact that man is all by himself, that there is no authority which gives meaning to life except man himself. Man represses the irrational passions of destructiveness, hate, envy, revenge; he worships power, money, the sovereign state, the nation; while he pays lip service to the teachings of the great spiritual leaders of the human race, those of Buddha, the prophets, Socrates, Jesus, Mohammed—he has transformed these teachings into a jungle of superstition and idol-worship. How can mankind save itself from destroying itself by this discrepancy between intellectual-technical over-maturity and emotional backwardness? (Fromm, 1965, pp. xiv–xv)

If, indeed, Fromm is right, a second insight is afforded us. Modern man feels overwhelmed with the immensity of the world and by the complexity of our civilization. Man's response is to join, to give up his individuality for membership in a group. By this he finds identity and stature.

> This particular mechanism is the solution that the majority of normal individuals find in modern society. To put it briefly, the individual ceases to be himself; he adopts entirely the kind of personality offered to him by cultural patterns; and he therefore becomes exactly as all others are and as they expect him to be.... But the price he pays, however, is high; it is the loss of his self. (Fromm, 1965, pp. 208–209)

Thus, so far, we seem to have a modern society which tends to change slowly in terms of social developments. At the same time, we have individual members who seek identity and individuality, but who must often do so at the price of primary relationships such as the family. Fromm's conclusion is that, psychologically, most persons cannot pay the price, and so they give up parts of their individuality to fit into groups—whether vocational or social.

The disabled in our society are caught in both these binds. They need, wish, and expect some rather quick social changes. It is impossible for them to wait the 100 years the blacks waited from the end of the Civil War to the 1954 Supreme Court decision. At the same time, psychologically, the disabled feel different enough, and they usually want to establish linkages, to establish relationships with groups of people with similar interests. Yet this is often so hard to do, for a multitude of reasons. Perhaps if the buses would kneel they would have a better chance at establishing and maintaining healthy relationships both vocationally and personally.

Lest the reader be given the impression that more recent authors are not writing on these topics, let me introduce a work published in 1970 by Charles A. Reich, *The Greening of America*. Reich speaks of a revolution he sees coming in our society. It is a quiet revolution of social ideas usually associated with the younger generation and their values. He speaks of a value system that is different from the two major value systems he identifies as totally integrated into our country's ethos. These three systems he labels Consciousness I, II, and III:

> Consciousness I is the traditional outlook of the American farmer, small businessman, and worker who is trying to get ahead. Consciousness II represents the values of an organizational society. Consciousness III is the new generation. . . .
> The great question of these times is how to live in and with a technological society; what mind and what way of life can preserve man's humanity and his very existence against the domination of the forces he has created. This question is at the root of the American crisis, beneath all the immediate issues of lawlessness, poverty, meaninglessness, and war. It is this question to which America's new generation is beginning to discover an answer, an answer based on a renewal of life that carries the hope of restoring us to our sources and ourselves. (Reich, 1970, pp. 16–17)

Consciousness I represents the Horatio Alger myth in America; that is, self-sufficiency, hard work, and individual sacrifice will ultimately win out. The independent businessman, the professional working alone can and will become successful on the basis of his or her individual tenacity and courage. Consciousness II represents much of what Fromm wrote about; it is the success of the individual who joins an organization. The citizen becomes a needed worker in a large organization, never standing on his own but sharing in the success of the larger unit. The worker also receives the security of being a part of a social unit, such as a union, while paying the price of conformity to the group. Reich asserts that Consciousness I was the dominant life-style in the early stages of our society, but that since the turn of the century Consciousness II has prevailed.

> Just as Consciousness I centers on the fiction of the American Adam, the competitive struggle, and the triumph of the virtuous and strong individ-

ual, so Consciousness II rests on the fiction of logic and machinery; what it considers unreal is nature and subjective man. Consciousness II believes more in the automobile than in walking, more in the decision of an institution than in the feelings of an individual, more in a distant but rational goal than in the immediate present. (Reich, 1970, p. 67)

Reich, however, insists that the revolution which is coming relates to a third view of social values.

> Consciousness III rejects the whole concept of excellence and comparative merit that is so central to Consciousness II. III refuses to evaluate people by general standards, it refuses to classify people, or analyze them. Each person has his own individuality, not to be compared to that of anyone else. Someone may be a brilliant thinker, but he is not "better" at thinking than anyone else, he simply possesses his own excellence. . . . Everyone is entitled to pride in himself, and no one should act in a way that is servile, or feel inferior, or allow himself to be treated as if he were inferior.
>
> It is upon these premises that the Consciousness III idea of community and of personal relationships rests. In place of the world seen as a jungle, with every man for himself (Consciousness I) or the world seen as a meritocracy leading to a great corporate hierarchy of rigidly drawn relations and maneuvers for position (Consciousness II), the world is a community. People all belong to the same family, whether they have met each other or not. . . .
>
> In personal relations, the keynote is honesty, and the absence of socially imposed duty. To be dishonest in love, to "use" another person, is a major crime. (Reich, 1970, pp. 226–227)

Clearly, Reich asserts that there is in our younger generation of adults an alternate to the two other, more traditional value systems found in our society. To this writer, Consciousness III represents an existential humanism in which the individual has supreme value and in which respect for others transcends the narcissism of individuality. Reich suggests that it will produce a third major value system. Perhaps it will balance off the ideas of slow and gradual change coupled with superiority found in Social Darwinism. Perhaps it will provide the identity that Fromm fears people lose when they give up their freedom to become a part of Consciousness II.

Several points can be made relative to the lives of the handicapped. In terms of Social Darwinism, the handicapped are placed in a no-win situation. They will never be judged to be part of the superior part of our society. They will never be a part of evolution toward excellence. Darwinists would consider them mutants, proof that nature is not perfect. The handicapped will never be, for the major part, members of the meritocracy of our modern world. We have accepted the idea of a person's value being tied to merit so fully that it has become an unconscious phenomenon.

It is hard to speak of the loss of individuality of handicapped persons; their uniqueness tends to reinforce their individuality. Very often social groups seem to have little need to reach out and include them as members. Part of the movement of mainstreaming seems to be a desire to be included, but hopefully not for the same reasons or in the same way as Fromm's men reach out to social groups as a result of a fear of freedom.

Reich seems to be saying that although there are some traditional groups in our society with more-or-less traditional value systems that fit into groups, there is a third value system growing in our culture. This new value system speaks of the innate worth of each individual. It speaks of a value system that is not tied to productivity at work, not tied to status, and not tied to upward mobility. Perhaps the disabled will have to fight for many years the battles of access to public transportation and access to productive jobs. It is reassuring to know that a value system may be emerging in our culture that says that individuals have value apart from and perhaps in spite of a lack of productivity.

Prejudice and Aggression

In the previous part I tried to outline the theme that some of the major problems the handicapped face in modern society relate to "value systems." Social Darwinism warns us that people's values change slowly. Fromm and Reich, from different perspectives, warn about man's acceptance of prevailing value systems. The handicapped seldom share in the rewards of these value systems. Fromm asserts that man loses his identity when joining larger social units. Reich describes two major value systems related to man's work and suggests that there is a saner set of values which are just emerging in our society.

The second major theme I would like to present involves two other major forces which impact on all disabled people—aggression and prejudice. Many would argue that aggression and prejudice are just two separate manifestations of the same human problems.

We seem to be experiencing a tremendous display of aggression or destructiveness in recent years. The American social dreams of peace and prosperity are not even talked about anymore. Within the past 20 years we have witnessed assassinations of public figures in our country. We have witnessed open riots between dissidents (mostly the young) and the establishment over Vietnam. We have witnessed various racial hostilities. We are observing innumerable "brush-fire wars" around the world, and the interminable strife in Ireland. Although we hope the threat of nuclear holocaust can be averted, it is impossible not to define these times as troubled.

Fear of personal attacks has modified many lifestyles in cities so that often streets in many parts are empty after dark. Should power failure occur, general looting destroys property indiscriminately—not just the property of the wealthy outsider but of the neighborhood resident as well. In recent months there has been a resurgence of open activity by the Ku Klux Klan. Destructiveness seems so commonplace that it no longer shocks the public. In a number of cases, violence and destructiveness seem tied to prejudice of one group against another. I would like to suggest two books which attempt to provide some understanding of these forces: Gordon Allport's *The Nature of Prejudice* (1958) and Erich Fromm's *The Anatomy of Human Destructiveness* (1973). My meaning should be clear—the handicapped must learn to deal with prejudice and aggression in their personal lives.

In his description of the nature of prejudice, Allport makes several important points. Primary is his assumption that prejudice is a result of many factors and cannot be explained away by one theory. Allport suggests that one of these roots of prejudice lies in man's tendency to establish and maintain groups. These groups then quickly become in-groups and out-groups, and close ties and allegiance naturally follow.

> Psychologically the crux of the matter is that the familiar provides the indispensable basis of our existence. Since existence is good, its accompanying groundwork seems good and desirable. A child's parents, neighborhood, region, nation are given to him—so too his religion, race, and social traditions. To him all these affiliations are taken for granted. Since he is part of them, and they are part of him, they are *good*. . . . (Allport, 1958, p. 28)
>
> We are now in a position to understand and appreciate a major theory of prejudice. It holds that all groups (whether in-groups or reference groups) develop a way of living with characteristic codes and beliefs, standards and "enemies" to suit their own adaptive needs. The theory holds also that both gross and subtle pressures keep every individual member in line. The in-group's preferences must be his preferences, its enemies his enemies. (Allport, 1958, p. 38)

The issue for our field is just this: as individuals, the handicapped have few valued groups of which they can be members.

More often they and their families face subtle pressures of non-acceptance—not strong drives for inclusion. Allport (1958) also asserts that stereotypes are typically attached to groups. He defines stereotypes as exaggerated beliefs associated with a category, and the stereotype serves to justify our conduct toward that group. Thus all handicapped people tend to be painted with the same brush, whatever their real abilities. People bring to individual disabled persons their own stereotype of a mythical group of all handicapped persons.

Also important is Allport's discussion of the "American dilemma" (Allport, 1958). He asserts, as others before him have, that we have a central conflict between our belief in the American dream of equality of opportunity and the very real awareness of our citizens that prejudices are very strong. We live in a state of collective guilt. We tend to approach people we feel prejudiced against with a high degree of uneasiness. Often the handicapped are aware of this basic ambivalence of others toward them.

Prejudice and aggression have, unfortunately, often gone hand in hand. It seems easier to be aggressive toward others who are the objects of prejudice. Erich Fromm's 1973 book on human destructiveness describes in great detail the destructiveness of Hitler and the Nazi drive to conquer the world. He attempts to give some reasons behind the incredible degree of cruelty which one group of men were able to inflict on another group. He also speaks of malignant aggression which is destructive and cruel, and which is usually not a part of the animal world. This unique form of destructiveness seems to have driven man to extreme lengths as civilization has progressed in its technology.

> We must distinguish in man *two entirely different kinds of aggression*. The first, which he shares with all animals, is a phylogenetically programmed impulse to attack (or to flee) when vital interests are threatened. This *defensive*, "benign" aggression is in the service of the survival of the individual and the species, is biologically adaptive and ceases when the threat has ceased to exist. The other type, "malignant" aggression, i.e. *destructiveness and cruelty*, is specific to the human species and virtually absent in most mammals.... (Fromm, 1973, p. 4)
>
> Malignant aggression, let us remember, is specifically human and not derived from animal instinct. It does not serve the physiology survival of man, yet it is an important part of his mental functioning. It is one of the passions that are dominant and powerful in some individuals and cultures, although not in others. (Fromm, 1973, p. 218)

Fromm goes on to explain that destructiveness is partially a result of our existential quest for meaning where meaning seems not to exist. It is founded in the feelings of loneliness and dread. It is partially founded in man's feeling of helplessness in a monstrous world of atomic destruction, or the threat of destruction. Destructiveness is man's attempt to control others rather than be controlled by others. This natural aggression becomes distorted and is manifested in an unending succession of inhumane acts visited on fellow men. It becomes easier to understand some of the attitudes of the public toward disabled persons from this frame of reference. Prejudice and hostility can be understood partly as social phenomena related to certain developments in any modern culture which produce isolation and fear.

The handicapped person, child or adult, needs to understand the roots of aggression and prejudice in our culture at this time in history. Probably more than most other groups, the disabled will face aggression and prejudice on a day-to-day basis. The causes will vary from person to person and from situation to situation. There are no easy solutions, and no easily taught defenses against these problems. The message is clear, however; the disabled should be trained to expect such attitudes and be given responses which can be applied to meet these dilemmas.

One other approbation should be discussed in this cursory description of attitudes of the public as they impose on the disabled person who is striving for inclusion in the American dream. It is the warning that society and social policy are often against individuals. As much as we believe in the rights of individuals in this country, we also believe in rule by the majority. Many of the present social and personal conflicts which are being worked out in the courts pertain to this theme. Does the government, in the name of the larger majority, have the right to infringe on the rights of the individual, and if so, to what degree and in what specific instances?

This natural conflict between an individual's rights and society's rights would appear to be one of the more critical issues to be faced by our court systems in the next 25 to 50 years. How do you safeguard the rights of the majority against seemingly inappropriate demands by individuals. Again, should every bus kneel? One of the factors which makes this controversy border on the tragic is that there is an obvious degree of "madness" on each side. There are individuals who will use the protection of individual rights to achieve some dubious accomplishments. The use of the legal processes to protect those engaged in drug trafficking, child pornography, and child prostitution makes even the diehard liberal sometimes question the supreme rights of the individual.

In a different vein, Jules Henry has been writing on this subject for years from a perspective of an anthropologist. He has spoken a message which the disabled should take to heart. That message is that culture is a two-edged sword, partially helpful but also very much antagonistic toward the fate of an individual man. His most urgent statement of that theme is found in *Culture against Man.*

> Ours is a driven culture. It is driven on by its achievement, competitive, profit, and mobility drives, and by the drives for security and a higher standard of living. Above all, it is driven by expansiveness. Drives like hunger, thirst, sex, and rest arise directly out of the chemistry of the body, whereas expansiveness, competitiveness, achievement, and so on are generated by the culture; still we yield to the latter as we do to hunger and sex. Side by side with these drives is another group of urges, such as gentleness, kindliness, and generosity, which I shall call values, and in our culture a central issue for the emotional life of everyone is the interplay between these two. (Henry, 1965a, p. 13)
>
> To say that culture "teaches" puts the matter too mildly. Actually culture invades and infests the mind as an obsession. . . to engulf the mind so that it will see the world only as the culture decrees that it shall be seen; to compel a person to be absurd. (Henry, 1965a, p. 297)
>
> If this book can be said to have a message it is that man wrings from culture what emotional satisfaction he obtains from it. (Henry, 1965a, p. 11)

Another fascinating book that Jules Henry wrote deals with the analysis of several family constellations in which one of the children suffered a severe form of mental illness. In this book, *Pathways to Madness* (1965), he attempts to describe the vast array of interfaces which constantly support or cause disintegration of family members. He writes of a variety of human rituals which are daily acted out and which help to protect each person's sanity. To be made constantly aware of the absurdities in any culture is enough to drive any person to despair. Thus we develop defenses to protect ourselves from our own insight as much as we need to protect ourselves from others.

One of these mechanisms is "sham" and would seem to be an important tool for the disabled to have in their response repertoires. An understanding of the concepts of what Henry calls black and white sham is critical for the maintenance of sanity in our society:

> One has to make a distinction—always fuzzy but always necessary—between black sham and white. Black sham is used to exploit and even to destroy people; white sham is merely socially necessary concealment and pretense. One uses black sham to sell a person down the river or to beat him out for a job, and white sham simply to get along with others—

even one's own mother. Black sham is killing sham—like black magic;
white sham preserves social relations. (Henry, 1965b, p. 100)

Sham is a combination of concealment and pretense; concealment
of how we really feel and pretense of feeling something different. . . .
Social life compels deception, for even the most truly innocent among
us are constantly compelled by fear to act as if they wished to do what
they would rather not do. . . . The real problem is not whether to be a
sham, but to understand when to drop the mask and when to put it on.
(Henry, 1965b, p. 99)

The lessons to be learned go beyond the fact that disabled persons need to understand the function of aggression and prejudice as
they operate in our social system. That is not enough. Needed also is
a heavy dose of skepticism—an awareness of the seeming antago-
nisms of society toward each and every individual. It is the nature of
any society to be against individual members at certain points, to be
ready to sacrifice one person's good for the good of many. It is also a
lesson that culture's basic antagonism toward individuals requires
that we firmly hold onto a perspective that allows us to survive
within our cultures. Jules Henry is not the first writer to point out
our need to make peace with society through the use of rituals such
as sham. Even the nondisabled must deal with the insanity of our
culture, its distortions, and its misplaced values which make everybody's life a little absurd at times.

The Unmeltable Ethnics: A Ray of Hope

The themes that I have tried to develop so far are twofold. First,
many of the value systems operating in modern America offer little
hope for success and satisfaction to the disabled, who simply cannot
compete and win any significant share of the rewards in open competition. Second, the disabled will always face a degree of hostility
and prejudice in our society. This is partly true because of the nature
of prejudice, and partly because in a number of ways our society is a
bit absurd. Societies that believe in majority rule ultimately must
side with the group and against any individual.

As a conclusion to this chapter, I would like to suggest a third
theme, knowing full well that all the themes have only been
sketched out and not fully developed and "proven." The third theme
is more optimistic for the future. It has been suggested by a book
written by Michael Novak, *The Rise of the Unmeltable Ethnics*
(1973). It is one of a number of recent books that have attempted to

break down another of our most enduring myths. This myth is that of the melting pot, the idea that America can absorb many different types of people. In this view a group of immigrants become Americanized and absorbed into the mainstream of America. Novak insists that this no longer happens, partly because the price is too high:

> What price is exacted by America when into its maw it sucks other cultures of the world and processes them? What do people have to lose before they can qualify as true Americans?
> For one thing, a lot of blue stars—and silver and gold ones—must hang in the window. You proved you loved America by dying for it in its wars. . . .
> I don't have other figures at hand. But when the Poles were only four percent of the population (in 1917–19) they accounted for 12 percent of the nation's casualties in World War I. "The Fighting Irish" won their epithet by dying in droves in the Civil War.
> There is, then, a blood test. "Die for us and we'll give you a chance." (Novak, 1973, pp. xxxii–xxxiv)

To become accepted as part of real America, many groups went through years of exclusion and years of melting before becoming Americanized. Often the price was great, often the melting did not occur. The land we live in advertises equal opportunity as a way of life and cultural pluralism as a reality. Novak is not convinced that we really have an existing cultural pluralism, even though we believe in it.

> No one has yet contrived an image, let along a political system, for living in a genuinely pluralistic way. The difficulties are obvious. How can each cultural minority be true to itself without infringing on the liberties of others? How can each person belong to a given ethnic group to the extent that he or she chooses, and be free as well to move into other groups? (Novak, 1973, p. 9)

What is seen as a positive leap by Novak is that we are beginning to find ethnic groups who wish to retain their ethnicity—their identity. This he suspects is the beginning of real cultural pluralism. Thus the Italians retain their fierce loyalties and ties to all the lore of Italian life as well as moving in the American mainstream. What makes this a critical movement, and a ray of hope, is that it signifies the beginning of an idea—that its melting pot is not only unnecessary; it is not helpful.

This is a very touchy point. Persons who have come from other cultures and who have worked hard to become acculturated are very proud of their accomplishments and speak fiercely about the sacrifices they made so that their children could share the good life. At issue for the handicapped is the simple fact that their handicaps will *not* disappear, will not melt in the melting pot. The handicapped will not succeed in becoming totally acculturated, totally Americanized. The message from Novak is that there is no reason to try.

Novak speaks of this movement in relation to European immigrants and asserts a need for real cultural pluralism. A good example of this is the movement toward bilingual education in our schools. The proponents of bilingual education state clearly that the child does not have to give up his native language. The schools should provide instruction in another language as well as English. Perhaps someday our culture will accept the concept of a multilingual society, just as Novak would recommend a real cultural pluralism.

The advantages to the disabled are becoming clear. If the melting pot is gone, then not everybody must be absorbed into the dominant superculture. Thus, perhaps the handicapped will not have to strive so hard to make it in our culture to be accepted, as so many generations of immigrants have done. A stronger commitment to cultural pluralism will lead to a healthier appreciation of the value of individual persons with a handicap.

One final note of caution from Novak: the struggle for an adequate place in the American scene is not always helped by those persons designated as the intellectuals in our society. Novak asserts that although the common man in our society believes that the intellectuals at colleges and universities are the most powerful in our society, those people firmly believe themselves that power really resides in businessmen (Novak, 1973). Leadership should not automatically be expected from the intellectuals in this quest.

> It goes without saying that the intellectuals do not love "middle" America, and that for all the good, warm discovery of America that preoccupied them during the 1950s no strong tide of respect accumulated in their hearts for the Yahoos, Babbitts, Agnews, and Nixons of the land. Willie Morris in *North Toward Home* writes poignantly of the chill, parochial outreach of the liberal sensibility, its failure to engage the humanity of the modest, ordinary little man west of the Hudson. The Intellectual's Map of the United States is succinct: "Two coasts connected by United Airlines." (Novak, 1973, p. 70)

Thus we are back at the starting point. The disabled will not find a "protector" within the ranks of most intellectuals, because they believe very firmly in a meritocracy. They compete and win and do not really understand what it means to be handicapped in our society.

Where, then, do the handicapped look for leadership in their quest for acceptance as an integral part of our culture? How do they fight value systems which are so productively oriented? What are good defense mechanisms for them to use against prejudice and hostility?

Perhaps I should have begun by admitting no special knowledge about the solution to those questions. The questions alone seemed important enough, and central enough to the future of our field so that the dilemmas should be described. Of one thing I stand firmly convinced; the next 25 years will force us to deal with these issues. They will become as important as adequate research data on reliability and validity of assessment instruments. They are fundamental because they speak of the way one person reaches out to another, of the way we strive to understand others, of the ways we can learn to appreciate others, and thus add value to our own lives.

References

Allport, G. W. *The nature of prejudice.* New York: Doubleday, 1958.

Fromm, E. *Escape from freedom.* New York: Holt, Rinehart & Winston, 1965.

Fromm, E. *The anatomy of human destructiveness.* New York: Holt, Rinehart & Winston, 1973.

Henry, J. *Culture against man.* New York: Vintage Books, 1965 (a).

Henry, J. *Pathways to madness.* New York: Random House, 1965 (b).

Hofstadter, R. *Social Darwinism in American thought.* Boston: Beacon Press, 1955.

Novak, M. *The rise of the unmeltable ethnics.* New York: Macmillan, 1973.

Reich, C. A. *The greening of America.* New York: Random House, 1970.

The New York Times, November 18, 1979.

3 The Disabled Face a Schizophrenic Society

Cynthia Griggins

"Do I want to go on like this?"

Counseling the spinal cord injured, I have more than once witnessed a quadriplegic struggle with this question. For the most part, my "counseling" in these situations has consisted of holding my breath and crossing my fingers, hoping he will decide "yes." So far they all have, and each time I have walked away with a vague, guilty sense of relief, much like the relief I experienced as a schoolgirl when I hadn't done my homework and the teacher called on me, but the bell rang before my ignorance was revealed. Being able-bodied, I have gotten by on some untested beliefs about the possibility of a "rich, full life" even as a quadriplegic. Later, among friends, I admit that I honestly don't know what I would do if I were quadriplegic, but it's left at that. No one ever really presses me for an answer.

There are, however, two recent plays that force a more serious look at some of the issues raised in counseling the disabled. In *The Elephant Man* (which has also been made into a movie), and *Whose Life Is It Anyway?* the protagonists are both severely disabled and both choose to die. Not that unbelievable, but the catch is, they are not "losers." John Merrick and Ken Harrison are both exceptional people—bright, insightful, spirited, capable. In the type of story we are most familiar with, these men would have struggled with their conditions and come out on top, winning the respect and love of those around them. Their stories would have had happy endings. These did not. Why did these men choose to die? How much of it

---

The author wishes to thank John Garwood, Astrid Schlaps, and Deborah Van Kleef for their criticisms and editorial comments, and Jay Adler for many long discussions of the ideas.

Extracts in this chapter from *Whose Life Is It Anyway?* by Brian Clark are reprinted by permission of Dodd, Mead and Company, Inc. © 1978 by Brian Clark.

had to do with the disability itself, and how much was related to society's response to their disability?

On the surface, in considering the situation of disabled persons in our society, one might think all is going well—or as well as can be expected. Are they not becoming more visible? Are not medical advances making more things possible for them? Don't we have welfare programs to help them financially and affirmative action to employ them? And aren't we passing legislation to ensure disabled people their full rights as citizens? As minority groups go, one might say the disabled are doing pretty well. But one does not have to look very far beneath the surface to see that something is wrong. The Rehabilitation Act of 1973 has still not been fully implemented; sheltered workshops, which employ a large percentage of the disabled, still often pay only one-half of minimum wage. Indeed, only an estimated 42 percent of the disabled are employed at all, even part-time, and the average income of a disabled individual is far below poverty level. One could go on and on with indications that all is not well with the "handicapped." Though on paper it seems that they are surging ahead in their struggle for equality, it does appear that society is somehow dragging its feet. Is it simply that the struggle is still in its early phases? Will the disabled, as blacks, women, and other minorities, simply need more time to be fully accepted and assimilated in the great melting pot? This may be the case; they are young in the sense of being a group, and new to most of us. Nevertheless, it seems that something is amiss. There is something contradictory and disturbing about society's attitude toward the disabled which is behind the foot-dragging, something that is causing us to push them forward with one hand and hold them back with the other. It is this problem that is explored in the two plays mentioned above, and which I would like to discuss in this chapter.

Although their stories are set nearly 100 years apart, a similar situation confronts Ken Harrison, the quadriplegic protagonist in *Whose Life is it Anyway?*, and John Merrick, the deformed title character of *The Elephant Man*. Both have been rescued from death by humane and caring individuals in the medical establishment. Ken Harrison suffered instant and total quadriplegia as a result of an automobile accident, and in the play we meet him in his hospital bed, recently stabilized medically and now facing rehabilitation. He can move nothing from the neck down, and though he was previously a talented, successful sculptor and art teacher, he knows that his long-term goals now can be little more than feeding himself with assistive devices. John Merrick, the Elephant Man, is a grossly deformed young man, a victim of neurofibromatosis, who is taken from

abject poverty and a freak-show existence into the protective envi-
rons of a London hospital, where he is cared for, educated, and
introduced to the high society of London in the 1880s. Although both
characters seem to have reasonably good lives ahead of them—
certainly the best that could be expected for people in their conditions—they both choose death. Ken Harrison chooses his very directly. In fact, the action of the play centers around his struggle to be
allowed to die. No one will let him—and only after the court orders it
does the hospital administrator finally withdraw medical supports
that are keeping Ken alive. John Merrick chooses his death indirectly, by sleeping not in his usual upright position (which was necessary in order to keep breathing) but lying down "like normal
people," causing himself to be asphyxiated.

   The situations of these two characters are metaphors for that
faced by all the disabled. In exploring the reasons for their deaths,
one might begin to see the confused and often destructive attitudes
we present toward the disabled, usually with the best of intentions.

   These attitudes are probably encountered in their clearest form in
the disabled person's relationship with the medical community. The
relationship is basically an authoritarian one, racked with problems in
control over decision making, the use of technology, and lack of concern for the quality of life. In part, these three problems seem to stem
from the medical community itself, but in most cases I think it is only
fair to recognize that professionals are only the media for cultural
attitudes and values. They are the people who carry out our wishes and
embody our moral confusions. Though morality, power, self-interest,
and charity are inextricably linked in these issues, I will attempt to
tease these apart sufficiently to discuss three areas of conflict between
the disabled and the medical community, each suggested by the plays
mentioned above. Consider first the problem of decision making.

   Although Ken Harrison's very existence depends on medical
technology, the choice itself to apply that technology has never been
presented to him. Indeed, even when Ken is in a position to make
such a choice, the physician will not allow it. This is how the doctors
perceive the situation:

Dr. Scott: It's his life.
Dr. Emerson: But my responsibility . . . .
Dr. Scott: No Clare, a doctor cannot accept the choice for death; he's
                committed to life. When a patient is brought into my unit, he's
                in a bad way. I don't stand about thinking whether or not it's
                worth saving his life. I haven't the time for doubts. I get in
                there, do whatever I can to save life. I'm a doctor, not a judge.

The issue is clouded by ethical questions about preserving life at all costs, which I will discuss below, but the point I would stress here is that the doctor is indeed playing judge, regardless of the content of his decision. He has decided Ken should live and takes appropriate action to this end. Now, it is obvious that an unconscious individual cannot make such a decision, and even if he could, he would in all likelihood choose to receive the necessary medical treatment until he is stabilized and could tell what his long-term condition might be. But even then, when such knowledge is available and quite definite, Ken still is allowed no choice. Dr. Emerson states: "just because our patient is conscious, that does not absolve us from our complete responsibility. . . ."

Most doctors, I am quite sure, would argue, as does Dr. Emerson, that this is a moral question and that they are compelled to save life by the Hippocratic oath. But when a patient espouses a different moral code, what is a physician to do?

Ken: . . . morally, you must accept my decision.
Dr. Scott: Not according to my morals.
Ken: And why are yours better than mine? They're better because they're more powerful. I am in your power. To hell with a morality that is based on the proposition that might is right.

The issue, in my mind, does indeed come down to power. The question of life versus death is of course the most extreme, and therefore the most dramatic. But I think the issue of the professionals' power and authority infuses nearly every aspect of the rehabilitation experience: when a patient should be treated, what type of treatment he should receive, what type of setting he should live in, when he should be discharged. The power of the disabled individual in these decisions is puny. Of course, he can always discharge himself "against medical advice," but there are punishments for this, like many hospitals' policy of denying subsequent admission for a certain period of time!

The implication behind the medical and rehabilitation establishment's position is "we know what's best for you." This statement is usually rationalized by the professional's superior knowledge and expertise. Ken Harrison admits to an examining physician that his knowledge of neurology, endocrinology, urology, and so on is inferior.

Ken: . . . and in so far as these bear on my case, I should be grateful for information so that I can make a proper decision. But it is *my* decision. If you came to my studio to buy something, and

look at all my work, and you say: "I want that bronze" and I
say to you: "Look you don't know anything about sculpture,
the texture is boring and it should have been made in wood
anyway. You are having marble!" You'd think I was nuts. If
you were sensible you'd ask for my professional opinion but if
you were a mature adult, you'd reserve the right to choose for
yourself.

Dr. Travers: But we're not talking about a piece of sculpture . . . but about
your life.

Ken: That's right Doctor. *My* life.

Dr. Treves, John Merrick's physician, is more clearly an oppor-
tunist serving to gain by treating the sensational "Elephant Man."
Nonetheless he is kind and caring toward his patient. Repeatedly
throughout the play he takes action which he explains to Merrick is
"for your own good." The effect of such a doctor-patient interaction
is clear: Merrick becomes more and more infantilized and stripped of
his dignity. And that is precisely the issue—the repeated denial of
choice to an individual robs him of his dignity and transforms him
into something less than human.

In the context of these plays, it is possible to understand why
dignity for some individuals might be choosing life, whereas for
others it might mean choosing death. It is the *locus* of the decision
making that is crucial—more crucial than the content of the decision
itself. Ken articulates this powerfully as he argues his right to choose
with the judge:

Ken: . . . I will spend the rest of my life in hospital . . . while I am here,
everything is geared just to keeping my brain active, with no real
possibility of it ever being able to direct anything. As far as I can
see, that is an act of deliberate cruelty.

Judge: Surely it would be more cruel if society let people die, when it
could, with some effort, keep them alive.

Ken: No, not more cruel, *just* as cruel.

Judge: Then why should the hospital let you die—if it is just as cruel?

Ken: The cruelty doesn't reside in saving someone or allowing them to
die. It resides in the fact that the choice is removed from the man
concerned . . . .

Judge: But wouldn't you agree that many people with appalling physical
handicaps have overcome them and lived essentially creative, digni-
fied lives?

Ken: Yes, I would, but the dignity starts with their choice. If I choose to
live, it would be appalling if society killed me. If I choose to die, it
is equally appalling if society keeps me alive.

Judge: I cannot accept that it is undignified for society to devote resources to keeping someone alive. Surely it enhances that society.

Ken: It is not undignified if the man wants to stay alive, but I must restate that the dignity starts with his choice. Without it, it is degrading because technology has taken over from human will. My Lord, if I cannot be a man, I do not wish to be a medical achievement.

If one examines the issue of choice in medical management today, at the dawning of the 1980s, one senses an even more disturbing development, which could compromise even further the dignity of the disabled person. Ken refers to the role of technology, the second of the problem areas mentioned earlier, at the end of the speech above. Used appropriately, with the full consent of the patient, modern medical technology is, of course, a godsend. I doubt if even the most adamant antitechnologists would reject an operation that could give vision to a blind man or movement to a quadriplegic. But the question which must be faced by the moral man is: How is modern technology affecting human will and decision making? How much medical treatment is delivered simply because the technology exists, and not because an individual has decided that he really wants it? And here I am talking not only about patients, but about physicians also. Does the physician make the decision to provide a certain treatment, or does he feel compelled simply because that treatment exists? Do we not act as if under a God-given mandate: if the technology exists, you must use it! Must we? Such a stance threatens to replace human decision—even that of the physician! And the disabled individual stands even less of a chance establishing his autonomy against an unquestioned technology than he does trying to oppose the decisions of another individual—even that of a physician.

I am by no means rejecting modern medical technology. It has offered millions of disabled people better lives, or life itself. However, the issue is this, the third problem area outlined earlier: regardless of who makes the decision regarding the treatment of the disabled individual, is the decision being made with consideration for the quality of life?

The answer to that question has traditionally been negative. Given the authority to save life or not, the medical community will almost always choose the former, regardless of consequences. This, of course, is only the reflection of a basic societal attitude toward life: that life (in the abstract) must be preserved at all costs (except in cases in which an ideal or belief is at stake). This is a Judeo-Christian belief firmly rooted in our culture for at least the last 2000 years. It is, of course, the same moral question being debated by the pro-abortionists and the Right-to-Life groups, and which has self-maiming, suicide, and euthanasia on the books as criminal offenses since feudal times. The philosophical bases of this question are complex, and I cannot pretend to offer any new insights into this controversy. But I do want to stress that our basic confusion and ambivalence over this issue profoundly affect disabled persons in this society.

Knowing the extreme suffering and hardship a severely disabled person will certainly face for the rest of his life, when life-saving measures are applied, the question must be asked—Why? What for? Certainly, the question of whether or not to survive is not the issue with the majority of the disabled, whose functioning is not so profoundly affected as Ken's in *Whose Life Is It Anyway?* (Or maybe it is the issue; I don't know how severely disabled one has to be to question the worth of going on.) But what must be questioned is decision making that blindly chooses life without regard to quality of life, decision making that does not consider that the quality of life is often cruel, and always unfair to the disabled person himself, decision making that does not struggle with the questions: Why? What for?

The end result of such blind decision making is that we often end up saving the lives of individuals whom we then don't quite know what to do with. So a total quadriplegic is kept alive—then what? What does our society have to offer him? Ken presses the point with the hospital social worker who was sent to improve his motivation:

Mrs. Boyle:	You'll be surprised how many things you will be able to do with training and a little patience.
Ken:	Such as?
Mrs. Boyle:	We can't be sure yet. But I should think that you will be able to operate reading machines and perhaps an adapted typewriter.
Ken:	Reading and writing. What about arithmetic?
Mrs. Boyle:	(Smiling) I dare say we could fit you up with a comptometer if you really wanted one.
Ken:	Mrs. Boyle, even educationalists have realized that the three r's do not make a full life.
Mrs. Boyle:	It's amazing what can be done. Our scientists are wonderful.
Ken:	They are. But it's not good enough you see, Mrs. Boyle. I really have no desire at all to be the object of scientific virtuosity. I have thought things over very carefully. I do have plenty of time for thinking and I have decided that I do not want to go on living with so much effort for so little result.

An entire rehabilitation system is built on this premise—that a human being is the sum of a number of functions. By definition, a fully rehabilitated individual is that person who can perform each and every function of which he is physically capable. If he can actually go out and work a job, be truly "productive," that is the ultimate victory. But even if he can perform "ADL" (activities of daily living, as our lingo goes), if he can feed himself, if he can get from his house to the grocery store, if he can somehow call up the plumber on the telephone without anyone's help, this is seen as success. How on earth did we get to this definition of a human being? What makes "functions" so important? And how does this affect our attitudes toward the disabled? Actually, I think it is quite simple. The goals and values we establish for the disabled are one and the same as those we hold for ourselves.

Consider how modern America is a highly technological, capitalistic society. It is a society that worships growth, expansion, productivity, and achievement. Thriving on competition, it cherishes its myths full of adventure-seekers and common men who work their way to the top in this "land of opportunity." The good and moral man is one who "makes a contribution to society." He is strong, not weak; healthy, not sick; beautiful, not ugly; self-sufficient, not dependent. He is John Wayne, vanquishing his enemies throughout his life, and denying his mortality and vulnerability even as cancer eats away at his body.

Recognizing these basic values, it would be dishonest (or schizophrenic) to say that America loves the cripple. How could she? To be crippled is almost to be un-American! So the only way we, as a society, can possibly deal with these anomalies is if they are actively engaged in denouncing and ridding themselves of those un-American characteristics. Somehow, a quadriplegic who is working and learning to dress himself (even though it may take him half a day) is more palatable than a quadriplegic who is doing nothing. It's bad enough that they can't contribute to society—at least they can *look busy!* "Being" has never been an act much favored by Americans. "Doing" is preferred. Actually it's our national passion. Men and women are measured by what they *can do.* So why should we expect any different from our cripples?

In keeping with these values, rehabilitation programs in this society are designed to eliminate as much as possible the undesirable aspects of disability (dependency, weakness, unsightliness, etc.), to keep the disabled looking busy, and to get them "doing" as much as possible, regardless of what it is. (This is roughly the same philosophy that sees working at a menial, degrading job, for far less than minimum wage as better than doing "nothing.")

These, I believe, are the attitudes which permeate the environment in which Merrick, Harrison, and all the disabled must live. They are contradictory and schizophrenic. We preserve life at all costs, then fail to consider the quality of that life. We treat the disabled with great kindness and concern, voice our respect for them, then despise them because they cannot live up to our values. We talk of full lives of dignity for the disabled, then deprive them of the choices necessary to maintain that dignity. Within the contexts of their respective plays, I believe Merrick and Harrison's deaths were a result, at least in part, of these schizophrenic attitudes. Both characters were sensitive and bright enough to be aware of the ambiguities, and both had enough integrity to say "No—I will not tolerate living under such conditions!"

Is suicide the only solution, however? Is it the disabled person's only alternative to a life stripped of its dignity? My experience with disabled people has shown me that this clearly is not so. I have met many who have survived—and done it with great dignity.

The secret seems to lie in the disabled person's reclaiming control over his own life. It involves wrestling back from the hands of others the power to make decisions for oneself, all decisions from the most important of whether to live or die, down to the least significant acts of daily life—what to eat, when to sleep, where to go today. It involves not only exercising control over one's actions, but being able to establish one's own goals, set one's own standards, and choose one's own values to hold dear.

The history of minorities in this country has basically been the story of "different" individuals struggling to achieve just this control over their lives. Blacks, women, Chicanos, and American Indians all have fought the same battle. What the disabled can learn from these other minorities is, first, that it is indeed a battle and, second, that battles are won by organized groups. No real progress was made by any of these people until they joined together and became a political force, assertively demanding control over their own lives. The majority guards the status quo jealously and does not change on its own. Until the disabled realize that they must become political creatures, that they must develop their own values and standards and actively demand power that is rightfully theirs—until they organize, their situation will not change substantially.

As for the able-bodied, specifically the rehabilitation and medical establishment who see themselves as the "helpers" of the disabled—they must realize that they can take away dignity, but they cannot give it. Therefore their role is circumscribed. They must focus on their own ambivalent attitudes and the ways in which they dehumanize the disabled by depriving them of decision-making power. They must relinquish such control and give the disabled the only true respect there is: respect for their ability to make choices and to live their lives as they see fit.

References

Clark, B. *Whose life is it anyway?* Derbyshire: Amber Lane Press, 1978.
Pomerance, B. *The elephant man.* New York: Grove Press, 1979.

4 Social and Psychological Parameters of Friendship and Intimacy for Disabled People

Constantina Safilios-Rothschild

Our era is one in which the right to intimate relationships has almost become a constitutional right to self-fulfillment and happiness. But this is also an era in which individualization and a narcissistic crisis make such intimate relationships strained and problematic (Lasch, 1979). Especially intimate relationships between men and women have plunged into new depths and impasses as old rules and hang-ups have not altogether disappeared, and new models have not been widely accepted (Safilios-Rothschild, 1977; 1980). Nonsexual friendships, on the other hand, have become increasingly important in people's lives, because they provide needed intimacy without heartbreaking complications as well as a reassuring continuity beyond breakups and divorces (Safilios-Rothschild, 1977).

There is, to some extent, a thin definitional line between the disabled and the nondisabled, but those with visible disabilities and those with chronic illnesses and disabilities that interfere considerably with their ability to communicate, to move about, and to function in everyday activities are rather clearly set apart from the so-called "nondisabled." For disabled people, the serious difficulties and dilemmas confronting the nondisabled in the area of intimate relationships are multiplied, and new problems are introduced by the presence of the disability.

Disabled People's Rights to Intimate Relationships

Probably the clearest indication that disabled people have second-class citizenship is the existence of a debate as to whether several categories of disabled people can or should marry or have children. Though the debate is becoming increasingly less relevant or powerful, many of the issues and dilemmas remain.

Rehabilitation has, until very recently, focused on and been legitimized by disabled peoples' return to gainful employment and to education and/or training to the extent that it was essential to gainful employment. No concerted effort was made to help disabled people maintain and re-establish satisfactory interpersonal relationships and intimacy, because it was not considered necessary (Greengross, 1976). After all, these were disabled people, and, as second-class citizens, they could not expect to have the same rights and privileges as others. It was believed and often written that "they should be grateful to be able to work and be financially independent," and the disabled were socialized to share these beliefs (Safilios-Rothschild, 1976). The lack of concern with the social and psychological well-being and rights of the disabled in the 1950s and 1960s was illustrated by the fact that rehabilitation success was measured by the disabled person's gainful employment and not by the extent to which the type of work they did corresponded to their education and experience or the extent of promotion and advancement possible (Safilios-Rothschild, 1970).

These trends continued as long as the nondisabled kept making the important decisions for the disabled and as long as the voices of the disabled, like those of other second-class citizens, such as the old, the poor, and women, were not heard. Nondisabled people in different types of positions and with different degrees of authority made *not only medical but also personal decisions for the disabled,* including decisions as to whether they could be "good" marital partners and responsible parents. The nondisabled used criteria, in making these decisions, that required levels of ability and responsibility that few nondisabled people could meet.

In the absence of a social movement for the disabled or of a strong identification among them with other disabled people, the well-educated and highly skilled among them did not become spokesmen for others with disabilities, but were integrated into the nondisabled world instead. The same has been true for all other minority groups. In the 1970s, however, the social movement of the disabled began to emerge with a different intensity in some states and cities, and many eloquent disabled people were heard. As soon as the disabled people started to talk about themselves and their wishes, it became quite clear that they wanted their full rights and that their criterion for successful rehabilitation is the ability to establish intimate relationships: friendships, love, marriage. In a sense, it is ironic that disabled people have now gained the right to intimate relationships when we are all groping for ways to establish rewarding, meaningful, secure relationships and very few, through trial and error, are succeeding.

Type of Disability and Degree of Stigmatization

Disabled people's ability to establish interpersonal relationships and intimacy is greatly influenced by the type of disability and the degree of stigmatization of the disability. There is considerable evidence that some disabilities are consistently more stigmatized than others among the disabled as well as the nondisabled. Autobiographical accounts by disabled people have clearly shown how those who are less stigmatized are quite prejudiced against those who are more stigmatized (Hunt, 1966).

One study has shown that the five least stigmatized disabilities are ulcers, arthritis, asthma, diabetes, and heart disease in ascending order of stigmatization (Tringo, 1970). It is interesting to note that these disabilities are quite prevalent and can afflict those with high social status, especially men. Ulcer and heart disease, after all, have been the disabilities of masculine occupational success. In addition, the high prevalence of these disabilities increases people's familiarity with them, since most people have probably had contact with an afflicted family member or close friend. This type of contact and familiarity has been found to be conducive to significant decreases in prejudice (Gaier et al., 1968). This may explain why they are not stigmatized and why the disabled persons can have intimate relationships as "normal" as their symptoms and their own self-definitions and reactions to their disability will allow them.

After those five least-stigmatized disabilities, the hierarchy goes as follows: amputation, blindness, deafness, stroke, cancer, old age, paraplegia, epilepsy, dwarfism, cerebral palsy, hunchback, tuberculosis, criminal record, mental retardation, alcoholism, mental illness (Tringo, 1970). What is quite peculiar in this hierarchy is that cancer, despite the fact that it is quite widespread and very often afflicts high-social-status males, is more stigmatized than blindness and deafness, disabilities which are very often congenital and seriously impair the disabled person's ability to communicate. A possible explanation is the fact that the data were collected in the late 1960s before facts and discussions about cancer became public, before prominent figures and their wives made their disability and treatment public, and before the prognosis for some types of cancer was improved.

Otherwise, the hierarchy of stigmatized disabilities shows that sensory disabilities are less stigmatized than visible disabilities that seriously impair people's mobility (paraplegia, cerebral palsy) or deforming disabilities (dwarfism, hunchback). Both types of disabilities are less stigmatized than those that are viewed as decreasing people's ability for rationality, self-control, responsibility, or morality such as mental retardation, alcoholism, and mental illness. Another series of studies has shown that facial disfigurements carry the greatest stigma among children and adults (Richardson et al., 1961), but because mental retardation, alcoholism, and mental illness were not included, we could hypothesize that facial disfigurement is still less stigmatized than the above disabilities. Obesity has also been found to be highly stigmatized (Cahnman, 1968; Richardson, et al., 1961), possibly as much as the most stigmatized of the above disabilities since the notion exists that obese people must lack self-control and must be, to some extent, weak and irresponsible people.

Within the context of this chapter, we will not discuss the least stigmatized, nonvisible disabilities. Instead, we will focus on stigmatized disabilities that interfere with the disabled person's ability to establish friendships and other intimate relationships. An earlier review of the relevant literature (Safilios-Rothschild, 1976) showed that, in the case of visible disabilities, disabled and nondisabled adolescents as well as adults attributed better qualities to, and preferred, nondisabled persons as friends. In fact, a study showed that a visible handicap was a greater deterrent to the establishment of friendship than race (Richardson & Royce, 1968). Clearly, therefore, not only the degree of stigmatization but also visibility of the disability are very salient characteristics with regard to the establishment of friendships and other intimate relationships. In addition, the onset of the disability is a very important factor. Congenital disabilities or those that occur during childhood or adolescence can be distinguished from those which occur in adulthood. The ensuing discussion will take into consideration these salient characteristics of disabilities.

The Role Played by Acquaintance on People's Perceptions of Disabled People

Visibly disabled people consistently experience a much greater strain in everyday interactions with nondisabled or less-stigmatized, nonvisibly disabled persons than those with nonvisible disabilities. There is considerable evidence that very often people do not want to enter unpredictable and, therefore, stressful interactions with visibly disabled people, and they avoid doing so by extending only "fictional acceptance" which does not go beyond a polite, inhibited, and overcontrolled interaction (Davis, 1961; Kleck, 1966; Kleck et al., 1966). The first impressions are difficult, and they can color the whole interaction. There is, however, some evidence that if this fictional acceptance stage is overcome, people's personalities can be more important than their appearance. One study has shown, for example, that children with normative values, that is, more conforming children, prefer nonhandicapped children as friends before they have a chance to get to know them more often than nonconformist children with atypical values. After they have a chance to get to know the children in a summer camp setting, however, the difference between conforming and nonconforming children disappears (Richardson, 1971). These results support the idea that contact on a voluntary, equal basis is conducive to the breakdown of prejudice.

The same study, however, also showed that visibly disabled children preferred nondisabled children as friends before they had a chance to interact with them, but they restricted themselves to the visibly disabled children after they had a chance to interact with both disabled and nondisabled children (Richardson, 1971). Other autobiographies of obese adolescents have shown mixed data in terms of friendships and dating with nonobese people (Cahnman, 1970). Before we can understand the dynamics of the impact that acquaintance has on chances for establishing friendships and intimate relationships, we need observation studies of interactions between disabled people with control of such important variables as dogmatism and self-esteem.

Some observations have shown that a nondisabled person's acceptance of a visibly disabled person is enhanced by his or her ability to establish one close friendship with a nondisabled person (Allen, 1976). It seems that the existence of such a friendship increases the desirability of the disabled person in the eyes of others and provides a possible model for other similar relationships by "normalizing," in a sense, the visibly disabled person.

When it comes to the nonvisibly disabled, we know even less how interpersonal dynamics operate once the stigmatized disability becomes known. The research on mentally retarded who can pass as "normals" up to a certain point cannot provide us with universally applicable cues because of the extremely negative stigma attached to the disability.

Options and Dilemmas about Intimate Relationships

Probably the most fundamental dilemma all minorities have to face is whether to try to establish intimate relationships within "their own kind" or to venture out to a wider circle of people. As Weinberg aptly summarized the results of the dilemma for the visibly disabled: the wider a visibly disabled person's social space (that is, the interactive network with those other than "his own kind"), the narrower his sociable space (that is, his field of intimate primary relationships— eligible dates and mates) (Weinberg, 1968).

The organizational solution to this dilemma has been recreational clubs matched by disabled people's associations, which have been serving similar recreational functions. Of course, there is a basic difference between recreational clubs established by hospitals or agencies for the disabled and associations controlled by the disabled. The second are clearly preferred by the disabled. But even becoming a member of the Association of the Little People of America or of deaf communities implies a more or less complete identification with other dwarfs and midgets or deaf people and abandoning the attempt to establish intimate relationships with nondisabled people or even people with different types of disabilities. In the case of deaf people, the identification with the deaf community is not only at the sociopsychological level. It has clear-cut behavioral consequences, namely, the use of sign language rather than speech and lip-reading to communicate (Higgins, 1979). Sign language as a communication strategy is clearly directed only toward other deaf people who use sign language and identify with other deaf people. In this way, the deaf cut themselves off from possibilities for interaction and relationships with the nondeaf, including those with other kinds of disabilities.

Although the example of the deaf is an extreme one, because basic communication is involved, the patterns are similar, though somewhat less drastic, for other disabled groups. For those who become disabled as adults, it is often more difficult to stop identifying with the nondisabled than for those who were socialized into disabled status, especially by going to special schools.

Those who refuse to identify with the disabled "of their own kind" may develop different social and psychological strategies to cope with their disabilities, especially when the disability is visible or when it interferes with everyday functioning. At the psychological level, they may still think of themselves as nondisabled by stretching the boundaries between disabled and nondisabled on the one hand, and by clearly differentiating themselves from other more severely or more stigmatized disabled people, on the other hand. At the social level, they may develop different sets of strategies to deal with important dilemmas such as the following:

1.   If they already have intimate relationships or a spouse, depending on the quality of the relationships and the reactions of the nondisabled spouse, the disabled person may emphasize or de-emphasize the disability.

2.   If they do not have an intimate relationship or a spouse (or have lost their partner because of the disability), they may put on an overconfident act and try to initiate relationships at the risk of being hurt. Or they may try to maximize the probability of succeeding by offering more than they receive or by selecting partners of lesser attractiveness or desirability. Of course, it must be noted that sometimes they may find themselves in a passive role. Some men and women may prefer and choose a disabled person for a friend, lover, or spouse for a variety of reasons. They may be insecure people who feel that there is less likelihood of being jilted and hurt in a relationship with a disabled person who has less options and would be "grateful" for the relationship. They may be idealistic people who need to help and love disabled people who are rejected by others and feel lonely and unhappy. They may be unattractive, or not very successful or socially desirable people who think that the other person's disability outweighs their own characteristics of low "market" value (the classical case is that of an attractive blind man or woman who marries an unattractive partner). But there are many other examples in which intimacy with a less desirable non-disabled person is clearly bartered for a variety of very desirable socioeconomic and sociopsychological characteristics of a disabled person.

3.   Under the influence of the increasing spirit of cynicism, some adult disabled people may opt for sexuality with or without rudiments of intimacy. For many disabled people, sexuality at a price may be the easy way out of the frustrations involved with trying to establish an intimate relationship. Other disabled adults may limit satisfaction of their needs for intimacy to same- and cross-sex friendships without venturing into the more agitated seas of love or marriage.

In the case of congenitally disabled people, additional problems and difficulties have to be faced because they often have not been able to develop the usual interpersonal skills and test them through friendships, play, and dating. This lack of socialization into intimacy with nondisabled as well as other disabled people is extreme for those congenitally disabled who were institutionalized at an early age, for those who had to attend a special school because their disability seriously interfered with their ability to communicate, or for those with a stigmatized visible disability such as facial deformity. For this category of disabled people, it is very comfortable and seductive to stay within their own community, where they are wholeheartedly accepted by people with whom they share many life experiences and where the probability of establishing intimate relationships is greater, and that of being rebuffed is smaller, than in the outside world.

This greater comfort, acceptance, and ease in finding friends and dates is, however, outweighed in the minds of many disabled people (with congenital as well as disabilities acquired later in life) by the realization that they are confining themselves to a "disabled ghetto." As has been true for ethnic or racial ghettos, its members as well as the larger society recognize that achievements and accomplishments within the ghetto do not count for much within the larger society and that, therefore, the only real accomplishments are those outside the ghetto. Disabled people know that having been able to establish intimate relationships, including marriage, within the ghetto-like community of people with the same type of disability is not rated a significant success. They may, therefore, develop different strategies to deal with this:

1. They may define as valid only intimate relationships achieved with nondisabled people. Thus either they avoid establishing intimate relationships with "their own kind" altogether by not interacting with other similarly disabled people, or they may intermittently find refuge in the disabled community when they are trying to recover from rejections and hurt from the nondisabled world. Although there are no exact data as to how many people within each kind of disability follow this strategy, there are some indications that there is a large number of them or even the majority (Higgins, 1979; Weinberg, 1968).

2. Some, though they define as satisfactory only intimate relationships with nondisabled, for a variety of reasons, do not dare or do not have an opportunity, or simply never succeed in establishing intimate relationships. They resign themselves to staying within the community of similarly disabled people. There are no data as to how many disabled people fall into this category or in what ways they reconcile themselves to the situation.

3. Some disabled people may define all intimate relationships as equally important, their satisfactoriness and significance depending on the nature of the relationship rather than the disabled or nondisabled status of their friend or partner. Such disabled people have been able to transcend their disability and view themselves and others as human beings—attractive or unattractive, interesting or uninteresting, compatible or incompatible—personalities, rather than disabled or nondisabled. More research is needed to understand what the factors are that help disabled (and nondisabled) people view the world in this way. Research in other types of prejudice, specifically, gender prejudice, has shown that a low degree of dogmatism significantly associated with a high degree of positive self-esteem are the most important variables distinguishing those who can view men and women in nonstereotyped ways and who can establish intimate, cross-sex friendships (Safilios-Rothschild & Wong, 1979). Most probably, the same variables would be important for disabled and nondisabled people's ability to see and relate to each other in a nonstereotyped, nondichotomous fashion.

4. Some disabled people choose to relate mainly to similarly disabled people, limiting their social life, their friendships, and their loves to the disabled community. They usually claim that their identification is only with the disabled world and that they measure their success and feel happy according to how well they do within the disabled world (Higgins, 1979). In recent years the ideological enthusiasm of the disabled people's social movement has helped disabled people redefine themselves and project a new image of themselves which is in no way inferior to that of nondisabled people. Thus their social movement can provide disabled people with much-needed self-confidence and self-esteem and the option to identify truly with other disabled people and not just those with the same disabilities. This may lead to their staying primarily within the disabled community as a transitory strategy until they are able to find new strategies to renegotiate the interpersonal basis of relationships with nondisabled people not solely on the conditions of the nondisabled (Safilios-Rothschild, 1972).

In the late 1970s it has been evident that the emerging social movement of the disabled has been making a significant impact. Although there has been no systematic study tracing the development and sociopsychological influences of the movement, there are many indications that the social structure has begun to change toward the accommodation of disabled people's needs for leisure, fun, and a variety of interpersonal relationships, from friendship to marriage. Individuals or groups of disabled people have begun to travel much more extensively, both nationally and internationally, testing the limits of barriers to disabled people and compiling useful travel guides for others (Annand, 1977; Couch, 1977; Weiss, 1977). Increasingly, television networks have responded to the new voices raised by disabled people by presenting during prime viewing hours several movies in which even severely stigmatized disabled people such as the mentally retarded are shown falling in love and displaying mixtures of tenderness, love, devotion, and everyday difficulties similar to those of everyone else. Even *Mademoiselle* magazine, in 1978, carried a fashion article in which a very attractive college student in a wheelchair was shown wearing different sets of clothes fashionable and appropriate for a girl in a wheelchair.

Is Marriage the Pinnacle of Intimacy?

There is considerable evidence that many disabled people with visible or congenital disabilities have been able to marry. Even mentally retarded people have married, although their marriage rates have been significantly lower than those for the entire population. Far fewer married retarded people have had children because of semivoluntary or clearly imposed eugenic sterilization (Bell, 1976; Hall, 1974; Floor, et al., 1975; Henshel, 1972). In the case of the mentally retarded, women have had a better chance to marry normal or mentally retarded partners than have men, because mental retardation affects men's ability to be successful breadwinners. Mentally retarded women, on the other hand, could fulfill, in its extreme, the traditional stereotype for women!

However, as marriage in itself has ceased to be considered the pinnacle of success in intimacy, disabled people will be able to explore among different avenues for the satisfaction of their intimate needs and find the ones that best fit them. With the reinforcement of their social movement and ideology, they will have to find their way out of segregation by settling their own conditions and by renegotiating interpersonal relations with other disabled persons as well as with the nondisabled.

References and Bibliography

Allen, B. *Interaction processes between the able-bodied and persons confined to wheelchairs.* Unpublished manuscript, University of Western Ontario, December 1976.

Annand, D. R. *The wheelchair traveler*. Milford, N.H.: Wheelchair Traveler, 1977.

Bell, N. IQ as a factor in community lifestyle of previously institutionalized retardates. *Mental Retardation,* 1976, *14*(3), 29–33.

Cahnman, W. J., The stigma of obesity. *The Sociological Quarterly,* 1968, *9*(3), 283–299.

Cahnman, W. J. *The stigma of overweight—six autobiographies.* Unpublished manuscript, Rutgers University, Department of Sociology, mimeographed, 1970.

Couch, G. R. Charting the unknown for those to follow. *Rehabilitation/ World,* 1977, *3*(2), 8–11.

Davis, F. Deviance disavowal: The management of strained interactions between the visibly handicapped. *Social Problems,* 1961, *9*(2), 120–132.

Floor, L., Baxter, D., Rosen, M., & Zisfein, L. A survey of marriages among previously institutionalized retardates. *Mental Retardation,* 1975, *13*(2), 33–37.

Gaier, E. L., et al. Contact as a variable in the perception of disability. *The Journal of Social Psychology,* 1968, *74*, pp. 117–126.

Greengross, W. *Entitled to have the sexual and emotional needs of the handicapped.* London: Malaby Press, 1976.

Hall, J.E. Sexual behavior. In J. Wortis (Ed.), *Mental retardation and developmental disabilities.* New York: Brunner/Mazel, 1974.

Henshel, A. M. *The forgotten ones: A sociological study of Anglo and Chicano retardates.* Austin, Tex.: University of Texas Press, 1972.

Higgins, P.C. Outsiders in a hearing world. *Urban Life,* 1979, *8*, 3–22.

Hunt, P. (Ed.) *Stigma: The experience of disability.* London: Chapman, 1966.

Kleck, R. Emotional arousal in interactions with stigmatized persons. *Psychological Reports,* 1966, *19*, 1226.

Kleck, R., et al. The effects of physical deviance on face-to-face interactions. *Human Relations,* 1966, *19*(4), 425–436.

Lasch, C. *The culture of narcissism.* New York: Norton, 1979.

Richardson, S. A. Children's values and friendships: A study of physical disability. *Journal of Health and Social Behavior,* 1971, *12*, 253–258.

Richardson, S. A., et al. Cultural uniformity in reaction to physical disability. *American Sociological Review,* 1961, *26*(2).

Richardson, S. A., & Royce, J. Race and physical handicap in children's preference for other children. *Child Development,* 1968, *39*, 467–480.

Safilios-Rothschild, C. *The sociology and social psychology of disability and rehabilitation.* New York: Random House, 1970.

Safilios-Rothschild, C. Social integration of the disabled: Toward another social movement? *Rehabilitation Digest,* 1972, *4*, 14–15.

Safilios-Rothschild, C. The self-definitions of the disabled and implications for rehabilitation. In G. Albrecht (Ed.), *The sociology of disability and rehabilitation.* Pittsburgh: University of Pittsburgh Press, 1976.

Safilios-Rothschild, C. *Love, sex, and sex roles.* Englewood Cliffs, N.J.: Prentice-Hall, 1977.

Safilios-Rothschild, C. Toward a social psychology of relationships. *Psychology of Women Quarterly,* 1981, 5(3), 377–384.

Safilios-Rothschild, C., & Wong, H. *The effect of dogmatism and self-esteem on attitudes toward military women.* Paper prepared for the Southeast Regional Conference on Changing Military Manpower Realities: Strategic and Organizational Implications for the 1980's. Maxwell Air Force Base, Alabama, May 1979.

Tringo, J. L. The hierarchy of preference toward disability groups. *Journal of Special Education,* 1970, 4(3), 295–305.

Weinberg, M. S. The problems of midgets and dwarfs and organizational remedies: A study of the little people of America. *Journal of Health and Social Behavior,* 1968, 9,(1), 65–71.

Weiss, L. *Access to the world: A travel guide for the handicapped.* New York: Chatham Square, 1977.

5 Claiming the Self

The Cripple as American Male

Leonard Kriegel

When I was first asked to contribute to this book, my initial reaction
was to question exactly what I might be able to contribute to a text
about problems faced by *Disabled People as Second-Class Citizens*.
I am not a physician; I am not a psychologist; I am not a sociologist; I
do not work in the health-care field. I am, however, an individual
who has lived 35 of his 46 years here on earth as a cripple, a word
which I prefer to either *handicapped* or *disabled,* each of which
seems to me a euphemism for the realities facing us. And I have,
during a writing career that covers 20 years, written rather extensively about my own struggle with disability. It occurred to me that
the only valid perspective I could bring to this text remained what I
had pulled from the rage, fury, and pride—and I ask here not your
indulgence but the empathy of your own pride—of having survived
as a cripple in America. For if I have, in my own eyes, anything to
boast of before my fellow men, it is that I have endured—and that I
know the price that my endurance has demanded of me.

Both as a writer and as a teacher of literature, I have long since
felt that perhaps the most powerful lines I have ever read were those
God addresses to Moses in Chapter 3 of the Book of Exodus. Our
purpose is not, I assume, to seek heaven's solace. But I will quote
two verses from that chapter. Moses has been ordered by God,
speaking through the burning bush, to go to Egypt and free the
Israelites in bondage there. From the text, we can infer that Moses is
less-than-eager to undertake the mission. And the following interesting exchange takes place at this point:

> 13 And Moses said unto God, Behold, when I come unto the children
> of Israel, and shall say unto them, The God of your fathers hath sent me
> unto you; and they shall say to me, What is his name? What shall I say
> unto them?

14 And God said unto Moses, I am that I am: and he said, Thus
shalt thou say unto the children of Israel, I am hath sent me unto you.

Now I have included this passage because I believe that in
God's answer to Moses we discover the unequivocal reality behind
all of our excursions into human psychology, the very essence of
what we somewhat glibly refer to as The Human Condition. For
each of us seeks to create a meaningful *I*, one who has been stamped
with his own distinct individuality. One is almost tempted to write
that our relationship with God is one of perpetual envy, for God
alone among us can absolutely and interminably identify the *I* he
embodies as belonging to him alone. It is the kind of affirmation we
seek in the lives of those men and women we assume exist beyond
our capacity, beyond our habits and virtues and will—but not beyond
our needs. For like God, each individual stakes his claim to an identifiable *I* that is his and his alone.

Of course, it is a tentative claim. It exists within the confines of a
world man is never truly at home in, a world he must shape even as
it shapes him. It is a man's capacity as an individual that is always
being tested, his ability to face those obstacles that stand in front of
him, to accept them as the inevitable burdens of a life he is in the
process of living. Everywhere, we seek to affirm the separate self,
the identifiable *I* who possesses the strength and courage to with-
stand whatever tests lie in wait for him. And no one, we soon discover—a discovery that never ceases to amaze me—has a greater
right to claim that *I* than the man who has wrested his sense of
himself from the very condition which declared his existence as a
man at an end. No one can claim the prerogatives of a manhood that
has been seized from adversity in quite the same manner as the
cripple can.

That the individual who must struggle hardest to declare himself
a man should become the very embodiment of manhood is a typically American paradox. But the cripple is forced to affirm his existence by pushing himself beyond those structures his handicap has
created. On a certain level it can be argued that this is what all men
and women do. After all, what else do we mean when we speak of an
individual's consciousness of his or her own humanity? But in a
culture which places such stress on the physical—however uncomfortable it may still be with the body—the cripple's insistence on
pushing beyond the restrictions imposed by his own physical limitations is an observable reality, that kind of violent joining together of
opposites that is so characteristic of modern life.

I do not mean by this that the cripple is envied by other Americans. Far from it. Were we to survey our fellow Americans, they would understandably reject the idea that the position of the physically handicapped is to be envied. And none of us would argue with that. Ask any man who must contemplate the prospect of spending his life in a wheelchair whether he would exchange that fate for a normal pair of legs, and the answer would, obviously, be a ringing affirmation. Ask me whether I would give up these braces and crutches to which I have been obligated ever since I was taught how to manipulate them as a boy of twelve, and I would accept without a moment's hesitation. To insist on one's capacity, to be willing to undertake the everyday risks that the cripple must confront simply in order to meet the world on relatively equal terms, even to enjoy the triumph and liberation that an *earned* mobility bestows on one—we can accept all of this and yet still hunger after what we are not. A man can believe in his own courage; a man can assume that his existence has been paid for by a price that would have broken so many others; a man can think of himself as having confronted his fate like Jacob wrestling with his angel. But a man *cannot* lie to himself.

The very title of this book, *Disabled People as Second-Class Citizens*, speaks of the everyday realities we are forced to face. It is not only our knowledge of those barriers the outside world imposes on us, however, that makes us think of our citizenship as second-class. It is also the inevitable pressure of what we know we have missed, of those elements in our lives whose significance is multiplied a hundredfold by contact with an imagination which knows what they are but which has not yet possessed them. For the hungers are invariably personal, the joys not tasted are joys not tasted *by me*. Those desires are *my* desires. And they are not abstract. However simple they may seem to others, they remain what I want. However absurd and childish they may be labeled by the world, they remain what I can feel myself reaching out for and touching in my imagination. And I find myself enraged that those the distinguished social-psychologist Erving Goffman has labeled the "normals" should be able to touch them so readily, so unconsciously. For my condition tells me that a man should earn what he possesses. And however successful the world may deem me—and in the world's eyes, I am a man who has, to use a phrase I believe should be cauterized from our language, "overcome his handicap to live a normal life"—I still know what it is I want. I stand before you a 46-year-old college professor, the author of a number of books, the father of two splendid sons, the husband of a lovely wife, the recipient of a number of academic awards and honors—and a man whose dreams at night still make him alien to what that world defines as success. How shall I tell my "normal" colleagues that I still dream about running on the beach, that even at the age of 46 I desperately want to swing a baseball bat once again, that I lie awake at night wondering what I would do with normal legs, only to discover that what I want to do is banal in the eyes of the normal. I want to run on the beach, I want to kick a football, I want to jump rope, I want to ride a bike, I want to climb a mountain—not a metaphor for achievement, just a real hon-est-to-God mountain—I want to ride a horse. I want to shop differ-ently; I want to make love differently; I want to walk to the movies differently; I want to drive differently; I want to know my children differently. The list could so easily be extended, but perhaps it is enough to note simply that I want to know the world differently.

These are not great feats of the imagination. They do not call for special skills or training. But they are what I want, what I have never tasted or else have tasted so long ago that the memory itself has become one with the desire, locked in a permanent embrace. And such memories, along with such desires, frame all that is absent from my existence at this present time.

We hear so much today about authenticity, the need to create an individuality which is both specific and personal. All through Amer-ica, men struggle not only to define themselves but to avoid being defined by others. And yet, when the cripple looks around himself, he discovers that he is defined from the outside. Our complaint against society—a complaint that lies at the very heart of this book—is not so much that society ignores our presence as that it ignores our reality, our sense of ourselves as human beings brave enough to capture our destinies against formidable odds. It is in this respect that the cripple and society are at war with one another. If we were satisfied to be objectified, to be infantilized on telethons, we would probably dis-cover that this America has a great deal of time for us, a great deal of room for us in a heart it wishes to hear praised. Our problem is not, to use Ralph Ellison's metaphor for the black man in America, that we are invisible. It is, rather, that the terms of our visibility have been created not by us but by those who will see what they want to see rather than what is there. If we look at our image in literature, what we discover is not ourselves but our condition—or at least what is taken to be our condition—which is portrayed for the world. We discover that our true selves, our inner lives, have been auctioned off, that we have been made palatable rather than real, that the world will continue to wish to see us as victim or demon, the object of its charity or the object of its scorn. Of one thing, however, we can be certain—the world will turn a blind eye and a deaf ear to our real selves until we impose those selves on the world. Years ago this recognition led me to write an essay entitled, "Uncle Tom and Tiny Tim: Some Reflections on the Cripple as Negro." There has been, I believe, a hopeful change from the analysis that essay offered of the cripple's position in society. What I hinted at—that the cripple might help to establish the terms of his existence in normal society only when he seized hold of the power to define who he was and where he was going—has increasingly been transformed into the terms of our situation today. It is not Tiny Tim whom we seize as a metaphor for our existence today. It is, rather, the authentic self, the *I* that has been wrested from adversity whom we now claim as our embodiment.

It is exactly here that the cripple discovers that society is more than a bit dubious about his achievement. It may even be afraid of that achievement. It is one thing for society to recognize our need for care: as a matter of fact, it is in meeting that need that society is most comfortable with us. It honors what it views as our suffering. But it retreats from what it sees as our growing ability to define our inner lives, to say who and what we are. For society seems to need that ability to define us in order to be comfortable with us. When I returned from a two-year stay in a state rehabilitation hospital at the age of thirteen, my mother was immediately asked by the neighborhood chairman of the March of Dimes (this was in 1946, before Dr. Salk's vaccine) to go from door to door to collect in the annual drive. Both he and my mother assumed that she would be more effective in this capacity than anyone else in our neighborhood, for she had been given a kind of subaltern authenticity as a mother of a cripple. Her presence was expected to remind our normal neighbors that she had *earned* their charity. Another individual going from door to door would simply not have been as "authentic."

That same society which was then at home with giving its largesse to my mother is now at home giving to muscular dystrophy telethons, to religious attempts to help children, to the efforts of such organizations as the Shriners to support hospitals. Perhaps the motives of all these groups and organizations are honorable. But they also serve to illustrate how society defines the cripple by seeing only his condition. And society manages to do this while keeping itself oblivious to the feelings it inspires in him. In January 1968 I was vacationing in Florida with my wife and children. While driving down the coast, we passed a large shopping center. Strung out on a huge white marquee in bold black letters was a sign that read: "Help Crippled Kids! See Stalin's Limousine! Donation: $1.00."

Now this is the material of absurdity, the kind of material that can be dealt with effectively by a novelist with the talents of a Kafka or a Nathanael West rather than by a social scientist, for it is a denial of the human. But it is also a form of definition society itself accepts. In fact, it is *the* definition that the cripple discovers stands in his path as he pushes toward the possibility of authenticity. He wants his realizable self; society wants to be made to feel good. Added to the cripple's problems as he reaches out for his authenticity is the resistance he must offer to what society tells him is properly his. He is, he discovers, a man whose conception of himself must be inflicted on society. His task is not only to say who he is but to point out to the world that his agony is not to be marketed as if he were a perpetual child being *told* what to do and how to behave. The authenticity he must insist on is what *he and he alone*—not his physicians, not his nurses, not his friends or relatives, but he alone—has created for himself. For no one knows the cost of his existence as he does. No one has lived with the intimacy of his fears as he has. And no one better understands that the self's true authenticity can be taken only from the self's resistance. It is not, finally, the crippled kids who will offer their souls for sale to feed our national need for charity. It would be better for them to laugh Stalin's limousine out of existence.

It is to his powers of resistance that one must address his admiration when he speaks about the situation of the cripple in America. This is particularly true now, when the mass of American men seem so torpid and confused. In fact, the cripple's situation may be a prototype for the general situation of men in this country. If part of me still hungers to perform those mundane tasks that define most lives, another part—the braver part, I suspect—insists that the mark of a man is that he permits himself to be formed by the very accidents that have made him what he is, that he can only be called a man when he openly embraces his situation. We have, after all, been formed by the passion with which we view the potential of our individual lives. In this the task of the cripple is to be brave enough to face what the normal can choose to ignore. The normal has that option, or at least he thinks he has, but those of us who have consciously chosen to take a chance at an existence pulled from disease or accident learn early on that we are isolated. Our condition turns out to be more intense than the rest of the world can afford to admit. Our isolation is massive. We cannot seize hold of those supports that give balance to the life of the normal. Society views us as both pariah and victim; we are pitied, shunned, labeled, analyzed, classified, and categorized. Sooner or later we are packed in the spiritual ice of a sanitized society in the hope that we can somehow be dealt with in some even more sanitized society of the future. Society will *permit* us everything—other, that is, than the right *to be* what we are—for without that right, it knows that we are nothing.

Society is uncomfortable with us. It is not uncomfortable with what it can do for us. Not at all. That sign in the shopping center was created by a *giving* society. Those telethons featuring a semi-maniacal Jerry Lewis are responded to by men and women who think they are *charitable*. Those well-meaning Shriners interviewed at halftime during the East-West football games they sponsor—let me remind you of the game's motto: "Strong legs run so that weak legs can walk"—do not believe that they have tampered with our reality. Disease and injury bring out the self-consciously charitable, even the sanctimonious, in other men. What we cripples discover we share is not so much a physical condition—the differences among us are far more pronounced than differences between white and black, gentile and Jew, Italian and German—as it is the experience of having been categorized by the normals. In their view we possess only a collective presence—for in their view we cannot be permitted a sense of individuality. If *we* prove ourselves capable of defining our own lives, then what explanation can they offer for *their* failure? If a cripple can break with the arbitrary paralysis of his existence, can say, "I am that I am because I have earned the right to be what I am," then what can a normal offer as an excuse for his failure? And if the cripple can point to the primacy of his performance, then how does the normal account for his failure? Finally, if the cripple can discover in his own combat with circumstance not only survival but even a form of heroism, then where does that leave the normal?

I do not wish to suggest that one is better for having suffered disease or disability. That is quite obviously nonsense. All that I mean is that we have no choice but to establish the terms of our existence, the boundaries of our authenticity, and in doing so we inevitably discover that society is not going to be too happy with us. Only by turning our visible stigma into a source of strength can we escape categorization by the normals. Only in this way can we define ourselves, speak to a world whose hostility is clothed in indifference and say, "Here I am because here I have created what I am." We can hold up the ragged ends of our existence and demand that the normals match our honesty. In this way we can point out how others might confront their own authenticity in a time of conformity, a time during which the very idea of an authentic self has more or less been buried beneath one dulled variation after another on the theme of doing one's own thing.

What makes the cripple's situation so difficult for the normal to deal with is that the control of one's own destiny—even having a voice in one's own destiny—is at best problematic for anyone. But the cripple approaches that destiny knowing that the element of chance is even greater in his life than it is in the life of the normal. Having already witnessed the power of accident, he knows that if the reconciliation of one's needs with the world's actualities can lead to maturity, it can also lead to madness and despair and suicide. Under the best of circumstances, maturity is temporary. But under those circumstances dictated by disease and accident, it is what a man is condemned to live with. It is not the cripple who needs to be told, as Sartre phrases it, that "man is nothing else but what he makes of himself!" Every step we take, every breath we draw, every time we make love, cross a street, drive a car, we live out the terms of that argument. The existential condition about which so much has been written is the situation to which fate has so closely condemned us. The terror and joy of performance is ours. The desire to measure, to prove capacity, haunts the cripple's everyday life. And all the time, the image of what one was crashes against the fantasies of what one might have been, for if what Sartre writes is true—and I obviously believe it is—then an unvoiced corollary to his argument is that the man who creates his authentic self against great odds runs the risk of what used to be called, in a more religious time, the sin of pride.

There is a point at which the acceptance of one's own wound, the living on an everyday basis with that internal enemy who, as the late Ernest Becker wrote in *The Denial of Death,* constantly "threatens danger," leads to a certain haughtiness. Perhaps it even points to an unspoken contempt for those who have not been called on to prove their capacity as we have been forced to prove our own. After all, everything the cripple does, every act of love or hate, every victory he claims or defeat he suffers, has been pulled from the fire. The true secret that he must acknowledge is the extent to which he can take pride in his performance and impose a meaningful presence on the world. When a man matches himself against his own destruction, it is virtually inevitable that the normal's frame of reference comes to seem comic, perhaps even banal. A man who lives on intimate terms with pain as a condition of daily existence must listen with a certain amazement to a sportscaster praising the courage of an athlete who earns a great deal of money for his aching knees.

But even as he acknowledges the magnitude of his achievement, even as he learns that he has earned through discipline and persistence what others hunger after, the cripple is reminded that the normal can diminish his reality. He is trapped by reality itself. Although a man may choose to create an authentic self out of his defiance of accident or disease, he cannot remake the truth of his existence. No matter what he demands of himself, dead legs cannot run. He can make of injury an acquisition; he can transform his handicap into a symbol of his endurance; he can accept his existence as an act of defiance; but he cannot change what has happened to him. He knows that he is now in a position in which he must recognize that his life is to be different in its essentials from the lives of normals, for he has been tested and discovered to be not wanting. He has come through, and he has learned the value of coming through. He has learned to look on the stigma itself as something he has somehow earned, to admit to having been set apart. This process has been powerfully captured by Karl Shapiro in a poem about a soldier who suffers an amputation during World War II. The soldier must at first struggle to accept the loss of part of his body. He must learn to adapt to life without the leg, even as the life he possesses becomes itself a defiance of the wound. Here is a stanza from Shapiro's poem, "The Leg":

> Later, as if deliberately, his fingers
> Begin to explore the stump. He learns
>   shape
> That is comfortable and tucked in
>   like a sock.
> This has a sense of humor, this can
>   despise
> The finest surgical limb, the dignity
>   of limping,
> The nonsense of wheelchairs. Now he
>   smiles to the wall:
> The amputation becomes an acquisition*

But even such acquisitions can be taken away by the society that seeks to define the cripple, for that society remains intent, let us remind ourselves, on shrinking his reality through its definition of his function and reality. Even the effort he makes to live honestly pinches his sense of his own courage, his ability to live on his own terms. What we remember is embedded in what we are. The first book I ever wrote was an autobiography, *The Long Walk Home.* What I set out to do in that book was to capture my life for myself. My purpose was to tell the story of one individual's struggle with polio, without either sentimentality or false piety—and without bravado, too. I was going to write a book that depicted the war between

---

*Karl Shapiro, *Collected Poems 1940–1978* [New York: Random House, 1979], p. 38. Reprinted by permission of Random House, Inc.

myself and the virus that had cut me off from my past, and I was
going to make it into a document that would match my conception of
what I had done with faultless honesty. It was a large ambition for a
young writer. But it was mine, and I knew that if I were not capable
of matching my fate with my honesty, I would ultimately fail as a
writer and fail as a man. When I first set down to shape the materials
of my past into a book, I assumed that what would prove to be
difficult were those scenes in which I relived the pain, the sense of
helplessness and loss of dignity that the onset of disease produces.
But these scenes proved easy to handle. They virtually wrote themselves. What proved difficult were those small defeats that made me
sweat as I relived them. I remember writing a scene in which I took
a young woman home from a date. I was eighteen; she was perhaps a
year younger. Embracing the young woman in order to kiss her good
night—which was all that custom permitted on first dates in 1951—I
slipped and fell. It is a memory that should at this distance be embraced with comic relief, but it still infuriates me, as it did when I
wrote *The Long Walk Home* some 16 years ago. If I am alive 16 years
from now, it will undoubtedly infuriate me then, for I still want to
right the balance for that moment, to make the scene more comfortable, more in keeping with the image of the man I know as myself.
As I wrote that scene, I could feel my rage at the injustice of my fate
spilling out of the typewriter. I hated not myself, but the circumstances which had trapped me from that moment.

I recently reread *The Long Walk Home*. It still seems to me an
honest book, but I can now also see how it speaks of my own limitations of vision, of how when I wrote it I was still viewing my life as
society told me it should be viewed, as the story of a man who has
"overcome a handicap to live a normal life." The last two lines of the
book read as follows: "At the cost of legs, I had won a self. How
much cheaper a price could I have expected to pay?" As I recall
these lines now, I wince, at least internally, for in a lifetime during
which I have written my share of sentences better forgotten, I can
think of no sentence as singularly untruthful as that last. I would give
a great deal to be able to take it back today. If I have learned nothing
else, I have learned how truly expensive all such "victories" are,
how fragmentary, how terribly short-lived, and how demeaning to
the legitimate and painful demands I had to make on myself in order
to survive to call the price cheap. Nothing I had ever before done,
and, I suspect, nothing I will do in the future, has cost me more or
has taken more out of me in my own quest for authenticity.

Fate manages to burrow beneath our illusions and to remind us
of who we are and what we are. A few months after *The Long Walk*

Home was published, I found myself living in a small Dutch fishing village. I was on a Fulbright year abroad, and I was, I confess, feeling rather smug about my life and rather vain about that self I had fashioned, like a man who draws for a five card inside straight in poker and discovers to his amazement that he has pulled a royal flush instead. I had my Fulbright, my book, my tenure at the college I still teach at today, my wife, my son, my "success" if you will. (As I speak to you in such possessive terms, I begin to feel like Mister Kurtz in Conrad's *Heart of Darkness*, although my "success" was not as ambitious as his. Still, it was mine.)

One day I was walking on the concrete embankment that paralleled the North Sea beach of *Noordwijk aan Zee*, the town in which we lived. My two-year-old son was walking with me, as he frequently did, holding onto the pinky that jutted out from the handle of my crutch and trying to keep up with his father's swing-through gait. Suddenly, he let go of my pinky and waddled on down the concrete incline of the embankment to the beach. He walked about 10 yards or so into the sand and then stopped. He waved to me, then waited for me to follow him. And I did follow him, for I was filled with a sense of selfhood captured that was so absolute that the illusion of power was greater than anything I had ever before experienced. It was an illusion so vivid that it literally devoured the reality of my past. I can phrase it in no other way than that I *knew* that I could run again, could pick my son up on my shoulders, cast braces and crutches aside, and run against that North Sea wind—a normal American father and his laughing American son—just like in the movies. For one brief moment the braces and crutches did not exist, the legs were not dead—even as I made my way down to the beach on those same braces and crutches.

Man makes himself, but he never remakes his circumstances, except, of course, in his fantasies. When my crutches hit the sand, reality once again hit me. My crutches sank, which is what crutches do on beaches when you try to walk. Not only would I not run with my two-year-old son against the wind, I was barely able to walk as I had been walking a minute earlier on the concrete. I had to give up the illusion, to allow it to be ripped from me and be replaced by a rage so pure, total, and all-devouring that it must have been that one step away from madness we speak about so often. It was a terrifying moment, for my mind was capable of such violence that I could have passed through that Dutch fishing village like a whirlwind of vengeance for my thwarted dreams. Instead, my wife arrived at my side and I retreated once again to the concrete.

No, the price is never cheap. And that authentic self is never really won. It recedes from the cripple's grasp, just as it can never really be won by the normals. It can be won only in fantasy, for fantasy creates the language of its own fulfillment. There a two-year-old boy can possess the patience and wisdom of Job. But when fantasy evaporates, we discover the final lesson that accidents and disease insist on. That lesson, too, must be absorbed, for no one knows better than the cripple that dignity as a man consists, finally, of the terms of the struggle he declares. No one knows better than the cripple that to live consciously is to live honestly, to acknowledge that his authentic self has been borrowed for a brief moment, borrowed for its own sake, and borrowed for the sake of all those sons he has left waiting on the beach.

6 Sex and Disability

Are They Mutually Exclusive?

Mary D. Romano

> Society creates handicaps. While most disabilities are products of birth and accident, the debilitating impact on a person's life often results not so much from the "disability" as from the manner in which others define or treat the person. (Gordon, 1974, p. 1)

In the interface between society and the individual there exist tacit expectations of behavior. These pre- and proscriptions affect every area of life; society expects the child to attend school and the adult to work, and, in turn, society is expected to provide opportunities for children and adults to do those things. Such behavioral expectations extend to areas of social and sexual interaction as well. In our society, for example, new acquaintance is sealed in a handshake; men, despite feminism, are generally expected to court women; adults are expected to marry and to function sexually to procreate as well as to use sexual activities as means of expressing feelings, of recreation, and of power and submission. These are prescribed behaviors. When the individual in the society happens to be disabled, however, that individual is confronted with a different set of prescriptions, many of which, in fact, are proscriptions, and nowhere is this more evident than in the areas of sexuality and social interactions.

What this chapter attempts is an exploration of those pre- and proscriptions. It will place them in an historical perspective, and it will explore avenues of remediation, for it is the posit of this chapter that it is time for those with disabilities to move out of second-class citizenship.

The author wishes to acknowledge her appreciation to Dr. James V. Romano for his editorial assistance.

Defining Sexuality in the Disabled

Sexuality as meant here is the complex aggregate of attitudes and behaviors that serve to express the manliness or womanness of each individual (Romano, 1973b). The attitude component of an individual's sexuality includes the person's self-image, the person's internalized values and expectations from his or her religious and ethnic backgrounds, and the degree to which the person has internalized those societal values and expectations that relate to manness and womanness. The behavioral component of sexuality includes a person's social interactional skills, the action and verbal manifestations of his or her attitudes, and sexual functioning which is here defined as the erogenous and genital components of sexuality (Trieschmann, 1978). Sexual functioning is thus a part of sexuality but not its whole; sexual functioning involves the physiological components of sexual expression, the logistics of sexual expression (coital positioning, contraception, varieties of sexual pleasuring, and so forth), and the purposes of sexual expression, among them procreation, recreation, and communication.

By disability, I refer in this chapter to a variety of conditions and illnesses—sometimes obvious, sometimes not immediately visible—that affect the way a person's body works. Thus a disability may involve difficulty walking, difficulty hearing or seeing, difficulty metabolizing sugar; it may involve a systemic malfunction, as in the mitotic processes of malignancy, and the therapeutic sequellae, be they surgical, chemotherapeutic, or radiological. Whatever the specific nature of a disability, however, it can be said that all disabilities have in common an impact on the individual in the way that individual lives. The peace, or lack thereof, that each individual who has a disability strikes with his condition may vary, and the acknowledgment of the condition becomes an issue in the person's self-image.

"Mutually exclusive," the issue raised in this chapter's title, is a descriptive term derived from probability theories in mathematics and logic; it describes states of events incapable of simultaneous existence (Hart, 1953; Kemeny, Snell, and Thompson, 1961). In looser parlance, mutually exclusive refers to incompatibility, to that which is inharmonious or antagonistic. Thus the question raised in the title of this chapter is whether sex and disability can exist simultaneously. Simplistically, the immediate answer is yes, based on the following syllogism: self-image is part of sexuality; disability is part of self-image; therefore, disability and sex are related. More germane, perhaps, would be to phrase the question in terms of antagonism or incompatibility, but to address that issue, one must consider the relationship between sex and disability as a process rather than a state.

From early times, disability has been perceived as a sign of moral weakness, as punishment for such weakness, and as justification for social discreditation (Goffman, 1963). This is seen in our earliest mythology. In the Greek myth of Hephaestus, for instance, Hephaestus was born lame as a punishment to his mother, Hera, for quarreling with his father, Zeus, and his mother, in disgust, threw Hephaestus out of heaven, in effect socially abandoning him because of his disability. Similarly, the Greek hero Philoctetes suffered a wound which grew so foul-smelling and painful that his companions could no longer stand the stench and his cries of pain; Agamemnon ordered that Philoctetes be abandoned in a deserted area, this action again illustrating the social isolation and discreditation that accompany disability (Tripp, 1970).

Even modern definitions of stigmata suggest a relationship between stigmata as marks indicative of disease or abnormality and as marks or tokens of infamy. This conceptual relationship has traditionally been socially manifested in patterns of social isolation of the handicapped. Institutionalized or hidden in back bedrooms, the disabled individual has historically been expected to accept social mirasmus as his due.

Language as an Impairment

The abrogation of personhood by virtue of physical handicap is clearly illustrated in the colloquial language of disability. Cripple, the lay label for an individual with a handicap, is a word not only suggestive of pervasive incompetence but is devoid of gender, and its use deprives its recipients of maleness or femaleness. Words such as cripple define their recipients by focusing on what is wrong rather than what is right with a person so that in addition to gender deprivation, which has significant and obvious implications in sexuality, the handicapped individual is deprived as well of all other identifying characteristics, both physical and characterological: tall/short, fair/dark, kind/mean, intelligent/stupid, generous/stingy, and so on.

It should be noted that this form of labeling is not confined to those whose experience with disabled people is limited. Health professionals use a form of deprivational labeling as well, and it, too, although more semantically sophisticated and specific, works toward the same effect as does its lay counterpart. Thus the health professional refers to an individual as an amputee, a cardiac, a diabetic, or a quadriplegic, and this label is used to define the person to whom it is applied.

If language is a mirror of society and culture, then it follows that implicit in society is the expectation that physical deviance subsumes other aspects of personhood and, to a considerable degree, negates them. However isolated people with handicaps and their families live in society, this societal expectation is often internalized by the disabled individual himself and by his family as well.

The implications of this in terms of the relationship between sexuality and disability are generally profound. Among them are the following:

1. To be disabled is to be asexual, or at best, half a person, with the remaining half asexual.

2. The disabled person should not be interested in anything sexual.

3. Disabled people are dependent and therefore childlike, and thus they require protection both "for their own good" and "for the good of society"; implicit in the latter is that if people with handicaps are permitted to function sexually, they will breed more handicapped people who will "burden" society.

4. Penile-vaginal intercourse ending in orgasm is the only form of "real" sexual function, and everything else is called "foreplay," suggesting, of course, that these other forms of sexual activity precede something else and are not in themselves "real" sex. When a disabled individual is unable to engage sexually according to these rules, the conclusion is that the disabled person cannot possibly have a satisfying sex life and might as well not even try.

5. If a nonhandicapped person has a sexual relationship with a disabled individual, it must be because the able-bodied person cannot find anyone else.

Exclusion of the Excluded

The belief that disability is a denial of personhood, sexual and otherwise, is not only manifested semantically but behaviorally in the alteration of usual interactive behaviors. Staring at a disabled individual is one such common behavioral manifestation, and intrusiveness is another; thus when the handicapped individual ventures out of his house, he becomes an object of visual attention and is considered fair game for such personal questions as What's wrong with you? How did it happen? Have you always been this way? Questioning is not the only form of intrusiveness, however. Suggestions and accusations—the former ranging from "You don't really want to go there, do you?" to recommendations of faith healers and the latter including imprecations of parental malfeasance and divine retribution—are frequently experienced by the handicapped individual, as is unsolicited help. Interactive behaviors such as these are virtually unique to those with disabilities and in our culture would be defined as highly socially inappropriate between able-bodied strangers. In that sense these behaviors are exclusionary, in that they demand that disabled people accept inappropriate interactions which are societally defined as unacceptable. This interactive model has an impact on the handicapped person's sexuality in many ways; it provides continuous validation for a belief in his "less than" status, forces him repeatedly to decide the degrees to which he will be self-revelatory and assertive, and denies him opportunity for reciprocal social interaction on an adult-adult basis. This interactive model requires constant internal attitudinal and external behavior struggles for disabled people to maintain a sense of personhood, competence, and desirability.

Inherent in this kind of interaction is the presumption that disabled people are children, that is, incompetent, needful of a measure of kindly protection coupled with firmness, and cognitively undeveloped. Behavioral manifestations of this presumption are pervasive in sociosexual issues for disabled people and are often accompanied by patronizing attitudes which put the handicapped individual in a one-down, defensive posture in relationship to others. One of the classic social interaction examples of this is the situation in which a disabled and an able-bodied individual are dining together in a restaurant, and the waiter asks the able-bodied person what the disabled individual would like to eat; the response hierarchy in this predicament ranges from capitulation, in which the able-bodied person does the ordering, to highly assertive, in which the disabled person bawls out the waiter. In the more sexual sphere, examples of this presumption might be that of depriving a handicapped person of sex education (What do you need that for?), of remarking on the "cuteness" of flirtatious behavior in a young disabled man or woman, or of denying contraceptive counseling to a handicapped woman (or, conversely, sterilizing her against her will).

Indeed, the assumption that disability is a tragedy—that to be disabled is to be sad, to be pitied, to be unusually courageous in the face of adversity—is one of the most exclusionary concepts in society. It seems obvious to say that people live with or in spite of handicaps and that, in fact, almost everyone will face disability as part of the life process. Yet reminders of our own frailty, rather than stimulating the empathy and behavior that we being able-bodied ourselves would want, more typically cause us to deny.

There is, of course, historical precedent for this, not only in the Greek myths mentioned earlier but also in biological and medical reality.

Medical, Physiological, and Sociological Developments

Until relatively recent years, many people who suffered disabling illnesses and injuries died with dispatch. Measles and poliomyelitis, common cripplers in the first half of this century, are now entirely preventable as the result of the development of vaccines; meningitis and other infectious processes are now treatable by antibiotics, the existence of which were unknown before World War II and which did not enter public usage until the late 1940s. Such medical advances have not only altered the careers of the sick but have made possible a degree of healthy survival previously unknown to mankind. In a related way, techniques of rapid medical evacuation and treatment, developed by the military for use in managing the wounded in combat situations, have been broadened to use in cases of civilian injury. Many major medical centers, for instance, now have helicopter landing pads, so that severely burned or newly spinal cord injured individuals can be quickly moved from the site of injury to medical care facilities. Such evacuation techniques, coupled with medical advances, have changed the course of disability by decreasing fatality as an expected outcome.

With this improvement in survival statistics has come increased knowledge and understanding of the physiology of disability so that heretofore routine complications of disabling conditions are redefined as preventable. Pressure sores (decubiti), upper respiratory infections, urinary tract infections, and renal calculi, all of which were once considered normal sequellae of mobility handicaps, are illustrative of this.

Medical and physiological advances such as these have been paralleled by sociological changes. Until the 1970 census, for example, there was no national attempt to ascertain the number of people with disabilities in the United States, and even in the 1970 census, the outcome was contingent on respondent definition, so that a person with diabetes or cancer or degenerative joint disease who did not identify himself as handicapped would not be counted as such. It must be presumed, then, that the actual number of people with handicapping conditions in the United States remains underreported. Similarly, the census reflects the number of people over the age of 65 but may well inaccurately reflect the reality that many disabling conditions are most prevalent in an elderly population.

Aside from these demographic issues, however, there has been a remarkable change in society's acceptance of an increased openness in dealing with sexuality. The so-called sexual revolution of the 1960s was manifested in the publication, and social as well as medical acceptance, of Masters and Johnson's research; in increased public attention to sexualized civil rights issues (e.g., feminism, gay rights, abortion); and in the social acceptability of overt as well as covert sexuality in media. This social redefinition of sexuality as a legitimate part of being, and of sexual functioning as a right and a joy rather than a duty has altered the courses of intrapersonal expectation and interpersonal relationship. And to the handicapped population, it has offered possibilities for research into the impact of various illnesses and disabilities on sexuality. It has also provided an opportunity to acquire social parity in terms of sexual issues and sexual being.

The outcome of these medical, physiological, and sociological developments vis-à-vis the handicapped population and sexuality has seemed to focus especially on those handicaps that are visible and that occur primarily in a young and/or young adult population, perpetuating in effect the mistaken idea that sexuality and sexual functioning are not of concern to a mature or aging population. The last decade has witnessed numerous articles, books, plays, and films relating to sexuality and spinal cord injury, among the more recent latter, for example: *Coming Home, The Other Side of the Mountain, Parts I and II,* and *Whose Life Is It Anyway?* All of this output has successfully conveyed the highly valuable concept of person first, disabled second. What is missing, however, is material that relates to the sexuality of the middle-aged or elderly handicapped person or to the individual whose disability is not readily and visually apparent; these people are thus left behind in an assumption either of asexuality or of nonconcern. That, as a result of successful media portrayal, spinal cord injury has cachet is sociosexually isolating not only to the quadri- or paraplegic but to amputees, those with rheumatoid and osteoarthritis and collagen diseases, those with cardiovascular and endocrinological disorders, people with malignancies, and so forth. *Love Story,* the most notable popularized account of someone with an invisible disability, manages to convey the dying person's need for intimacy but fails to deal realistically with the relationship between the disabling condition, in this case leukemia, and the sufferer's sexual being; the heroine is young, pretty, articulate, and witty to the end, attributes which make her an object of sympathy and pity rather than empathy.

In actuality, the person with an invisible disability such as heart disease, diabetes, or cancer may feel a constant stress in mediating between the disease and the sociosexual presentation of self (Goffman, 1959, 1971). For people with these disabilities, the issue of passing versus telling is a constant one. In *First, You Cry,* her book about mastectomy and its impact on her being, Betty Rollin writes of her need to announce her condition at dinner parties. Her anger, her anxiety, and the anxiety engendered in others by her proclamations and self-revelation are very much facts of her life and of the lives of others with similar health problems (Rollin, 1976). The dinner guest with hypertension who requires a salt-free diet and the dinner guest with diabetes who needs a sugar-free diet are hard-pressed not to define themselves and be defined as "problems" in social interaction. And in their sexual interactions lurk the questions of possible rejection on the basis of infirmity if it is discovered, and of pity as a motivating factor in the sexual relationship.

Cataloguing these issues and problems, however, requires consideration of their resolution, and in order to consider remediation, it is necessary to review the current state or process of the art of dealing with sexuality and disability (Daniels, Cornelius, Chipouras, and Makas, 1979; Robinault, 1978).

Remediation: The State of the Art

The current state of the art reflects the integration of increased medical knowledge, increased information on the number/incidence/nature of disabling conditions, the increased long-term survival of handicapped people with their resultant growth of interest in quality of life issues, and societal attitudes. Also reflected is the impact of consumerism, the extent of which has not been measured but which promises to play a significant role in future remediation.

At the present time, programs relating to sexuality and disability are directed primarily to adults and fall into two major categories: therapeutic and educational. Included in the therapeutic approaches are individual, conjoint, and group counseling, and surgical management of genital function. The educational approach most documented is the Sexual Attitude Reassessment, a format designed to desensationalize sexual issues and to enhance self-awareness.

Of the therapeutic approaches, direct, one-to-one counseling seems to be the most prevalent. The proponents of this method describe the advantages of offering highly personalized attention to the individual's needs, but this method also has several drawbacks. It is time-consuming, reaches a small population, and depends for its efficacy on both the consumer's ability to articulate his concerns and the professional's ability to perceive the latent and manifest content of these concerns and their implications for total functioning and the professional skill to respond accurately and comfortably without moralizing or temporizing (Hohmann, 1972). Conjoint approaches, in which the handicapped person and his or her sexual partner are seen together by a counselor or pair of counselors, are valuable in that they deal with the sexual concerns of both the disabled individual and the partner. However, these too are time-consuming, reach a small population, and neglect the disabled individual without a sexual partner whose concerns relate to the problems of making sociosexual contacts as well as knowing what to do in sexual situations (Tomko, 1974).

Group counseling programs, usually bringing together people with similar disabilities, have been developed in a number of rehabilitation centers (Eisenberg & Rustad, 1976; Holden & Meier, 1975; Romano, 1973a; Romano & Lassiter, 1972). Advantages to this method include economy of time, safety in that no one has to speak until ready, familiarity (the bull-session concept), and the opportunity provided to model adaptive behavior. Disadvantages to this method can be that in a given area there are not enough people with a common bond to form a group and that a leader trained both in group leadership skills and in sexuality and disability is not available.

Surgical management of sexual problems in the disabled has become more common in recent years. In the past, sterilization through vasectomy or tubal ligation was not uncommon and was, on occasion, performed not because the handicapped person requested it but because the physician or the individual's family believed such a procedure to be in the best interests of society, if not of the individual. In light of recent legal action, it is to be hoped that sterilization will be available to the disabled population on the same basis on which it is available to the able-bodied, that is, voluntary rather than forced.

Surgical management of erectile impotence is a burgeoning form of therapeutic intervention. The two most common devices in use are the Small-Carrion penile prosthesis, a semi-rigid prosthesis which is implanted bilaterally into the corpus cavernosa and which results in permanent erection, and the Scott-Bradley prosthesis, which is a totally implanted, hydraulically operated unit that permits its recipient to control erection through a pump system (Berkman, 1979; Furlow, 1978; Lange & Smith, 1978; Melman, 1978; Small, 1978). Surgical indications, long-term effects, and complications are still under study. Clearly, however, such devices may help some men to cope more effectively with the impact of their disabilities on sexual function when they have access to such devices (Stewart & Gerson, 1976).

The Sexual Attitude Reassessment, as noted previously, is basically an educational model designed to desensationalize sexual issues and enhance self-awareness. It makes use of an intensive time frame in which a multimedia presentation of a variety of explicit sexual activities is coupled with periods of small group discussion. This model encourages an accepting, experimental attitude toward sexual activity and can open communication between health professionals and handicapped participants, in so doing changing the relationship to a more collegial, collaborative one (Cole, Chilgren, and Rosenberg, 1973; Halsted, Halsted, Salhoot, Stock, and Sparks, 1977). Its disadvantages are its expense, its limitation to a specific setting in that it requires extensive audiovisual equipment and meeting space, and its possibility of being used to the exclusion of other approaches, with the implication that it is a form of therapy rather than an educational approach.

What is striking about all these approaches is the absence of measurement in a behaviorally specific way of program effectiveness or outcome, of cultural variables, and of therapists' knowledge and skills. Typically, these approaches are offered under the auspices of health care delivery settings, notably within the Veterans Administration (VA) Hospital system and at teaching medical centers such as the Texas Institute for Rehabilitation and Research, the Moss Rehabilitation Hospital in Philadelphia, and the University of Minnesota's hospitals. Help in resolving problems related to sexuality and disability through the provision of factual information, counseling, and education is rarely offered outside such settings, that is to say, in family agencies, schools, community mental health settings, or in private doctors' offices. The location of existing programs, in fact, gives evidence of being person-dependent, and program existence appears to be without particular regard to disabled population loci. The person-dependency of programs refers to the unfortunate reality that many programs seem to depend on the presence of a person committed to maintaining the program through personal endeavor and skill. When that person leaves, the program tends to disappear (even if it was previously well-integrated with other programs) (Cole, 1978; Zirinsky, 1979). Equally unfortunate is the latter program reality, that of existence without regard to population loci. Relatively few ongoing

Hincker Memorial Library Concordia

programs exist in major population centers or in areas where people dependent on the fixed income of Social Security or veterans benefits can find moderately priced housing and reasonable costs of living. Those handicapped people who live in areas far from centers where therapeutic or educational programs exist must do without services.

If in fact the relationship between sexuality and disability is a process, changing with specific knowledge and general attitudes, then this relationship is a mutable one. It is open to remediation and enhancement, with goals of parity in social acceptance, sexual opportunity, and equal access to educational and therapeutic programs that relate to sociosexual interaction. Change being inherently anxiety producing, its impetus will come, at least in part, from the people who feel trapped by the past and the present. These people will include helping professionals who will use their facilitative skills to develop therapeutic programs and who will work at attitude change. Included as well will be politicians and policymakers concerned with maintaining political power by responding to the needs of their disabled constituency. The media can be tapped to portray disabled individuals realistically, not as automatic heroes or victims but as people. Educators will be involved through the mainstreaming of handicapped children with able-bodied children and through the development both of sex education curricula for all children and of courses relating to sexuality and disability in professional schools of medicine, nursing, physical and occupational therapy, rehabilitation counseling, and social work. Ultimately, if remediation is to occur so that to be handicapped is no longer to be asexual, consumers—men and women with illnesses and disabilities and their families—will advocate for their rights to acceptance, to educational and therapeutic services, and to sociosexual equality in interpersonal relationships.

References and Bibliography

Berkman, A. *Issues in the use of penile prosthesis.* Paper presented at the Annual Convention of the American Psychological Association, New York, 1979.

Cole, S. Personal communication, 1978.

Cole, T., Chilgren, R., & Rosenberg, P. A new programme of sex education and counseling for spinal cord injured adults and health care professionals. *Paraplegia,* 1973, *11,* 631–638.

Daniels, S., Cornelius, D., Chipouras, D., & Makas, E. *Who cares? A handbook on sex education and counseling services for disabled people.* Washington, D.C.: George Washington University, 1979.

Eisenberg, M., & Rustad, L. Sex education and counseling program on a spinal cord injury service. *Archives of Physical Medicine and Rehabilitation,* 1976, *57,* 135–140.

Furlow, W. Surgical treatment of erectile impotence using the inflatable penile prosthesis. *Sexuality and Disability,* 1978, *1,* 299–306.

Goffman, E. *The presentation of self in everyday life.* Garden City, N.Y.: Doubleday, 1959.

Goffman, E. *Stigma: Notes on the management of spoiled identity.* Englewood Cliffs, N.J.: Prentice-Hall, 1963.

Goffman, E. *Relations in public.* New York: Basic Books, 1971.

Gordon, S. *Sexual rights for the people. . . who happen to be handicapped.* Syracuse, N.Y.: Center on Human Policy, 1974.

Halsted, L., Halsted, M., Salhoot, J., Stock, D., & Sparks, R. A hospital based program in human sexuality. *Archives of Physical Medicine and Rehabilitation,* 1977, *58,* 409–12.

Hart, W. *College algebra.* Boston: D. C. Heath, 1953.

Hohmann, G. Considerations in management of psychosexual readjustment in the cord injured male. *Rehabilitation Psychology,* 1972, *19,* 50–58.

Holden, B., & Meier, R. Sex and coffee—a sexual counseling approach. *Archives of Physical Medicine and Rehabilitation,* 1975, *56,* 543.

Kemeny, J., Snell, J., & Thompson, G. *Introduction to finite mathematics.* Englewood Cliffs, N.J.: Prentice-Hall, 1961.

Lange, R., & Smith, A. A comparison of the two types of penile prosthesis used in the surgical treatment of male impotence. *Sexuality and Disability,* 1978, *1,* 307–311.

Melman, A. Development of contemporary surgical management for erectile impotence. *Sexuality and Disability,* 1978, *1,* 272–281.

Robinault, I. *Sex, society and the disabled.* New York: Harper & Row, 1978.

Rollin, B. *First, you cry.* Philadelphia: Lippincott, 1976.

Romano, M. Sexual counseling in groups. *Journal of Sex Research,* 1973, *9,* 69–78. (a)

Romano, M. Sexuality and the disabled female. *Accent on Living,* 1973, *18,* 27–34. (b)

Romano, M., & Lassiter, R. Sexual counseling with the spinal cord injured. *Archives of Physical Medicine and Rehabilitation,* 1972, *53,* 568–572.

Small, M. The small-carrion penile prosthesis: Surgical implant for the management of impotence. *Sexuality and Disability,* 1978, *1,* 282–291.

Stewart, T., & Gerson D. Penile prosthesis: Psychologic factors. *Urology,* 1976, *7,* 400–402.

Tomko, M. Facility role models. In National Paraplegia Foundation (Ed.), *Sex: Rehabilitation's Stepchild.* Chicago: National Paraplegia Foundation, 1974.

Trieschmann, R. *The psychological, social, and vocational adjustment in spinal cord injury: A strategy for future research.* Washington, D.C.: Rehabilitation Services Administration, 1978.

Tripp, E. *The Meridian handbook of classical mythology.* New York: New American Library, 1970.

Zirinsky, J. Personal communication, 1979.

II

Institutional and Bureaucratic Contributions to Discriminatory Practice

Society has successfully created institutions and bureaucracies that are unresponsive to the needs of the disabled and embody its prejudicial feelings about them. This has been accomplished by establishing a transportation system that is inaccessible, by creating a medical community that, intentionally or not, remains ignorant of and unresponsive to the special medical needs of this group, and by endorsing architectural designs that effectively exclude the disabled from free and equal access. Institutional and bureaucratic attempts to provide benevolently for this population have, in fact, created a compensation system that prevents them from entering society's mainstream. Once established, these institutional and bureaucratic entities have assumed a life of their own and, as is the case with any life form, make alterations or modifications only to assure their own survival. In this section nearly all the authors acknowledge that change is occurring to help reduce these institutional and bureaucratically created barriers. Whatever the origins of this change—zeitgeist, expediency, or plain charity—a shift is occurring in the way in which they are willing to make accommodations for a disabled population.

The purpose of this part is to examine the means by which discriminatory practices of specific institutions and bureaucracies existing within the context of the larger social system are exercised. It has been designed to investigate the extent to which institutional and bureaucratic systems work in the direction of the disabled's deterioration rather than his rehabilitation. Such analysis must precede the presentation of remediative programs, although many of the chapters in this section do suggest ways in which discrimination can be combated. The chapters in this section attempt to achieve objectivity in their descriptions of current practice by trying to keep *theoretical interpretations of facts apart from biases. Schroeder (Chapter 7) reviews the status of legal enactments which have been designed to guarantee justice for the disabled and suggests amendments to the Civil Rights Act of 1964 which could assure the disabled an opportunity for full participatory citizenship in American society. Lifchez and Davis (Chapter 8) consider architectural barriers confronted by the disabled and attempts to create a barrier free environment. Dunham (Chapter 9) examines the impact on and consequences of inaccessible transportational systems for the disabled, while Sims and Manley (Chapter 10) present the argument that pension and compensation programs as currently conceived present disincentives to total integration into the community. Falconer (Chapter 11) delineates obstacles often encountered by the disabled person in his independent search for responsible medical care. Finally, Goldiamond (Chapter 12) considers the family's role in the rehabilitation process and discusses discriminatory practices directed toward the family with a disabled member.*

The extent to which these institutional and bureaucratic systems can be altered is a question that will ultimately be answered only with the passage of time. If, however, the change we currently observe is not accompanied by change in the larger social context (the subject of Part I of this text), the permanency of our present efforts will be as futile and elusive as the labors of Sisyphus.

7 The Law Speaks

Disability and Legal Practice

Oliver C. Schroeder, Jr.

In America, law is the people's tool to achieve justice. The people make the law directly, through public service as jurors in civil and criminal cases, through petitioning by initiative or referendum the enactment of legislation, through the exercise of the First Amendment rights to speak and write freely or to assemble peaceably by which public opinion can be molded into action for the public good. Indirectly, the people also make laws by voting for their legislators, executives, and, in some state governments, judges. Legislators in turn enact statutes; executives then issue regulations under the statutes; judges finally interpret the statutes and regulations in specific legal cases involving aggrieved human beings who seek to use the law to acquire justice. Justice is the goal, and law must always be made and used to achieve that goal.

What is American justice? Justice is: (1) a belief by an individual citizen that his or her relationship with all other persons in the United States is founded on personal integrity, a common respect one for the other; (2) a belief that he or she can seek and find a life of fulfillment, happiness, and dignity. American justice is based on a relationship between and among human beings which exalts fairness; equality of opportunity; justness in economic, political and social relationships; and rational reason in categorizing differences between and among persons. Fair, equal, just, rational, and reasonable are human concepts which explain the true meaning of American justice. Therefore, fair, equal, just, rational, and reasonable are the basic requirements for the law's operation as it struggles to effect a true justice for all persons in America.

How goes the struggle for the handicapped or disabled as he or she seeks to achieve the inalienable legal rights guaranteed to each person by the Declaration of Independence—the right to life, liberty, and the pursuit of happiness? Has justice been achieved? Is the law fashioning American society to enhance the disabled's opportunity for a just, fair, equal, rational, and reasonable relationship to his or her fellow citizens? These matters demand attention not only to determine where we are but, more importantly, where we must go.

Law for the handicapped or disabled person really came into prominence with the Congressional enactment of the Rehabilitation Act of 1973 (29 U.S.C. Sec. 701, et seq.). Prior to that time, legislation of benefit to the handicapped or disabled did exist at both federal and state levels, but the philosophical concept of these laws was to aid the handicapped or disabled because he or she was different from the "normal" citizen. Public funds were appropriated and public programs were executed on the basis of helping second-class persons to lead better lives. These laws for the disabled were conceived to be acts of charity, not laws to enhance the lives of normal citizens.

So the 1973 act with its 1974 amendments did not merely reshape old laws as tools for the handicapped and disabled. The 1973 act has provided a new tool, a new concept. The disabled person is conceived to be a first-class citizen. Any attempts to make him or her a second-class citizen through discriminatory acts is now to be illegal. We are not to help a second-class citizen to live a little better through acts of legal charity, as past laws were designed to do. We are to recognize the disabled as first-class citizens and to protect and serve them in that noble relationship by legally prohibiting the discriminations that relegate them to second-class citizenship.

The federal act of 1973 used the power of the public purse to create that protection and security. Sec. 504 of the act states:

> No otherwise qualified handicapped individual in the United States, as defined in section 706(b) of this title, shall, solely by reason of his handicap, be excluded from the participation in, be denied benefits of, or be subjected to discrimination under any program or activity receiving Federal financial assistance.

The legislative history emerging with the 1974 amendments explains further this new law tool:

> Section 504 was enacted to prevent discrimination against all handicapped individuals regardless of their need for, or ability to benefit from vocational rehabilitation services, in relation to Federal assistance in employment, housing, transportation, education, health services, *or any other Federally-aided programs* [italics added].

What has been expressed by this new law which can explain today's legal struggle to achieve justice for the disabled? The legal literature has exploded with scholarly writings seeking to explain and develop new uses for this tool, to identify growing needs for the better justice due the disabled citizen. For those interested, the bibliography's titles will suggest specific areas of concern and interest in the new laws for the old problems confronting the disabled citizen. These old problems coalesce in a simple question: How can I, a disabled person, secure my legal right to be a first-class citizen so that I can relate to my fellow-citizen in a fair, just, equal, rational and reasonable manner?

Legislative enactment of the 1973 Rehabilitation Act was originally conceived to present in plain meaning the rights of the handicapped. Executive promulgation of more specific regulations to implement the statutory rights was considered not necessary. The federal judiciary in the case of *Cherry* v. *Mathews*, however, ordered the Department of Health, Education and Welfare to issue executive regulations under the legislative statute. These regulations appeared in 42 Federal Register 22676–22685.

Once the 1973 Rehabilitation Act was fully perceived, other federal statutes and appropriate agencies took cognizance of the new era of legal rights for the handicapped to assure and encourage first-class citizenship. A listing of these other legal efforts will aid in more fully understanding the legal action generated by the 1973 Rehabilitation Act:

1. *§2122 of the Tax Reform Act of 1976.* I.R.C. §190 grants a tax credit for the removal of architectural barriers to disabled persons access and has implementing regulations in Treas. Reg. §§7.190–1.190–3.

2. *§51 of the Tax Reduction and Simplification Act of 1977* recognizes a handicapped aspect of granting a tax credit for hiring new handicapped employees who have completed government programs.

3. The Department of Labor's Office of Federal Contract Compliance Programs (OFCCP) has issued regulations on §503 of the Rehabilitation Act. 41 *Code of Fed. Reg.*, §§60–741.1 to .54 (1977) Executive Order No. 11, 758, 39 *Fed. Reg.* 2075 (1974).

4. The Vietnam Era Veterans' Readjustment Assistance Act of 1974 has spawned regulations on the handicapped. 41 *Code of Fed. Reg.* §60–250.1 to .54 (1977).

5. The Small Business Administration has regulations on the Rehabilitation Acts §504. 43 *Fed. Reg.* 9488–9493.

6. The Treasury Department has regulations for §122 of the State and Local Assistance Act of 1972, as amended, 31 U.S.C.A. §1242(a) (i) (West Supp. 1977) and Treas. Reg. 51.50 has regulations to prohibit discrimination to otherwise qualified handicapped. 42 *Fed. Reg.* 18362–18372 (1977).

7. The Urban Mass Transport Act of 1964, as amended, 49 U.S.C. §§1601–1613 (Supp. V, 1975) has also produced regulations. 41 *Fed. Reg.* 18233 (1976).

The speed of legal action on behalf of full citizenship for the disabled leaves much to be desired, however. A quotation from *U.S. News and World Report* (1979) reveals the dismal delay:

> Only five of the 29 agencies affected have adopted regulations to implement the ban on discrimination against the handicapped in federally aided programs. The newest rules, issued by the Transportation Department on May 31, are seen by the disabled as much too weak. (p. 10)

New legislative dimensions were added in 1975 to the handicapped individual's legal rights to full citizenship. The Education for All Handicapped Children Act, 20 U.S.C. §1405 (Supp. V, 1975) with regulations in 45 *Code of Federal Regulations* §84.11(a) (2) and the Developmentally Disabled Assistance and Bill of Rights Act, 42 U.S.C. §§6001–6081 became law. Once again the basic concept was to assure and encourage that mentally handicapped children were to be blessed with full citizenship in the mainstream of American education. As far as educationally possible, a mentally handicapped child was to be in a common classroom with the child not mentally handicapped. Note that the Developmentally Disabled Assistance Act also carries the crucial legal designation of "Bill of Rights Act." The law is moving slowly but surely toward recognizing an inherent constitutional right to full citizenship for the handicapped and disabled.

Numerous legal problems have emerged since the original 1973 act was enacted.

Confusion over the terms handicapped and disabled is serious. Both are frequently used interchangeably in statutes, regulations, and decisions. Technically, disabled refers to a medical condition. Handicapped refers to an individual's status due to the disability. Some preference is shown for disabled, because it reflects that the person need not be considered as handicapped in his or her job performance. In reality, both words are laden with negative values. The law needs a term that can center more on the individual's capacity and not his impairment.

Difficulty in legally defining the handicapped person has been a second serious problem. The original 1973 act provided this definition: handicapped individual means any individual who (a) has a physical or mental disability which, for such an individual constitutes or results in a substantial handicap to employment and (b) can reasonably be expected to benefit in terms of employability from vocational rehabilitation services. The emphasis on benefit by training really was inapplicable to several aspects of the Rehabilitation Act, so the definition was supplemented in 1975 to read: A handicapped individual "(a) has a physical or mental impairment which substantially limits one or more of such person's major life activities, (b) has a record of such impairment, or (c) is regarded as having such an impairment."

This broad definition was ultimately scrutinized by the U.S. Supreme Court in the very recent case of *Southeastern Community College* v. *Davis*. The Court concluded in footnote 6:

> A person who has a record of or is regarded as having an impairment may at present have no actual incapacity at all. Such a person would be exactly the kind of individual who could be "otherwise qualified" to participate in covered programs. And a person who suffers from a limiting physical or mental impairment still may possess other abilities that permit him to meet the requirements of various programs. Thus it is clear that Congress included among the class of "handicapped" persons covered by §504 a range of individuals who could be "otherwise qualified."

In contrast to this definitional problem, the legal definitions of physical impairment (any disorder of the enumerated body systems—musculoskeletal, cardiovascular, etc.) and mental impairment (any disorder based on mental illness, mental retardation, and specific learning disabilities) have posed less difficulty in the law, probably because these definitions are very broad. In contrast, state laws are often much more specific and stringent in such definitions.

Severe difficulty in applying the 1973 Rehabilitation Act to protect a handicapped person's right to the education and employment of his or her choice has emerged as the result of the recent landmark decision cited above, *Southeastern Community College* v. *Davis*. Excerpts from the syllabus of the case on the facts and the law are illuminating:

> Respondent, who suffers from a serious hearing disability and who seeks to be trained as a registered nurse, was denied admission to the nursing program of petitioner Southeastern Community College, a state

institution that receives federal funds. An audiologist's report indicated that even with a hearing aid respondent cannot understand speech directed to her except through lipreading, and petitioner rejected respondent's application for admission because it believed her hearing disability made it impossible for her to participate safely in the normal clinical training program or to care safely for patients. Respondent then filed suit against petitioner in Federal District Court alleging, *inter alia,* a violation of §504 of the Rehabilitation Act of 1973, which prohibits discrimination against an "otherwise qualified handicapped individual" in federally funded programs "solely by reason of his handicap." There was no violation of §504 when petitioner concluded that respondent did not qualify for admission to its program. Nothing in the language or history of §504 limits the freedom of an educational institution to require reasonable physical qualifications for admission to a clinical training program. Nor has there been any showing in this case that any action short of a substantial change in petitioner's program would render unreasonable the qualifications it imposed.

(a) The terms of §504 indicate that mere possession of a handicap is not a permissible ground for assuming an inability to function in a particular context, but do not mean that a person need not meet legitimate physical requirements in order to be "otherwise qualified." An otherwise qualified person is one who is able to meet all of a program's requirements in spite of his handicap. HEW's regulations reinforce, rather than contradict, this conclusion.

(b) Section 504 does not compel petitioner to undertake affirmative action that would dispense with the need for effective oral communication, such as by giving respondent individual supervision whenever she attends patients directly or by dispensing with certain required courses for respondent and training her to perform some but not all of the tasks a registered nurse is licensed to perform. On the record it appears unlikely that respondent could benefit from any affirmative action that HEW regulations reasonably could be interpreted as requiring with regard to "modifications" or postsecondary educational programs to accommodate handicapped persons and the provision of "auxiliary aids" such as sign-language interpreters. Moreover, an interpretation of the regulations that required the extensive modifications necessary to include respondent in the nursing program would raise grave doubts about their validity. Neither the language, purpose, nor history of §504 reveals an intent to impose an affirmative action obligation on all recipients of federal funds, and thus even if HEW has attempted to create such an obligation itself, it lacks the authority to do so.

(c) The line between a lawful refusal to extend affirmative action and illegal discrimination against handicapped persons will not always be clear, and situations may arise where a refusal to modify an existing program to accommodate the needs of a disabled person amounts to discrimination against the handicapped. In this case, however, petitioner's unwillingness to make major adjustments in its nursing program does not constitute such discrimination. Uncontroverted testimony established that the purpose of petitioner's program was to train persons who could serve the nursing profession in all customary ways, and this type of purpose, far from reflecting any animus against handicapped individuals, is shared by many if not most of the institutions that train persons to render professional service. Section 504 imposes no requirement upon an educational institution to lower or to effect substantial modifications of standards to accommodate a handicapped person.

Several federal lower courts have fashioned a modicum of constitutional legal protection to aid the handicapped person who has been deemed unqualified for education or employment because of his or her disability. An irrebuttable presumption has been created in the law. When the handicapped person has been denied employment or education, such denial is presumed to be based on illegal discrimination. The door of opportunity cannot be slammed in the face of the handicapped. However, nothing in this legal doctrine of irrebuttable presumption affirmatively aids the handicapped to walk through the door. And often when he or she seeks to do so, discretionary decisions by executive agencies legally can deny first-class citizenship rights.

Other constitutional protections such as the equal-protection clause or the recognition of the handicapped as a suspect class being discriminated against have not been utilized as yet by the law. Discriminations based on race, sex, national origin, religion have all been favored by the suspect-class doctrine and the equal-protection clause. So if these persons are discriminated against, the law immediately suspects illegal discrimination. There is an expressed feeling in the law that race, sex, national origin, and religion discriminations are rooted in pure prejudice. Handicapped discrimination has not only prejudice but also is rooted in incapacity. This very view, however, is reason enough to apply a high and clear standard of scrutiny for the handicapped. The law must focus away from the disability and on the actual capacity of the individual.

Many legal cases are not filed in court because plaintiffs are poor or are enured to discriminating treatment. Many lawyers shy away from the litigation because the law is unclear, the legal standards are obscure, and the expense is great. Gathering data takes enormous amounts of man-hours. Often the needed proof is of a mechanical, technical, or structural nature that calls for expert testimony in what is technically or medically possible. After a showing is made, the court's order may only be nominal—to sensitize the employer to the problem, not to grant the disabled his or her desired relief.

The final legal decision has not yet been rendered on two important points of law concerning the disabled. Can a disabled individual bring a private lawsuit to assert his constitutional, statutory, and regulatory rights as a handicapped person? Must that person exhaust all of his or her administrative legal remedies before bringing such a lawsuit? A U.S. Supreme Court decision or a Congressional statute clearly answering these two questions in the affirmative would be most valuable.

The handicapped today have no legal right to affirmative action to assure and encourage their equal opportunity to education and employment. In the wholly private sector of American society untouched by federal tax dollars, the handicapped have at most minimal legal rights.

In regard to the growing visability of disabled persons and the public's growing awareness of the need to provide access for the handicapped to public facilities one should consult *Resource Guide to Literature on Barrier Free Environments* (Jan. 1977) published by the Architectural and Transportation Barriers Compliance Board, Washington, D.C. 20201.

For those persons interested in a source which specializes in the litigation and legal problems of the handicapped contact The National Center on Law and the Handicapped, 1235 Eddy Street, South Bend, Indiana 46617.

Today legal concerns for the handicapped are channeling more and more on the virtues of taking the word handicapped and inserting it into the 1964 Civil Rights Act. The language of §504, Rehabilitation Act of 1973 is almost identical to the language in Title VI of the Civil Rights Act of 1964 which assures protection for blacks in federal programs. Title II of the Civil Rights Act could also be amended to protect the handicapped person's access rights to public accommodations. Title VII of the 1964 Act could guarantee employment rights for the handicapped. In short, the Civil Rights Act could supersede the Rehabilitation Act of 1973 and related statutes. An amended Civil Rights Act could prohibit discrimination in regard to race, color, religion, sex, national origin, or *handicap*. This legal advance could be the cornerstone for a more potent legal right to assure the handicapped or disabled an opportunity for full citizenship in American society.

Bibliography

Access to buildings and equal employment opportunities for the disabled: Survey of state statutes. *Temple Law Quarterly*, 1977, 50, 1067–85.
Cherry V. Mathews, 419 F. Supp. 922 (D.C. 1976).
Civil Rights—handicapped discrimination—private college required to pro-

vide interpreter services for deaf student under Section 504 of the Rehabilitation Act of 1973. *Cumberland Law Review*, 1978, 8, 979–89.

Constitutional law—irrebuttable presumption doctrine—right of blind
teacher to take teacher's examination. *Wayne Law Review*, 1977, 23,
1295–1304.

Development of equal employment opportunity for the handicapped: An
overview and analysis of the major issues. *University of Baltimore Law
Review*, 1977, 7, 183–278.

Discrimination against the handicapped in federally funded state services:
Sub-part F of Rehabilitation Act regulations. *Clearinghouse Review*,
1978, 12, 339–44.

Employment of the handicapped—the Rehabilitation Act of 1973. 29 U.S.C.
Sec. 793 - Sec. 503, *Duquesne Law Review*, 1977–78, 16, 481–92.

Employment rights of the handicapped. *Clearinghouse Review*, 1977, 11,
703–12.

Ending discrimination against the handicapped or creating new problems?
The HEW rules and regulations implementing Section 504 of the Rehabilitation Act of 1973. *Fordham Urban Law Journal*, Winter, 1978, 6,
399–412.

Enforcing Section 504 regulations: The need for a private cause of action to
remedy discrimination against the handicapped. *Catholic University
Law Review*, 1978, 27, 345–63.

Foreword—The specter of equality: Reflections on the civil rights of physically handicapped persons. *Temple Law Quarterly*, 1977, 50, 944–52.

History of unequal treatment: The qualifications of handicapped persons as
a "suspect class" under the equal protection clause. *Santa Clara Law
Review*, 1975, 15, 855–910.

Historical overview: From charity to rights. *Temple Law Quarterly*, 1977,
50, 953–60.

Is the Constitution handicapped? *Trial*, June, 1978, 14, 52–55.

Law and handicapped persons: Achieving equality through new rights. *Journal, Kansas Bar Association*, Fall, 1978, 47, 181–9.

Potluck protections for handicapped discriminations: The need to amend
Title VII to prohibit discrimination on the basis of disability. *Loyola
University Law Journal* (Chicago), 1977, 8, 814–45.

Rehabilitating the Rehabilitation Act of 1973. *Boston University Law Review*, 1978, 58, 247–74.

Rights of the physically and mentally handicapped: Amendments necessary
to guarantee protection through the Civil Rights Acts of 1964, *Akron
Law Review*, 1978, 12, 147–63.

Southeastern Community College v. *Davis*, 47 L.W. 4689, June 11, 1969.

Symposium on employment rights of the handicapped. *DePaul Law Review*,
1978, 27(4), 943–1148.

Toward equal rights for handicapped individuals: Judicial enforcement of
Section 504 of the Rehabilitation Act of 1973. *Ohio State Law Journal*,
1977, 38, 676–708.

U.S. News and World Report. June 25, 1979, p. 10.

8 What Every Architect Should Know

Raymond Lifchez and Cheryl Davis

When confronted by some particularly inept handling of the design of a building, making it inaccessible, have you wondered how the architect could have been so negligent? What happened? Oversight, economics, misunderstanding of the fundamental requirements of accessibility? Or—it begins to dawn on you—was it a matter of personal willfulness? Did the architect survey the situation, know what needed to be done, but could not bring himself to do it? Did he avoid the real issues to be confronted by this particular design solution by diverting his attention to matters with more personal appeal?

Architecture as pure design has, in the last decades, become a rubric behind which creative talents have sought new and daring architectural forms, uncompromised by attention to human behavior. In the practice of architecture as high art, the humanity constraint on the design is seen as minor or negligible. Interestingly enough, the results are not always poor and do satisfy a range of human needs. But the question emerges: how ethical is it to practice this profession—licensed to build buildings and other places of assembly—without a convincing demonstration of being intellectually and emotionally grounded in the subject of people?

It is informative to take a moment to look at the attitude toward the federal requirements when they were first enacted to regulate access for the handicapped. Though some architects have begun to awaken to their mandate, little overall progress toward the goals set forth in the law has been made. Professional schools of architecture are still reluctant to teach a perspective of disability to students, and practitioners have expressed little enthusiasm for embracing this cause. (It is so interesting to compare the profession's attitude toward energy conservation—solar technology—which has been enormously

This article is drawn from a larger work "Architectural Design Education with the Handicapped User in Mind" sponsored by the Exxon Education Foundation.

positive and imaginative and the postion—or nonposition—that has been taken toward access.)

In 1977 the pulse of the profession was epitomized in a short, thoroughly negative article devoted to the subject which appeared in the *San Francisco Bay Architects' Review* (1977, pp. 12–13):

> Protection of public safety and health keeps taking on an ever expanding definition. Can public codes really serve everyone's special needs and still be responsive to the general public's values? Provisions to help the handicapped trip the blind where the curb is cut away. The San Francisco State Student Union Building is forced to abandon altogether some spaces that were approved but were inaccessible to those in wheelchairs. What does this suggest for the fate of future preservation and reuse projects? Architects have used stairs as a design element through history and are we now to outlaw them even where they are integral in our old buildings, if they are open to the public? *Let's hope that the success of the handicapped lobby doesn't inspire the hayfever sufferers to a similar program to require the defoliation of grass and trees in public open spaces* [italics added].

Clearly, the word was out that the physically disabled of the world would, if they had their way, turn the environment into one giant appliance with ramps and grab bars everywhere! And what, of course, was not openly expressed was the fear that all those handicapped people who had until now stayed so nicely out of sight would be free to compete for a place in the sun. How unseemly. And how uninspiring to the designer.

What Every Architect Should Know

Access is not just another constraint on architectural design but a major perceptual orientation—to humanity. To achieve it, architects must confront a range of human issues for which there are no simplistic architectural solutions. The first step in this process is for the architect to learn how to be very self-aware so as not to (unconsciously) stigmatize handicapped clients—be they the physically disabled, the elderly, or even children.

Renovating society's house, which is one way to perceive the built environment, is a profound work. To restructure the environment so that it responds better to the needs of all requires that a significant number of people—not only architects but clients and managers and all others who are concerned with the build environment—re-evaluate their thinking. All must come to believe that an environment which is more responsive to the needs of "real people" is not only possible but desirable. Designers operate within a political context, and to implement real change they must be more sensitive and forward thinking than others. The architect must be prepared to point out to others that the new standards and code provisions intended to ensure that buildings become accessible to and usable by people with disabilities should not be perceived as unusual but only the latest requirements placed by consensus on the environment. The architect as visionary must remind others that architecture reflects how society feels about itself, that this is a dynamic process, and that architecture is always a major expression of societal aspirations and ideals.

This has not been the case, however. Disabled people have hailed these laws affecting new building with something resembling a fanfare of trumpets. Designers, by and large, have responded to them with hostility. Economics, building codes, technologies, all are seen as valid constraints, if not altogether pleasing, but this one is different. The concept that the built environment should respond to people's needs, that it should not diminish, humiliate, or unnecessarily reduce a person's capacity of living in the world, is often attacked as a fetter to productivity, an enemy of architecture as high art. There are millions of disabled people in the United States, yet the feeling is widespread among designers that the new standards are the result of a small and vociferous cabal of disabled people and a few well-intentioned advocates.

Bridging the gap between the law and practice is where architects are today, and the struggle has begun to produce some reasonable buildings. It has become perfectly clear in this process that one cannot convince people by putting a codebook in their hands, nor does one produce accessible design with the code alone. Small wonder that the conscientious designer feels hemmed in and even confused by a statistical approach devoid of professional goals.

The promulgation of accessibility codes may be seen, to some extent, as an attempt to generate quickly an environment that—if not beautiful and visually exciting—at least responds to some of people's personal needs and does not deprive them of their civil rights. It represents a short cut. In the long run, however, the way to produce an environment that neither excludes disabled people nor makes them uncomfortable is to include in the designer's thinking that along with everything else an architect must know must be added a more profound approach to people, their behavior, the things they bring to their environment and by which they interpret it.

There are a number of ways to get at this problem, which needs to be tackled both in the education and practice of architects. Curiously, since architects teach architecture students, the effort that needs to be made is even more important. Let me explain.

A central theme in teaching students architectural design is that of client accommodation. It is against a perspective of the client (flesh-and-blood characters or ones created for the role)—their way of life, values, expectations—that the design is judged as suitable. Nonetheless and oddly, this theme of the client, central as it is to teaching students to become professionals, is the one least articulated, least developed as a teachable subject. Unlike other architectural subjects about which certain standards have emerged among schools, there is no such consensus in schools about how people—the clients—fit into the process of designing the built environment. But obscuring this vital subject obscures the very context in which design is grounded and thus makes all other standards of evaluation dubious. If a design is not a suitable accommodation, no matter what it may look like or how it is constructed, does it meet its societal purpose? The profession has not taken this issue on in a serious manner.

One way to offer the designer, in education and in practice, insight into the social and psychological dimensions of the relationship of the nonaverage user to the built environment is, quite simply, to expose the designer to representatives of that user group. Through an empathetic approach, the designer quickly loses his stereotypes and begins to get a feel for the actual substance of another person's life, a person whose story may be very different from the designer's own but whose feelings and responses may be readily understood. A common result of the designer's authentic effort to enter into the subjective experience of the disabled person and into the social and historic context of disability is heightened responsiveness to disability-related issues and, more importantly, a respect for the intent underlying the codes, standards, and criteria.

Workshops where one temporarily "tries on" a disability constitute attempts to give the designer an entry into the subjective experience of disability. Trying on a disability for a day offers the designer a sense of the physical issues involved, but it often backfires, as it can generate so much anxiety that the designer overreacts, unable to understand or even believe that any but "supercrips" venture out alone at all. Trying on fails to offer the designer any sense of the way in which the environment affects, feeds, and is sustained by social and cultural prejudices and expectations. A more powerful tool for dealing with these issues meaningfully is autobiography.

Autobiography can be used to obtain an understanding of the individual in an environmental context. It is a way of approaching a person's life as an environmental history, conveyed through discussion and personal anecdote. The person telling the story may share experiences of the houses she has lived in, the schools attended, the places worked in. The feelings which emerge convey to the designer an interpretation of the environment very different from what he or she may expect. For example, stairs function objectively as a means of vertical circulation. Yet when a wheelchair user talks about living upstairs (as in one of the vignettes in this chapter), a complex and intriguing picture emerges. The stairs become a stage on which certain things may happen. Indeed, the environment becomes both a theatre for human drama and a Felliniesque director which feeds the actors their lines. The stairs are not merely physically difficult: they are a source of family conflict and profound emotional discomfort; they are a signpost saying, "Disabled people excluded." Going through such distress day after day is devastating, but disabled people do it all the time. Through autobiography the architect and the student designer can begin to understand that for millions of people the existing built environment is a harsh and unforgiving place which both limits their lives and diminishes their perceived capacity to function in the eyes of society.

   In architectural practice, consulting, and teaching, the authors have found the life experiences described by Ms. Davis to be powerful in changing people's perceptions. In a certain way, they seem softly discursive, but they are packed with the kinds of insights, subjective reactions, and information that must be shared between disabled persons and designers if the latter are to become truly sensitized to the issues and difficulties facing the disabled user in the environment. And we mustn't discount the softly discursive style, for herein lies the human presentation which is very difficult to ignore.

A Disabled User's Perspective

My sensibility is shaped by disability as much as by the society, economy, culture, and times in which I live. I could tell you the bare facts of my life, but they would tell you little about me. To know me as one whose consciousness has been profoundly shaped by the experience of disability, you must loosen your grip on the everyday world of your objectivity and enter the realm of subjective experience.

   In the objective world, you would learn that I went to a special school. In the subjective realm, you would learn what it felt like for me every morning as the bus drove into the schoolyard, past the sign at the front door which read, School for Crippled and Deformed

Children. In the objective mode you would not know how that sign stabbed me to the core five days a week, how different it made me feel. For me, the sign meant that society labeled me "other," and as I was being taught that I should be "happier with my own kind," I was also learning that able-bodied people did not consider me their kind.

When disability is reduced to the need for grab bars and wide doorways, it becomes a subject of little interest, relegated to the technician or practitioner. The social theorist, the historian, the psychologist most often do not regard disability as a fertile subject for investigation. The myth of objectivity blinds us to a whole realm of human experience which cries out for serious study. The "children of crisis" are blacks, they are women, they are children. They are not disabled people. It is as if the study of disability were reduced to vocational counseling or rehabilitation medicine. Imagine confusing gynecology with the study of women in society, or dermatology with the study of racism!

Disability is a social idea as much as it is a physical fact. Our conception of what constitutes an appropriate social niche for disabled people affects the way we create our environment. Our conception of disability is partially based, however, on the way in which our predecessors created our environment. This is the environment-as-found: fixed, immutable. Thus the facticity of environment and the concept of disability are mutually interactive.

The following autobiographical vignettes will communicate some sense of the way in which the built environment shapes the experience of disabled people, their self-concepts, the way they relate to others, and their sense of place in the world. In my writing, the environment is an arena in which social conflicts—often generated by the environment itself—are played out.

The vignettes may be painful to read; they were painful to write. I offer them not to bare old wounds and battle scars but to demonstrate the value of the subjective mode, best entered through the analysis of experience, as a tool for understanding the interactive effects of society and the environment on the development of the disabled individual.

Living Upstairs

When I was seven years old my family moved from Boston to Milton, Massachusetts. Although it coincided with the great outflux of Jews from Roxbury, and the simultaneous influx of Southern blacks, our relocation probably had less to do with that migratory phenomenon known as "white flight" than with my physical disability. The Jews of Cheney Street worried about their changing neighborhood, but my parents' greatest fear was that as I grew older and, therefore heavier, they would one day soon be unable to carry me up and down the stairs. They had reason to worry.

Our apartment building lay more than halfway up Cheney, a steep slope leading to the summit of Elm Hill. Until I was three, we lived in number 58 on the third floor. To reach our apartment, one climbed a full flight of exterior stairs and two more inside, making about 45 steps in all. My mother and father slung me over a hip, or "sat" me on a crooked arm and then huffed and puffed the way up, a climb which left them increasingly weary and ill-tempered. I never surmounted my fear of being dropped, and my consequent fretfulness annoyed them, as if, even so young, I was supposed to appreciate their efforts. After four years of this routine, when it was time to think about sending me to school, my parents must have realized that they could not carry me down every morning and up every afternoon five days a week (to say nothing of taking me on Saturdays to grandmother's house and on Sundays to Franklin Park). Accordingly, we moved next door to number 60, where we lived for two years on the second floor. There, my parents had to contend with only four exterior steps and one flight inside: an improvement, relatively speaking.

For me, the move next door changed nothing. At an age when my peers were allowed to run downstairs to play with their friends, I depended on the willingness of my parents to "lug me up and down" (their phrase). When they carried me, I felt myself to be, in the most literal sense, a burden. I knew I tired them out. I resented their fatigue, for they groaned, as if insisting I admire their martyrdom on my behalf. I had one flight less of complaining to listen to, but I was still a captive audience and while, up and down the block, I saw children who were free, insofar as seven year olds are free, I was not.

After seven years of climbing hill and stair, my parents accepted the inevitable, and we moved to Milton, first renting for two years, then moving into our own home. My parents took me along on some of these house-hunting expeditions. They claimed they wanted it to be easier to carry me in and out of the house, not that they wanted me to be able to get myself in and out of the house. (I am not sure that they would have understood the difference between these two objectives.) Many of the houses seemed to my childish eyes to be nothing *but* stairs. I looked at those stairs and, sensing that this was critical, made my opposition to these prospective homes as relevant to my parents' way of looking at them as I could manage. Thus, I never pointed out that I couldn't get myself in and out; I reminded my mother of the last time she had strained her lower back carrying me up the steps. The one they finally purchased was as far from a model of accessibility (we didn't then know the word) as can be imagined; yet it was superior to several they had considered.

The new place on Houston Avenue was a two-family house, with a first floor apartment six steps above grade. The lower unit had only two bedrooms, which meant, if we occupied it, that my sister and I would have to share a room. Three years older than I, Karen wanted her privacy; on this she was quite vocal. The upstairs unit offered access to several additional rooms in a finished attic. My sister could have a lot of privacy up there; I would have to crawl up yet another flight of stairs to invade her personal space.

My parents explained the options, as they saw them. Either we could have less stairs for me (and less space for the family), or we could have "a few more steps" for me (and ample space for the family, as well as a sister who wouldn't hate me for making her share a room). Then they said to me, an eight year old child, "*You* decide."

I should decide? What was going on here? What were they asking of me? I was eight years old; who was I to say where we should live? If I said, "Downstairs," they might go along with it—and then complain about and forever resent the fact that I had "made" them live in quarters too tight for comfort. They might *not* go along with it, and then I would see what I suspected was in fact the case: that they had already made the decision to live upstairs, that the choice was false. If I said, "Upstairs," my parents would love me, congratulate each other for parenting such a "mature" child, and, most importantly, be able in good conscience to answer any complaint about the stairs I might make in future years with the response, "But the decision was *yours;* we gave you the choice." So with an air of, "We only want what you want, dear," they ostensibly left it to me to determine where we would live. Feeling that I had been manipulated, without at the time being quite able to explain how, and feeling that I had no choice but theirs, I said, "I want to live upstairs." They praised my maturity, and I knew that, in some important way, I had been had.

My parents compounded still further the bind in which they had placed me when they asked me if I wanted a ramp up to the porch on the first floor. They pointed out that it would enable me at least to go from the driveway to the level of the porch, some 42 inches above. "Still," my mother added, almost as an afterthought, "you'll still have the flight inside to cope with, so it doesn't really offer so much, does it?"

"No," I thought, "but if we had occupied the lower level apartment, it would have got me right inside." I knew what my parents wanted me to decide. They reminded me how terribly expensive a ramp was and how hard my father worked and how little income the family had and how much my last stint in the hospital had cost. . . . Again, it was not hard at all for me to make a "mature" decision, one which I privately resented but for which I had ostensibly no cause to complain. After all, my choice had been "freely made."

Leaving Home

I left home when I was 22 years old. I would like to say that my reasons for leaving were the same as anyone of my age, but it wouldn't be true. "I want my independence," everyone says when moving out on their own, but what it meant for me as a disabled person was not quite what it meant for an able-bodied woman. It was not merely that I wanted to be closer to my job, or that my parents were putting a damper on their daughter's sexual activity (the absence of which was then so total that I regarded myself as nearly neutered). I left because I envisioned myself living with aging parents possibly for the rest of my life, simply because I feared to find out whether or not I could take care of myself.

I lived and quarreled with my parents in an inaccessible home, unable to get in and out unaided. I couldn't afford a car; father was always reminding me how expensive "under-25" insurance was and expressing doubts that I could get a wheelchair in and out of a car myself, despite my telling him that I had, in fact, done it. (It never occurred to anyone to equip the family car with hand controls.) Taxis were financially disastrous alternatives, and obviously, I couldn't get a wheelchair on a bus. I went places if and when my parents were willing to drive me; they drove me everywhere I wanted, as long as I wanted what they wanted.

My mother believed that I couldn't minister to my own bowel care needs without her; she had convinced me, too, for a long time, but I was beginning to question this. The idea that she might be mistaken was intensely disturbing. It seemed as if she needed to feel needed so badly that my independence would be sacrificed. I was coming to resent her participation in my care as a gross and humiliating instrusion on my body, as an assault to my spirit. In the most basic physical sense, I had no privacy and I felt as if I were being repeatedly violated.

Suffice it to say we did not get along. Our household was perpetually engaged in an undeclared civil war. The only way to break the Gordian knot of our conflict was for someone to leave or die. Until I convinced myself that I might be able to live on my own, the only way out I could see was suicide. I was beginning to think of it continually, and it terrified me. When I realized that anything had to be better than this, I finally found the courage to plan the move.

Eventually, my parents realized that I was right; I had to go. My relatives were astonished that they would "let me go," as if it were their duty to compel me to stay. In reminding them that I was a reasonably intelligent adult, my mother reminded herself. Before too long, my parents (with who knows what internal conflicts) were helping me to look for an apartment.

As a low-income wheelchair user (salary of a junior secretary), my requirements for a dwelling were quite specific. The rent had to be $125 or less. The place had to be within a few blocks of Boston University, where I worked, since I was determined to push to the office, except in bad weather, when I would have to pay for a cab. (Incidentally, cabs were very had to get for such short runs, since the drivers thought the effort of getting my wheelchair in and out was not adequately offset by the low fare. In winter, I would wait for up to an hour.) I had to be able to enter the apartment unaided and be able to maneuver in the kitchen and bathroom. Realtors told us only the size, the location, and the rent; therefore, we had to run around to all prospective apartments, a colossal waste of time.

This was 1967, and most of the buildings in Boston's Back Bay were hopeless. None of them had accessible front entrances. Most landlords refused to rent to me, saying, "What the hell do you think I'm running, a nursing home?" Finally, Mr. Greenblatt rented me a basement studio near Kenmore Square and let my parents pay to have the back door ramped, "conditional upon the approval of the other tenants." Success! Let me describe this palatial abode.

To get to the rear entry, I had to push down an alley running between a nightclub-disco-bar and a movie theater. The alley, which had about a one-in-eight gradient, culminated in an expanse of fractured blacktop and loose dirt, which was deeply rutted and pocked by water-filled holes. I would never lose my fear of falling into them. I wasn't afraid of getting wet; I was petrified of being unable to get back into my chair in such a lonely spot, since the place was alive with rats. These weren't just any rats; they were Back Bay rats, enormous, sleek, and fearless. In daylight they stood in your path and watched you approach, as if appraising your edibility. The route disgusted me, but it led to the only semi-affordable, partially accessible place I could find in the area; therefore, in the absence of choice, I suspended judgment.

Inside, the studio was wood-paneled and dim. Some of the darkness was caused by the filth on the windows, the outside of which were uncleanable, because of the burglar screens bolted onto the frames. A front burner on the stove didn't work and, since I couldn't reach the rear burners, it necessitated my cooking one-dish meals until I bought a hotplate (Mr. Greenblatt never did repair the stove). Although the bathroom door was wide enough, I had to remove it, since it blocked access to the tub; this was all right for me, but I thought it would disconcert any company I might have.

My parents let me take several pieces of furniture, some dishes and glassware, and their apprehensive blessings for the new venture. They moved the furniture in for me, cleaned the place up, and got a carpenter to build a ramp, under which the rats subsequently made a fine home of their own. I could see that my parents were far from pleased with the place. I wondered if they thought I liked it or hated it. This, my first apartment, was small, dark, roach-infested, hard to get around in, and surrounded by an army of vermin, but I loved it. It was *mine*. The door had dead-bolt lock, and I could have all the privacy I wanted.

That first night, as my parents left me at my apartment, they assured me that I could call them any time of day or night; I had only to say the word and I could come home. I thought they were hoping my independence would be temporary, but I realize now how anxious they must have been. I've seen the same pattern when disabled friends leave home. I must say, my mother could hardly have been reassured when I asked her, "How do you know when water's boiling?" To everything they said, I nodded and answered yes. Yes, yes, yes. They knew I could hardly wait for them to leave.

The next morning was Sunday. I awoke at nine and lay there in bed, blissfully surveying my books, clothes, couch, walls, floor, ceiling, and door, luxuriating in my spendid squalor. I could let people in or not. I could buy the food I wanted, eat when I wanted to, go to bed or stay up when I wanted, go out when I wanted . . . *I* would choose. I didn't have to come home early because my parents didn't like to stay up late. I didn't have to ask my father to drive me anywhere. I could experience whatever presented itself, without asking my parents if it was all right with them. That was real independence. I thought of all that freedom and the new life I had begun. As I threw back the covers—I remember as if it were this morning—an incredibly wide grin stole across my face.

At the Moscow Circus

I was excited to learn that the Moscow Circus was coming to Boston. Perhaps I was moved by nostalgia; many years ago, I had seen a pair of Russian dancing bears perform on the *Ed Sullivan Show* and I had never forgotten it. Besides, European circuses struck me as being much more fun than the three-ring American variety, which dazzled the eye but divided my attention. Whatever the reason, I was eager to go.

My life, at the time, revolved around disability. I was actively involved in several disability rights organizations and working for a state agency on a program to develop housing for low-income disabled people. I wrote, advised, consulted, and did research on disability-related issues. Sometimes it seemed as if I did nothing else. In a way, I think I looked at the circus as a chance to get away from it all. This was going to be an offnight for disability. No axe-grinding, no politicking. I would go back to worrying about civil rights and human services later. For one lovely evening, though, it would be cotton candy and Pavlov's performing dogs.

A circus is best enjoyed in company, so I invited two friends, Kent and Marsha. Kent bought our tickets, advising the ticket office that one of us used a wheelchair and that we wanted to sit together. Once inside the Gardens, we traveled up several ramps and into an employee's elevator off the usual path of travel. My friends were shown their seats, which were several feet beneath the level of the aisle, while I remained in my wheelchair, since a transfer to the regular seat below was too difficult for me. With their heads at the same level as my footrests, conversation was awkward, but at least we were together.

More than six feet wide, the aisle left plenty of room, as long as I sat sideways, for people to pass me (my chair being less than 23 inches in width). The arrangement offered uncomfortable viewing, but I was willing to put up with it. The management, unfortunately, was less willing to put up with me. The usher, a rather self-important looking youth, advised me that "wheelchairs are supposed to sit over there," indicating a spot only slightly closer than Moscow.

"That's fine," I said, "but I'm with two friends who walk; they haven't brought their own chairs."

"You have to move; you're a fire hazard," he said.

"I'll move if you'll put folding chairs down there for my friends," I thought that sounded reasonable; Marsha and Kent seemed agreeable.

"Impossible!" he snapped. "I have other things to do."

"Then I'm afraid I can't move," I replied.

"Well," said the usher, "I'll let you stay, but the chief usher will be along soon. If your refuse to move for him, he'll throw you out; he won't be so nice." I wasn't aware he had been nice.

Inevitably, the chief usher materialized, a red-nosed, pudgy man of about 60. I observed him reprimanding young children a few rows below me. He looked like a man who chose to vent his rage on everyone else's children because he didn't get any respect from his own. He enjoyed his authority as chief usher and he meant to use it. "You'll have to move," he fairly barked at me.

His bearing reminded me of my father, making me feel tiny, vulnerable, and very young. I actually trembled. Then I stiffened, enraged that he should treat me in this way. Why the hell should I move? We paid for these seats. I was here with my friends, and no one would separate us. "No," I quavered in a small voice.

Face purpled, the veins on his forehead stood out. He shouted, "I'm gonna get a policeman to throw you out," and left. I sat there shaking. My friends were angry but calm; I, in contrast, was intensely upset. They urged me to hold my ground and not permit him to bully me. What did that usher think this was, Kent joked, Russia? Despite my friends' support, I found the situation hard to endure. The ushers were making me feel as if I didn't have a right to see the circus with my able-bodied friends. They were wrong, I thought, wrong, but a small part of me was not so sure. I had spent 12 years attending a special school where I could be with what they said was "my own kind," and I wasn't always quite sure what my own kind was. Thus, I was easily intimidated. As the chief usher pointed a hostile finger at me, people had stared at us. The commotion embarrassed me, and although my rage demanded I stay, other feelings screamed at me to leave. Seeking a compromise, I noticed that I could, with difficulty, maneuver myself into the seats behind me. I asked a woman if she and her children would like to swap their seats for ours, which were more expensive and offered a better view. Suspicious at first, she traded gladly when I explained that it was probably the only way my friends and I could sit together. I think I also hoped that sitting in a regular seat would render me invisible.

While the chief usher summoned the law, I performed my own circus act in the stands. Dropping from my wheelchair to the floor, I crawled beneath the barrier, swung from it, and clambered up into a regular seat. Then I folded the wheelchair and brought it flush against the barrier. It now took up less than a foot of aisle space. Surely, I thought, the chief usher would be satisfied. I sat there regaining my breath, embarrassed to have had to crawl in public ("like a monkey," a relative used to say), but also feeling very capable, because of my improvisational use of the barrier to complete the transfer. Before my self-satisfaction had settled in, however, a policeman appeared. "That does it!" cried Marsha, "I'm calling my photographer friend at the *Boston Globe*." She and Kent sailed off in search of a telephone, leaving me alone with the law.

"Ma'am," he said softly, "I'm afraid you'll either have to move the chair, or leave." He was respectfully courteous, and I resolved to respond in kind.

"I'm not willing to sit apart from my friends," I said, "but I may be willing to park the wheelchair elsewhere, if it's in a safe place."

"You can park it over there," he said, indicating an exposed area. Anyone could steal it there, I decided. I wouldn't dream of positioning it out of close reach in an arena like this unless it were under lock and key and I told him so. "Why?," he asked gently.

"Would you leave your legs somewhere else?" I asked. "If my chair is stolen, I have no way of leaving this seat. It cost six hundred dollars, it's uninsured, and I can't afford a new one. I am a working person; if it's stolen, the state won't get me another. Without it, I can't work, shop, make dinner— or leave the Gardens. Do you really want me to park it there?"

"But your chair is a fire hazard. You have to move."

I looked around us. From higher up in the stands, about 20 people dissatisfied with their seats had trickled down to sit in the aisles, on the stairs, anywhere they could. If any people were creating a potential hazard, they were, not me. "If you make me move, Officer, that would be discrimination." He clucked his tongue and drummed his fingers, impatient and annoyed. "Do you see all those people sitting in the aisles?" I asked. He did. "Well, if you make me move, without making all of them move, that's discrimination."

Puffing out his cheeks, he lifted the bill of his cap, then expelled the air. Cheeks deflated, he looked depressed. "I'm sure not going to be the one to make you move," he said, as he walked away. The chief usher returned just then, and so did my friends. The old man began to hector and bully me afresh. I had resisted all efforts to move for nearly an hour. The circus had been going on for half an hour and I hadn't seen any of it. I was tired, angry, and humiliated, and suddenly all I wanted to do was leave. Without even looking at the old man, who continued to shout, I told my friends I was tired and wanted to leave; did they mind?

As we rose from our seats, a little girl in a wheelchair entered, escorted by her mother and a girlfriend. She was crying, and from her mother's words, it was clear that she too had been told that she had to "sit with the wheelchairs," apart from her mother and friend. I was appalled. The little girl and I weren't the first people who had had trouble here. I remembered the experience of my friend Vivienne, who had come here with her five-year-old daughter. They had taken Viv's wheelchair away and forgotten to return it. As the Gardens were closed and cleaned up for the night, she had sat marooned in the stands for an hour, her child clinging to her in tears. The memory of that little girl in the wheelchair preyed on me for a long time.

One more thing happened that night. It's a pity O. Henry couldn't have been there to record it. On the way out Kent went to the ticket office to demand our money be returned to us. He was advised that this performance was a fundraiser; no refunds were ever made for benefit performances. Where were the proceeds going? They went, Kent was told, to the Muscular Dystrophy Association "to help the handicapped."

In Conclusion

First, we must recognize the significance of the autobiography as a way into others' lives, of the great potential it offers architects who sincerely seek understanding of issues of access in order to create a world that is barrier-free. Ms. Davis, though speaking very personally, is actually speaking for a host of people. What she says is more significant than a story about a private life. She opens wide a door and reveals to us experiences different from our own, with which we immediately empathize, from which we as architects take more than information, we take reason and a desire to act. It is only when confronted by this whole image that the built environment takes on the meanings attributed to it by others and which the architect must understand to build environments that are truly accessible.

Second, we must recognize that the architect is actually less powerful than one imagines to affect change. Search as architects may for an approach to a barrier-free environment—to desired change—they alone do not create buildings. If architectural solutions addressing certain social needs are not the most appropriate for society's good (e.g., the segregation of the infirmed and elderly into custodial environments or children onto "playgrounds"), it is not entirely the architect's fault. It is the rare citizen or professional who can single-handedly demonstrate through individual works a more humane, socially appropriate point of view when the majority values other things.

Bibliography

Brickner, R. *The broken year*. New York: Doubleday, 1972.
Brickner, R. *My second twenty years*. New York: Basic Books, 1976.
Chevigny, H. *My eyes have a cold nose*. New Haven: Yale University Press, 1962.
Goffman, E. *Stigma: Notes on the management of spoiled identity*. Englewood Cliffs, N.J.: Prentice-Hall, 1963.
Goffman, E. *Relations in public*. New York: Basic Books, 1971.
Lifchez, R., & Trier, P. The university as a half-way house. In M. R. Redden (Ed.), *New directions for higher education: Assuring access for the handicapped*, No. 25. San Francisco: Jossey Bass, 1979.

Lifchez, R., & Winslow, B. *Design for independent living: The environment and physically disabled people.* New York and London: Whitney Library of Design and the Architectural Press Ltd., 1979 (cloth); Berkeley: University of California Press, 1981 (paper).

The handicapped lobby. *San Francisco Bay Architects' Review*, May 1977, pp. 12–13.

9 Transportation and the Needs of the Disabled

Jerome R. Dunham

A large portion of the population in the United States cannot use public transportation. These include the very young, the very old, the very poor, and many who are severely disabled. As Larsen (1979) says,

> Impaired physical ability and fixed or limited incomes are two of the major problems facing elderly and handicapped (E&H) persons. These problems interact to make the transportation needs and usage requirements of the E & H unique. Studies, both national and local, demonstrate that this segment of the population will increase in the future, and this, in turn, will place a special importance on planning and implementing transportation projects which serve the needs of the elderly and handicapped. (p. 1)

It is interesting to look at some of the characteristics of the disabled population. A survey prepared for the Urban Mass Transit Administration states that there are 7,440,000 transportation-handicapped people in the urban United States. Affecting one out of every eight urban households, the population ranges from 5.4% in mass transportation areas to 4.4% in nonmass transit areas. The study defines the disabled population according to problem areas and functional problems:

Problem areas:

1,938,600 who use mechanical aids (26.1% of transportation-handicapped people)

1,572,800 with a hearing dysfunction (21.1%)

I wish to single out the following people for their significant contributions to this chapter: John Michaels, Carolyn Feiss, Kent Hull, Marlyn Minkin, Michael Hughes, Dorene Witt Urell, Richard Fredrick, Michael Hardisty, Beverly Juntti, Anne Waltz, and Louis Sternberg.

1,566,000 with a visual dysfunction (21.1%)
409,200 who use a wheelchair (5.5%)
3,502,300 (47.1%) who have other problems

Functional problems
Difficulty going up or down stairs (64.9%)
Difficulty stooping/kneeling/crouching (60.9%)
Difficulty walking/going more than one block (56.9%)
Difficulty waiting/standing (56.2%)

Some of these categories overlap, particularly visual and hearing dysfunctions. When an individual is multiply handicapped, the resulting problems are geometric rather than additional.

Despite the charming picture of the crippled child in the cart drawn by dogs or goats, in the past very little attention has been paid the transportation needs of the disabled. The first governmental intervention to remediate these problems occurred in 1970. Most people concerned with transportation never considered the transportation problems experienced by the disabled, and the disabled neither envisioned the possibility of their having transportation rights, nor realized that they could make demands to change the transportation system. A first step in precipitating change is to make the appropriate persons aware that there is a problem; there is, however, resistance to acquiring this awareness.

Thus, although adequate funding is essential for bringing the level of transportation service to a point where it will meet the needs of disabled people as well as those of the general population, the underlying problem is still one of awareness and what is inadequately expressed as attitudinal. Solutions to transportation and other problems require a basic belief in the expanding potential contribution of disabled persons and a prolonged intimate knowledge of the precise skills and limitations in different situations for each disability group.

Not only is there attitudinal resistance and a low level of awareness of the transportation needs of the disabled, there also seems to be a resistance to innovative design of vehicles or systems to meet these needs. The modern city bus is not radically different from the old horse-drawn wagon with planks thrown across to sit on. The wheelchair (so far as this author can discover) was not originally the result of an inspiration for a transport device for the nonambulatory individual but, rather, a gradual adaptation of the two-passenger Bath chair in which the rich were pushed about in Bath, England, for entertainment. It would be interesting to know if a rich invalid ever thought through the chair's applicability to travel problems. The motorized wheelchair has been beset by design problems for years, and there seems not to have been any fallout from any recent technological advances.

Innovative design and coordinated research are important, but it appears these must be coupled with subsidization and a better understanding of how industry can respond to the challenge of making a better wheelchair or transbus. One area that would not require large sums of money, but does require both awareness and the capacity to implement a program, is the training of transportation personnel to more sensitively interact with disabled persons. A one-time, half-day orientation of bus drivers or airplane cabin attendants to a half-dozen disability groups is not adequate training. But a long-range plan involving the interaction of transportation personnel and a variety of disabled persons in a task-oriented set of problem-solving experiences would help clarify issues in selected transportation situations. This would provide a base on which practical solutions could be built and would make travel more practical and a richer experience for a larger number of disabled persons.

Some disabled persons cannot make a single move without confronting some barrier to their mobility. To surmount these barriers requires a combination of motivation, ingenuity, mechanical aids, money, and in some cases, the help of a second party. A person who has been disabled for a long period has, by necessity, developed methods of dealing with mobility problems; the newly disabled will benefit from these advances made by others, but they will have to tax their own resources as they begin to establish mobility and transportation options.

It would be easy to be lulled into complacence by the great progress in the last decade. National mandates now require access to all forms of public transportation, but as yet the actual public transportation available to the disabled does not compare in adequacy to the services available to the able-bodied.

Recently issued Department of Transportation regulations require wheelchair accessibility on buses, subways, and other mass transit modes. The technology for accomplishing this is new, and cost estimates run very high to include them in the mainstream of public transportation. However, the experience of the municipality of metropolitan Seattle demonstrates that an excellent wheelchair lift, the Lift-U of Seattle, can be installed on a new bus for under $6000. Several other manufacturers also have wheelchair lifts for use on buses. Among them are: General Motors, Travelift by the Vapor Corporation, Environmental Equipment Corporation, Translift of Canada, and Transportation Design and Technology, Inc. These lifts are passive and do not interfere with normal passenger use. The two basic models are a front-door lift which is formed out of the steps the able-bodied passengers use. When the lift is not in use, it is stored as the front steps. The General Motors lift uses the same type design but is mounted at the rear door. The Lift-U lift is a solid platform which serves as the bottom step of the front doorwell and stores under the bus; when in use it is deployed from under the bus.

Programs to improve mobility between the home and the bus stop and the bus stop and the final destination must be implemented to make use of buses an alternative. Curb ramps must be installed and other barriers removed before main-line buses can be effectively used by the disabled.

The disabled must rely primarily on the private automobile for their transportation needs. With improved hand controls, wheelchair lifts for vans, and steering systems, many severely disabled are able to provide their own transportation. Amputees, hemiplegics, paraplegics, quadriplegics, and others with disabilities that diminish strength and movement can now safely control their own cars or vans.

Hand controls are available that fit nearly every type of car or van. Also available are foot controls for those without functional arms or hands. They are attached to the vehicle after it is delivered, and most models of hand controls do not interfere with the standard operation of the vehicle. Lifts or ramps for vans are becoming more popular; there is an increasing variety of models available, and dealerships are proliferating rapidly to install lifts and make other needed modifications and conversions of vans to suit individual needs and tastes. The best sources for information on hand controls, wheelchair lifts, and van conversions are magazines written for the disabled consumer, such as *Paraplegia News* and *Accent on Living.* Information can also be obtained from local rehabilitation centers, or centers for independent living.

Disability Types

Each type of physical disability imposes special handicaps for use of transportation. Assessment of the actual needs of each disability group in specific situations is essential to proper planning and implementation of affirmative action in the broad area of transportation.

Blindness

Since most persons designated as blind have varying amounts of useful vision, the problem for many partially sighted persons is a matter of training themselves to use those visual or auditory cues they can perceive. For many partially sighted persons, even those with many years of living with limited sight, it is mandatory that they receive this training from a low-vision clinic and a mobility instructor in order to form new habits of noticing visual patterns.

The totally blind person moves about in an invisible environment. If newly blinded, the individual must retain old abilities as well as learn new techniques of movement and keeping in contact with the environment. The newly blinded person, the elderly blind person with some hearing loss, and the deaf-blind person primarily proceed through their environment by physical contact. Called "following a shoreline," this means following the wall or the edge of the carpet with the foot or the tip of the white cane, or touching lightly along the furniture from bed to washroom. Outdoors, it may mean following the wall of a building, the line between grass and sidewalk, or the line between level and slight descent as, for example, in front of a gas station. Those well-trained blind persons with good hearing utilize auditory cues for most of their orientation and only slip back to the "shoreline" technique when in the presence of loud, sustained noise. The pounding of a jackhammer, a very high wind, a combination of heavy traffic noise, a jet flying overhead, or a suburban train moving past are all highly salient to the blind.

In a complex, unfamiliar environment, the blind person is usually forced to rely on the help of another individual, a dog guide, a long white cane, or an electronic device. To use these effectively, the blind person should receive training from a qualified instructor. The majority of blind persons use canes; only a small percentage use dogs, and even fewer use the new electronic devices whose beams reach out and bounce back from wall or tree and change back into detectable sound, so that the blind person can learn to identify the textures and distance of an object. As a general rule, the blind person should first go through a regular mobility training course with a cane, only then going on to guide-dog training or an electronic device.

The first difficulties encountered in traveling independently by bus, rail, or air are the unfamiliarity and size of the terminal, depot, or airport. When the facility is used often, the blind person can memorize its floor plan, whatever its size. If the blind person is moving through a strange city for the first time, however, he or she will probably ask for the help of a passerby, although many persons with a guide dog or cane will follow the rush of people by sound. The way to the street is thus found with only a vague notion of the area through which he or she traveled. Sometimes, a well-trained blind person can operate in the following way: he calls a cab and enters it at his New York apartment; the cab takes him to the limousine terminal; cab driver helps him to counter; personnel at counter assist the blind person into the limousine; limousine driver assists the blind person to skycap at airport; skycap eventually delivers the blind person to airline attendant. In other words, by not letting go of one helper until the blind person has secured a new person on whom to be dependent, he has established the capacity to be a world-wide traveler. Those using dog guides usually achieve greater independence and are seldom refused admittance because of the dog. Most dog users eventually have to interpret the law, however, to some restaurateur or bus driver.

Deafness

The transportation needs of deaf people vary, depending on the degree of verbal and auditory communications necessary. Private transportation requires little or no dependence on verbal communication. Deaf drivers have excellent driving records.

Difficulties do occur for hearing-impaired persons, however, with the use of public transportation. Railroad stations, bus terminals and airports often provide travel information and changes over public address systems. Ticketing agents and information personnel often have little patience for written communication, especially during peak travel hours. It is not uncommon for the most crucial travel information to be given by an agent while looking down and writing or turning around to handle the luggage. This eliminates the possibility of lipreading. Taxicabs are available mainly via telephone contact which constitutes inaccessibility for deaf people.

As more public information agencies are equipped with special telecommunication devices (TTYs) used by hearing- and speech-impaired people, public transportation will become more accessible to them. The availability of TTYs provides the deaf with information that hearing people have been able to receive by phone, such as city bus schedules and arrivals and departures of planes, trains and buses. The increasing use of visual communication devices has provided deaf individuals with additional accessibility to public transportation.

Deaf-blind

It is difficult for most people to conceive how a deaf-blind person can travel independently. Among the vision-and-hearing impaired there are many gradations of limited vision and limited hearing which may confuse the bus driver or the public at large. In the home and yard, many totally deaf-blind persons accurately interpret vibrations in the floor, airflow, changes in terrain, and the angle of the sun. Some have devices such as vibrators that help in determining when the doorbell and the telephone are ringing; some use a braille compass for orientation.

The greatest problems for the deaf-blind in city travel are communicating with people in the community and dealing with traffic. These problems are unique to the combination of visual and hearing loss. In terms of communication, if a deaf-blind person wants to talk with someone who doesn't know sign language, it becomes necessary to rely on the print alphabet spelled into the hand, write notes if the person has enough vision to read them, or use a portable device called a tellatouch machine, which has a conventional typing keyboard and gives feedback to the deaf-blind person in braille. For example, when applied to bus travel, a deaf-blind person has to prepare a written or typed sign requesting the correct bus information and show it to the driver of each bus until the correct bus arrives. Then the person must rely on the driver to tell him when to get off. This can be cumbersome and is only effective if the person reading the sign is willing to be of assistance. It is not uncommon for the driver to forget and miss the person's stop. Another example involves the deaf-blind person attempting to cross a street in a downtown area. The person prepares a card ahead of time requesting help to cross the street. He must then rely on someone passing by to read the card and offer assistance. It may be a while before help is offered, and it may be extremely difficult to get the proper help. Many times the person reading the sign will not understand what is being asked, which usually leads to confusion.

In dealing with traffic, if the deaf-blind person has enough vision to notice the cars, there is usually no problem learning to interpret traffic flow. However, if the person cannot see the cars, he then must depend on people passing by, using cards as explained above. This usually works fairly well in an area with a number of people available. In a quiet residential area, however, it is another story. The person is literally stranded, because there are often no people available to offer assistance.

In considering possible solutions to these problems, community education immediately comes to mind. This could begin with in-service training programs for professionals working with disabled persons, as well as bus drivers, and could extend even to brief spots on a local or national television network. To help solve the problem of crossing streets in a quiet residential area, especially on the way to and from work, volunteers who know sign language could be orga-nized, or carpools established in which the deaf-blind person pays a specified amount instead of taking a turn at the driving. There now are laws enforcing accessibility, but a lack of public awareness of the needs of the deaf-blind will surely render these laws ineffective.

Mental Retardation

The individual with borderline intelligence may have learned vari-ous bus routes and how to handle money; those who are moderately retarded may have more serious difficulties. It is possible for the young adult, even with serious limitations, to learn a city bus route, but it may take a year for the learning to be foolproof. Problems arise when there is a change in the schedule (particularly at transfer points), changes in routes, as well as buses that are late or early. The ability to deal with airports, bus terminals, or train depots depends in part on the complexity of the facility. The three primary barriers are signs, schedules, and telling time correctly. Inability to read signs and not being certain how to ask the right questions can lead to much uncertainty and a number of errors. Reading travel schedules can be a difficulty for many people and is impossible for the non-reader. Many moderately retarded persons can learn to tell time on the hour and half-hour, but most lack the ability to tell time more precisely, a skill necessary for a number of travel situations. Making contact with Travelers' Aid prior to the trip makes it possible for the retarded person to travel with some comfort and safety.

Arthritic Disease

Arthritics, like all other people, need the emotional and mental stimulation of getting out in the world. They also have the necessary trips to the physician and physical therapist and, for some, employ-ment. Without some mode of transportation this is impossible. Se-verely afflicted arthritics often cannot drive by themselves, so they are dependent on salaried drivers or volunteer drivers who are often friends. Many arthritics are maintained on a limited income, restrict-ing them to older vehicles which are in constant need of repair. Rheumatoid arthritics cannot usually maintain their vehicles because of increased loss or range of motion and constant pain. Those who suffer with rheumatoid arthritis can be of any age. Most of them need and want to be as active as possible in spite of continuing loss of physical strength. Many severely afflicted arthritics use a van, as transferring from wheelchair to car seat is a real problem. The van has either a hydraulic lift or a double trough-like ramp and tie-down devices that secure the chair so the arthritic can remain in the chair itself. Since rough riding can produce much pain, it is important that the vehicle have good shock absorbers and run smoothly, and that the arthritic passenger wear a support collar around the neck for protection. It is extremely difficult for an arthritis victim to find a vehicle completely suitable without employment or some type of subsidy.

Cardiac Disease

The cardiac patient is confronted with both the psychological and emotional stresses that relate to his transportation to and from work, the store and other destinations within the community. The stress of driving and parking in a busy city environment can be alleviated by proper public transportation.

The greatest challenges to a cardiac patient who uses either public or private transportation is to safely walk the distance from the bus stop and/or parking spot to the intended destination. The degree of difficulty is increased significantly if this distance involves walking up noticeable grades and/or walking in extremes of heat or cold. Since coronary heart disease is the leading killer in America today, evaluation of public transportation modes and routes should give consideration to these factors.

Pulmonary Disease

Those individuals with chronic obstructive pulmonary diseases such as asthma, bronchitis, or emphysema have some additional problems. A person with severe asthma can become breathless just standing in a cold wind waiting for a bus, and going uphill half a block to the bus stop may be extremely difficult for some individuals with chronically obstructed lungs. The emphysema victim who has to carry oxygen with him may find it is illegal to carry liquid oxygen in his vehicle through a tunnel, and the airlines will not allow the private oxygen supply to be brought on the plane. If the person is afraid he will need oxygen, the airline will sell it to him at considerable cost which he must pay even if he doesn't use it. Another problem, both in the airline supply of oxygen and in ambulance and aid cars, is that sometimes the oxygen provided is too rich, and the individual's regular breathing response is interrupted—he simply stops breathing.

Cerebral Palsy, Mental Illness, and Alcoholism

Lastly, there should be mention of three populations—the cerebral palsied, the mentally ill, and the alcoholic. The severely involved cerebral palsied person may be intellectually able to cope with the complexities of travel but may not have any feasible way to be transported on a daily schedule to a work situation where his abilities can be utilized.

Many persons with psychiatric disabilities are overwhelmed by the complexities of urban transportation. Advocacy is needed to secure bus passes and to teach patiently the routes and transfer points. Reduced cost of transportation is also an important support to successful adjustment of the psychiatrically disabled to community life.

In the case of alcoholism, the urban transit system needs a firm and enlightened policy. With sensitive training, its transit operators can learn to discriminate between the people with alcohol on their breath and those who are sufficiently inebriated to be out of control.

People with many other kinds of disabilities have similar experiences and difficulties with travel. Some people with multiple sclerosis (MS) report a variety of problems when their condition has advanced or when they are not in remission. For instance, some have visual problems and cannot see to drive, a few have to sit close to the restroom on the bus because of bladder and bowel incontinence, and sometimes it is the frustration of not having a simple bar to hang on to in an airline washroom. Some airlines will not transport a motorized wheelchair or the batteries for them, in which case a power source at the destination must be located. When they do take a folding wheelchair in the luggage compartment, the wheelchair user may have to wait for half an hour before an attendant with an airport chair comes to deliver the traveler to the baggage compartment where he can pick up the chair. If the person with multiple sclerosis or rheumatoid arthritis does not have a driver's license because an attendant is used as a driver, and if the individual does not have credit cards or other identification, it may be difficult to arrange for easy car rental at the destination.

Almost all disabled people have to plan far ahead, informing transportation personnel of their disability and needs. The disabled person may have to double-check arrangements at the destination to be sure that any special needs will be met. It may take strict regulation of food intake or deliberate abstinence from fluids for a matter of hours if the transportation washrooms are inaccessible. Some individuals with communicative disorders may have great difficulty in making their needs understood and need to plan for this contingency. As one person with MS related, "I look normal, but when I get tired my voice is very weak and people don't understand me."

Travel for Recreation

An increasing number of disabled persons are traveling around North America as well as the rest of the world. Some of the individuals writing about what's possible are excited and optimistic. For example, Russek writes in his foreword to Gutman's *A Travel Guide for the Disabled* (1967):

> Travel by the physically handicapped has been increasing in recent years. One sees them everywhere in wheelchairs, on crutches, wearing artificial limbs (or braces) in every major airport, railroad station and ship embarkation area. Travel facilities, as well as hotels, have provided ramps, wheelchairs, attendants and structural modifications to accommodate these travelers. (p. 3)

And Bruck, in her book *Access* (1978, p. 225), writes, "The world has opened up for disabled travelers. Airlines, railroads, interstate buses, highways, accommodations, places of interest are becoming accessible and willing to serve this newly emerging sector of the traveling public."

Although travel is simpler than it once was for most disabled people, many barriers of attitude and architecture still survive. Airport facilities in small developing countries can still provide hair-raising experiences. Many historical antiquities, such as the Acropolis or Great Pyramid of Cheops, have to be seen from a distance. Information about travel can be secured from:

> *Access Guides for Cities and States*, Rehabilitation World, Travel Services Department, 20 W. 40th St., New York, N. Y. 10018.
>
> *Access New York*, N.Y.U. Medical Center, Institute of Rehabilitation Medicine, 400 E. 34th St., New York, N.Y. 10016.
>
> *Access Washington*, Information Center for Handicapped Individuals, Inc., 1413 K. St., N.W., Washington, D.C. 20005.
>
> *A List of Guidebooks for Handicapped Travelers*, The President's Committee on Employment of the Handicapped, Washington, D.C. 20210.

Dialysis Worldwide for the Traveling Patient, NAPHI, 505 Northern Blvd., Great Neck, N.Y. 11021.

Easy Wheelin' in Minnesota, Robert R. Peters, One Timberglade Rd., Bloomington, Minn. 55437; Education Services Department, The Minneapolis *Star* and the Minneapolis *Tribune,* 425 Portland Ave., Minneapolis, Minn. 55488.

Flying Wheel Tours, 148 West Bridge St., Owatonna, Mich. 49201.

Grand Travel Consultants, 427 Broad St., Shrewsbury, N.J. 07701.

Gutman, Ernest M., Encar Publications, Fort Lauderdale, Fla. 33308: *Cape to Cape by Wheelchair, Middle Europe by Wheelchair,* and *A Travel Guide for the Disabled.*

Handicapped Visitor Services Booth, Union Station, 50 Massachusetts Ave., N.E., Washington, D.C. 20002.

Handy-Cap Horizons, 3250 East Loretta Dr., Indianapolis, Ind. 46206.

Highway Rest Areas for Handicapped Travelers. The President's Committee on Employment for the Handicapped, Washington, D.C. 20210.

Hill Travel House, 2628 Fair Oaks Blvd., Sacramento, Calif. 95813.

Kasheta Travel, 139 Main St., Far Rockaway, N.Y. 11690.

National Park Guide for the Handicapped, no. 2405-0286, Superintendent of Documents, U.S. Government Printing Office, Washington, D.C. 20402.

Rambling Tours, P.O. Box 1304, Hollandale, Fla. 33099.

The Wheelchair Traveler, Douglas R. Annand, Ball Hill Rd., Milford, N.H. 03055.

Travel for the Patient with Chronic Obstructive Pulmonary Disease, Rehabilitation Research and Training, George Washington University Medical Center, Ross Hall, Rm. 714, 2300 Eye St. N.W., Washington, D.C. 20037.

Travel Information Center, Moss Rehabilitation Hospital, 12th St. and Tabor Rd., Philadelphia, Pa. 19141.

Vacationlands N.Y. State, Supplement for Handicapped and Senior Citizens, The Easter Seal Society, 2 Park Ave., New York, N.Y. 10016.

Where Training Wheels Stop, Paralyzed Veterans of America, Washington, D.C. 20014.

Public Policy

Excluded from reference in the civil rights and transportation legislation of the 1960s, the right to access to transportation by disabled was mentioned in a 1970 amendment to the Urban Mass Transit Act (UMTA) of 1964, Section 16(a):

> It is hereby declared to be the National Policy that elderly and handicapped persons have the same right as other persons to utilize mass transportation facilities and services; that special efforts shall be made in planning and design of mass transportation facilities and services so that the availability to elderly and handicapped persons of mass transportation which they can effectively utilize will be assured; and that all federal programs offering assistance in the field of mass transportation (including the program under this Act) should contain provisions implementing this policy.

This new section tied disabled people's right of access to public transportation to public funding, a first step toward improving the mobility of the disabled population.

The next major piece of federal legislation that carried this concept forward was the Rehabilitation Act of 1973. Section 504 of this Act states:

> No otherwise qualified handicapped individual in the United States shall, solely by reason of his handicap, be excluded from the participation in, be denied the benefits of, or be subjected to discrimination under any program or activity receiving federal financial assistance.

Although Section 16 of the UMTA amendments covered only the transportation programs funded by the Urban Mass Transportation Administration, Section 504 touched all transportation programs with *any* federal funds. According to a 1977 report of the Comptroller General of the United States (General Accounting Office, 1977), 114 federal programs provide financial assistance to human service agency-operated transportation programs serving various disadvantaged people including those with disabilities. In addition, federal funds assist a large number of other transportation programs, including the airline regulatory programs; airport, train, and other terminal construction; the Amtrak system; highway construction; and of course, public transit. Section 504 applies to all these programs.

It is important to recognize that the passage of the UMTA amendments and Section 504 of the Rehabilitation Act did not automatically open up transportation for disabled people. Today, little headway has been made, except on paper. What has occurred is a growing awareness on the part of the transportation industry and some public officials that these laws mean expensive changes in both equipment and standard operating practices (estimates in 1977 ranged from $1.8 billion to $5 billion to implement the 504 regulation for UMTA alone). The transportation industry's reaction to these regulations has been delay and more delay. This can be illustrated by looking at the history of the Transbus. The design was begun in 1971, after which there was a series of rules published, hearings conducted, rules amended. Finally, in May 1979 when bids were put out there was no response. At this writing Transbus is still in the requirements, but it appears not to be a viable issue.

Changes in federal policy covering access to other transportation modes have taken place with considerably less publicity, but frequently as much controversy, as the Transbus issue. Until the publication of the DOT regulations implementing Section 504, architectural barrier removal and changes in policy to improve access to transportation by disabled people occurred in a somewhat disjointed manner.

The leader in the field has been Amtrak which adopted a policy to provide special assistance to "Aged and Handicapped Passengers" (Amtrak Executive Memorandum, 1972). "It will be Amtrak policy to consider the special requirements of aged and handicapped persons in our passenger service policies and in the design of passenger cars, stations, and terminals." The policy goes on to say that "as special barriers now exist which, in a sense, discriminate against these passengers, special efforts will be made by Amtrak through employee training, passenger information programs, station design, passenger assistance, and in all aspects of vehicle design and renovation."

Commenting on *The Source Book for the Disabled* (Hale, 1979), Feiss states:

> Enlightened as these arrangements are, certain practical difficulties remain. Passengers are not permitted to travel in wheelchairs. On short-distance runs, the special toilet for the handicapped, which is large enough for wheelchair entry, is in the food service car, of which there is only one, and at the most two, on each train. But given the basic restriction that no passenger may occupy a wheelchair, the disabled traveler must first retransfer to the wheelchair and then again out of it onto the train seat.
>
> The solitary passenger cannot expect more than minimal help from an Amtrak employee in transferring to a regular train seat, and the only seat on each train which has a removable arm to facilitate transfer from a wheelchair is also in the food service car. On most short-distance runs,

including those from Boston to New York to Washington, there is no reserved seating—not even for the special seat in the food service car. Nevertheless, given advance notice, Amtrak staff claim that every effort will be made to accommodate the handicapped passenger.

Feiss continues by saying that the DOT's May 1979 regulations implementing Section 504 provide, in great detail, specific design and program standards covering all aspects of Amtrak's services and setting time limits for their implementation. The implication of these new standards is that the 1972 policy was not adequately effective as a means for improving access for disabled travelers.

Most of the United States population lives in urban areas, making rapid transit systems especially important to the transportation needs of the disabled. Concerning these systems, Bruck (1978) states:

> In subways, accessibility is severely limited. Only cities with new systems are accessible to mobility-impaired individuals: Atlanta's MARTA (Metropolitan Area Rapid Transit Association), San Francisco's BART (Bay Area Rapid Transit Association), and Washington's Metro. New York, Chicago and Boston systems remain almost totally inaccessible. Even the accessible systems require disabled persons to traverse long distances between the train platforms and accessible elevators. Vision- and hearing-impaired passengers need clearly marked destination signs on the trains and audio announcements about destinations on platforms and about stations within the trains.
>
> At Washington's Metro the elevator buttons are identified by raised printing and in Braille. Half-fare rates apply twenty-four hours a day. Routing and scheduling is available for deaf citizens on a TTY service. Metro is also the first subway designed to warn deaf passengers of incoming trains. Every time a train comes, a row of lights on the edge of the platform grows brighter, warning deaf people to step away from the edge, and lights dim after the train leaves the station. (p. 225)

It should be noted that, in the case of the Washington, D.C. system, it took a rather drastic legal action to halt the commencement of service until the subway was made accessible.

The airlines pose a different set of problems. Unlike Amtrak which is owned and operated through the federal government, the commercial airlines are privately owned and operated, although federal funds support their regulation and the construction and operation of airports. Controversy about the rights of disabled passengers on commercial aircraft has raged for years. Until recently people in wheelchairs were regularly denied the right to travel by air. Even now, one often hears reports of people "being treated like baggage."

The safety of the passengers and the plane has been given as the reason that wheelchairs, white canes, and other assistive devices have been refused on board. In 1977, the Federal Aviation Administration amended its rules establishing a policy covering denial of service to passengers needing special assistance:

> No certificate holder may refuse transportation to a passenger on the basis that, because the passenger may need the assistance of another person to move expeditiously to an exit in the event of an emergency, his transportation would or might be inimical to safety of flight. . . .

However, these rules allow the airline to refuse service if the airline has "established procedures (including reasonable notice requirements) for the carriage of passengers who may need . . . assistance" to exit quickly, but only if the passenger fails to comply with the notice requirements in the airline's procedures, or the passenger cannot be carried in accordance with the airline's procedures. The rules go on to require that the airline provide its local FAA office with a copy of the procedure it adopts for review by the FAA administrator. The significance of this rule is clear. There are few, if any, guarantees of equal treatment of disabled people among the airlines. The burden of knowing all the varying rules falls squarely on the disabled person.

The DOT Section 504 regulations seek to standardize and clarify the rights of disabled passengers using federally financed airport facilities. Speaking to "each operator at an airport receiving any federal financial assistance," the regulations specify that all fixed facilities, services, and amenities at airports (terminals) must be fully accessible to disabled people, regardless of their disability. Of special interest are sections covering the provision of assistance and specially designed jetways and passenger lounges for the enplaning and deplaning of passengers. Where such equipment is not available, lifts, ramps, or other suitable devices not normally used for the movement of freight can be used to board passengers in wheelchairs. The implication of these new regulations, when read in their entirety, is that if they use any federally funded airports, airlines will not be allowed to deny access to passengers who are disabled, thus nullifying the FAA policy described above.

While UMTA-funded public transit and paratransit systems around the country have been subject to Section 16 of the UMTA, as amended, efforts to provide adequate accessible public transportation for disabled people have been uneven. Uniformly, all public transit operators receiving Section 5 operating assistance from

UMTA have provided half-fare programs for elderly and disabled riders. A number of cities including Los Angeles and Seattle have adopted policies of full accessibility, but have been unable to find fully reliable wheelchair lifts and are only replacing a small part of their inaccessible fleet each year, so accessibility is spotty, at best.

In some communities, plans have been made to pool a number of vans and minibuses to form a paratransit system or to form a service where nothing else is available. However, these coordinated efforts are hard to implement over a large region so that, at this writing, only the small state of Delaware has a state-wide authority for special transportation (DAST).

Many people have planned federally financed "dial-a-ride" systems, which were discontinued after the federal funding period expired. However, many cities operate a limited service which picks up passengers at their doors and delivers them to their destinations. Such services are usually popular with recipients, but they are expensive. Door-to-door services usually require advanced booking, ranging from a matter of hours to a matter of a few days. Some providers may require trip prioritization, such as medical first, work second, then shopping, recreation, and so forth. They are rarely operated the same hours as regular bus services, and many services are not provided on the weekend. Some systems, as in Tacoma, Washington, have planned a mixed program—accessible standard transit plus a fleet of dial-a-ride vans serving people who cannot realistically use the transit system.

The potential effect of Section 504 on the nation's public transportation systems is tremendous. New regulations mandate that transit and paratransit vehicles purchased after May 31, 1979 be wheelchair accessible and that all terminals and support facilities and services must meet specific standards for accessibility. The key phrase in these sections of the DOT implementing regulations is "the system, when viewed in its entirety, must be accessible to wheelchair users." This phrase means that the entire system does not have to be accessible. For example, secondary commuter or rapid-rail and subway stations do not have to be accessible to wheelchair users as long as "key" stations are. Key stations are defined as transfer points, major interchanges with other modes, and end stations. The entire fixed-route public transit system (bus) does not have to be accessible either, according to the regulations: program accessibility is achieved when one-half of the peak hour fleet is accessible to wheelchair users.

Public policy is only as good as the efforts to carry it out. In stating that disabled people have the right to use publicly funded transportation, the federal government has set the ground rules for the future. A major problem occurs, however, in sectors where federal programs do not exist or where federal programs are of limited scope. For example, most DOT programs focus on the urban areas with few programs designed to serve rural communities or benefit the disabled people in these areas. In addition, federal funding to support these new policies or establish new programs does not appear to be readily available, and growing pressure to reduce taxes and cut public spending does not suggest that this situation will be remedied soon.

Litigation

In the litigation brought by physically handicapped individuals to secure access to public transportation systems, courts have taken three different approaches. First has been the purely passive approach of deferring entirely to the decisions of administrators of the transportation companies. Not only have courts shown great deference to the administrators, they refused to interpret Section 504 to require extensive affirmative efforts on behalf of handicapped riders. An example of this judicial conservatism is *Snowden* v. *Birmingham-Jefferson County Transit Authority:*

> Although it is necessary for persons handicapped in this manner (wheelchair users) to arrange for someone to help them board and alight from the bus, these persons are allowed to use the transportation vehicles in question. Thus, it cannot be said that persons who ambulate by wheelchair are excluded from use of the defendant's transportation system. For this reason, the court finds no violation of the Rehabilitation Act of 1973 (by the defendant), and hence that Act provides plaintiff and the class she represents with no cause of action.

Had this interpretation of Section 504 been widely accepted by courts, it would have gutted the implementation of the statute in transportation accessibility matters. However, a second approach by courts, although somewhat passive, has been more activist because it relied on administrative regulations promulgated by the Urban Mass Transportation Administration as guidelines for determining appropriate transit services and viewed the principal function of courts as enforcement of those regulations. In *United Handicapped Federation* v. *Andre,* the Court of Appeals for the Eighth Circuit took this approach to the UMTA regulations:

On the basis of record before the district court, if it were not for the subsequent promulgation of the administrative guidelines and regulations, we would agree with the district court's result. However, we feel that the denial of relief to the plaintiffs cannot be justified in light of these recent definitions and guidelines. Although the buses in question have been purchased and placed in service, because of the recent developments the defendants now have the burden to take affirmative action to conform to the regulations and guidelines. It is difficult to assess the record and statutes in any other light. . . . The district court, upon receiving further evidence, should reappraise defendant's compliance with the statutes, regulations and guidelines, and fashion whatever equitable relief it deems necessary.

This approach is limited in the sense that it appears to ratify and use as a basis for further proceedings the UMTA regulations (which many handicapped people and their advocates have considered inadequate). At the same time, it at least recognizes the obligation of public authorities to make affirmative efforts to remove the barriers in the transit system and to design the system in a way that some degree of access is provided for handicapped passengers.

The third approach has been taken by courts which have gone beyond the *Andre* holding and attempted to assess the actual performance of transit authorities in specific situations. In *Vanko* v. *Finley* the federal district court assessed the operation of the Cleveland Transit Authority in terms of compliance with the UMTA guidelines. The court concluded that compliance by local transit authorities with the UMTA regulations was sufficient to satisfy the requirements of both Section 504 and the Urban Mass Transportation Act "special efforts" provision. Likewise in *Atlantis Community Incorporated* v. *Adams,* the court also was unwilling to go beyond the provisions of the UMTA regulations in requiring federal or local defendants to provide accessible transportation for handicapped people.

Thus although handicapped people have been able to persuade courts to go beyond the very restrictive approach exemplified by *Snowden,* judicial activism has been quite limited. Courts have shown extraordinary deference to the judgment and role of administrative agencies in defining what constitutes appropriate public transportation for handicapped people, even against contentions that the levels of effort provided for in the regulations are inadequate. Overall, the judicial response to suits brought in the transportation area reflects a cautious approach. Currently, there is not a great deal of promise for major litigation attempting to challenge inadequate public transportation policies at either the federal or local level.

References and Bibliography

Amtrak Executive Memorandum, No. 72–4, Washington, D.C.: March 15, 1972.

Architectural and Transportation Barriers Compliance Board. *Resource guide and literature on barrier free environments*, with selected annotations. Washington, D.C.: 1977.

Atlantis Community Incorporated v. *Adams*, 453 F. Supp. 825 (D. Col. 1978), *appeal docketed* no. 78–1963 (9th Circuit, Dec. 14, 1978).

Bruck, L. *Access, the guide to a better life for disabled Americans*. New York: Random House, 1978.

Buyer's guide, Bloomington, Ill.: Accent on Living Magazine, 1978.

Department of Transportation, Urban Mass Transit Administration. *Technical report of the National Survey of Transportation of Handicapped People*, Washington, D.C.: 1978.

Federal Aviation Administration. *Regulations*, Chapter 27, Section 121–586, Washington, D.C.: effective 4/24/78.

Feiss, C. Personal communication, 1980.

General Accounting Office. *Report of the Comptroller General of the United States: Hindrances to coordinating transportation of people participating in federally funded grant programs*. Washington, D.C.: USGPO, 1977.

Goldenson, R. M., Ed.; Dunham, J. R. & Charlis S., Assoc. Eds. *Disability and rehabilitation handbook*. New York: McGraw-Hill, 1978, pp. 120–126.

Gutman, E. M., *A travel guide for the disabled*. Springfield, Ill., Charles C Thomas, 1967.

Hale, G., Ed., *The source book for the disabled*. New York: Paddington Press, 1979, p. 53.

Hall, K. Personal communication, 1980.

Handicapped Americans Reports Magazine, 1979, 2, (17).

Larsen, F. *Transportation for the elderly and handicapped*. Unpublished Master's thesis, University of Washington, 1979.

Michaels, J. *Transportation: An overview of laws and service models for people with disabilities*. Olympia, Wash.: Governor's Committee on the Employment of the Handicapped, 1978.

Snowden v. *Birmingham–Jefferson County Transit Authority*, 407 F. Supp. 394 (M.D. Ala. 1975), aff'd *per curiam*, 551 F. 2d 862 (5th Cir. 1977), reh. den. 554 F. 2d 475 (5th Cir. 1977).

United Handicapped Federation v. *Andre*, 558 F. 2d 413 (8th Cir. 1977), reversing and remanding 409 F. Supp. 1297 (D. Minn. 1976).

Vanko v. *Finley*, 440 F. Supp. 656 (N.D. Ohio 1977).

10 Keeping the Disabled out of the Employment Market

Financial Disincentives

Bonnie Sims and Scott Manley

There is increasing reference to the role financial disincentives to employment play in the total psycho-social-vocational rehabilitation of the disabled. The disincentive problem is not to be confused with malingering, because in many instances the individual may be physically, mentally, and psychologically ready for employment. Here the disincentive problem is the realization by the disabled individual that benefits may be lost once employment is secured. Thus, in reality, the social compensatory systems are designed to compensate disablement rather than assist productivity.

Financial disincentives do not always manifest themselves in cash-in-hand benefits, nor do they necessarily equal or exceed pre-injury financial status. An individual receiving Social Security Disability Insurance and Medicare, for example, may also be entitled to food stamps, rent subsidy, and educational and social service benefits. A combination of these indirect benefits represents significant cash value.

> If employment following rehabilitation is to be successful, it must produce income that would generate utility as great as the utility generated by benefits in order to be worthwhile to the client. In addition, a labor income would need to cover employment costs such as clothes, transportation, food on the job, and taxes. Under Title XVI (SSI) the cash benefits are lower, so incentive to work is presumably higher unless other welfare provisions such as food stamps, rent and subsidies reduce that incentive. (Carley, 1975, p. 8)

This chapter deals primarily with disincentives to employment faced by the spinal cord injured, persons who acquired their injuries traumatically, often as the result of their active life-styles. Individuals affected are for the most part between the ages of 19 and 39, have a high school education or less, and were employed pre-injury in blue-collar positions. Their vocational experience is mainly in fields requiring physical and manual dexterity; they literally made their living off the "sweat of their brow." Thus, following an incapacitating total and permanent injury, they do not have the skills and training necessary to secure sedentary vocational positions. In most instances, financial compensation for their labor would not exceed disability benefits. Further compounding problems associated with their vocational rehabilitation is the widespread endorsement of a psychology of entitlement wherein the individual feels he has literally paid his premium for disability benefits and is entitled to reap the returns.

Financial benefits available to the disabled can be grouped into four major categories: (1) Workers' Compensation, (2) Social Security/SSI, (3) private insurance (including no-fault insurance), and (4) coordinating benefits.

Workers' Compensation

An individual injured on the job is entitled to Workers' Compensation benefits, including medical coverage and weekly indemnity payments as compensation for lost wages. In recent years greater emphasis has been given to the provision of rehabilitation benefits as well. The Department of Labor indicates approximately 80% of the workers nationally are covered under state and/or federal compensation programs. However, there is considerable variability in individual state laws with regard to the extent of coverage, benefits paid, and insurability requirements. Individuals addressed under Workers' Compensation programs are those classified as totally and permanently disabled. According to the State Workers' Compensation Laws (1969), they are presumed to be unable to work or unable to work steadily in the labor market.

Some state plans, such as those in Minnesota and California, may statutorily determine who is permanently and totally disabled. Such people would be entitled to receive lifetime indemnity benefits regardless of changes in employability. In other states indemnity payments are limited to a time and/or dollar maximum (i.e., $200/week for 400 weeks) with no penalty imposed for re-employment. This amount is, in fact, a settlement on the disability paid out over a period of weeks. In the majority of states, however, the individual may be rated as having a permanent partial disability which would result in the termination of benefits once employment is again secured. In all states unlimited medical coverage is provided. This benefit insures that if medical care is needed, it will be made available to the disabled individual regardless of post-injury employment status.

Knowledgeable and enlightened Workers' Compensation insurance carriers have developed creative benefit packages which assist the disabled individual in re-employment with the returns being a reduction in medical costs. This is a significant feature when it is learned that the lifetime care of a paraplegic may approximate $900,000 (El Ghatit, 1978). Consider, for example, the following case:

Mr. S. was rendered paraplegic while working on the job as a manual laborer. He was of average intelligence but lacked formal schooling beyond the eighth grade. He was married and had two children. Mr. S.'s insurance company was involved with his case from the onset of the accident. They explained the insurance benefits available to him and, in addition, indicated they would pay costs associated with air transportation and living arrangements for the patient's wife while she learned the various aspects of her husband's rehabilitation program.

During Mr. S.'s rehabilitation program the insurance carrier requested from the rehabilitation staff specific recommendations for housing modifications. Although this was not a specific benefit of his policy, the insurance carrier realized the importance of allowing Mr. S. the freedom to be as independent as possible. The insurance carrier also recognized that the long-term medical costs of Mr. S.'s case would probably be significantly higher if he were confined to his home, where he could become depressed and deteriorate physically. An automobile with automatic transmission was also purchased and delivered to the rehabilitation facility so that Mr. S. could receive driver's training in his own vehicle. At the completion of his rehabilitation program, he and his wife drove to their recently modified home in their new car.

The scene was set for the insurance carrier to approach Mr. S. about returning to employment. He was well informed of his benefits and had a high level of trust in the insurance carrier. If he returned to work, the insurance carrier would remain responsible for ongoing medical costs, which they felt would be minimized as a result of Mr. S's improved self-concept as a contributing member of his community. Mr. S. was enthusiastic about returning to work, and therefore the insurance carrier initiated vocational testing and exploration. Mr. S. wanted to operate a laundromat, so a market analysis was conducted to determine the need and potential success of a laundromat in his community, with positive results. The insurance carrier advanced the necessary funds to purchase the land, build the laundromat, and provide the necessary equipment. Mr. S. would be responsible for cleaning and general operation of the facility. His net income the first year was over $20,000. Mr. S. continues to do well medically and vocationally. The insurance carrier has been able to keep medical costs to a minimum and has already recovered its initial investment.

Insurance carriers recognize that cost effectiveness is achieved through medical management and that indemnity benefits may account for only a fraction of the potential lifetime cost of a catastrophically injured person. Farsighted companies recognize that adequate medical management and acquisition of rehabilitation skills are not in themselves sufficient to ensure reintegration into the community if the environment prohibits an active life-style or relegates the individual to domiciliary care. Realizing that total rehabilitation requires the necessary equipment, housing, and transportation, compensation carriers may revamp the environment, purchase nonmedical convenience items, and equip vehicles with the proper controls to ensure driving independence. In some instances the carrier may advance indemnity benefits to allow purchase of an accessible home, a useable vehicle, or self-owned business, as seen in the preceding case example.

Although case management by the Workers' Compensation industry could serve as a model to various social agencies, there is no conclusive proof that a Workers' Compensation recipient is more likely to return to employment than someone with alternative sponsorship. Problems preventing re-employment may be circumvented through the provision of adequate housing, transportation, medical coverage, and attendant help when needed, but there still remains an unknown quantum which severely curtails vocational involvement.

Most importantly, the individual needs full information of his benefits under state law. Often there is confusion (as well as suspicion) on the part of the disabled individual as to whether his benefits will be discontinued should he seek re-employment. He is often unsure as to the extent of medical coverage and the willingness of the carrier to provide assistance beyond the letter of the law.

Negligence on the part of the carrier to provide this information about benefits can be exemplified by the case of a young quadriplegic male receiving unemployment benefits at the time of injury. Under the law he was entitled to indemnity benefits based on his unemployment income, a precedent set in his state of residence. Since he was not informed of his potential claim, he could well have sought counsel in settling this matter. The attorney could have sued for punitive damages from the carrier in addition to securing lost wage benefits for his client.

Although in many states there is entitlement to full benefits or a settlement as such, attention should be paid to provide offsetting indemnity provisions, wherein the individual continues to receive indemnity payments despite employment. Thus if he returns to work at a lower salary than that earned prior to injury, he would be compensated by an additional sum to equal his prime employment level. As an individual progresses in his employment and his salary status improves, the offsetting amount would be decreased.

Referring again to the psychology of entitlement theory, consideration should be paid to terminology associated with disablement. Terms such as "total and permanent," "lost wages," and "disability insurance" only encourage and reinforce the inability to perform. Substituting the term "continuation of salary" without taxation or continuation of full salary with deductions for a period of one or more years might reassure the individual that he remains an integral member of the work force. Use of such terms would also impose an obligation on the individual to return to his vocational duties. Although a study conducted by Sims and Manley (1979) indicates that employed spinal-cord-injured individuals who have returned to their former employer receive greater salaries than spinal-cord-injured individuals who return to a different job and/or a different employer, it is not always feasible for the disabled to return to their former positions. In such cases, employers may have to consider other positions for these employees to assume. Motivation to re-employ the disabled worker may be increased if the employer is required to subscribe for reimbursement through various compensatory systems, such as Social Security or Workers' Compensation.

Certainly, potential employers should be informed that individuals with Workers' Compensation coverage are entitled to full medical coverage for their specific injury and any concomitant complications. They should be made aware that the cost of ongoing medical needs met through group health and accident plans need not rise as the result of increased utilization by handicapped employees. Employers should be notified that the Second Injury Fund is available to the handicapped employee should he incur additional injuries on the job. Finally, employers should be alerted to tax incentives, such as deductions for modifications to work site and the availability of funds for initial salaries paid to handicapped employees. The employer may also call on the state vocational rehabilitation agency to assist with modifications to the work environment.

Social Security/SSA–SSI

Prior reference was made to an unknown quantum severely curtailing compensation recipients from becoming re-employed. It is the assumption by these authors that the major disincentive contributing to this phenomena is Social Security Disability Insurance (SSA).

If the disability is presumed to continue for at least 12 full months, after a waiting period of five full months of disablement, the individual may receive SSA benefits based on his work history. These benefits may comprise the greatest income possible, especially if the person has an active work history, received a substantial salary pre-injury, and has several dependents.

As previously stated, many spinal-cord-injured persons are not equipped physically or educationally to secure sedentary jobs paying a salary comparable to pre-injury rates. Basically, the Social Security Disability Insurance/Supplemental Security Income (SSI) program is based on an all-or-none theory regarding substantial gainful activity. A family of four may receive maximum benefits amounting to approximately $966 per month tax free. Despite a trial work period of nine months wherein the disabled individual continues to receive benefits along with income derived from employment, this amount is discontinued if the individual is able to earn as little as $330 per month. Prudent individuals will not risk losing the security of a maximum insured income in order to become employed in a position that may gross only $600 per month.

Compounding the disincentive to work is the added benefit of Medicare, for which one is eligible two years following onset of benefits. Though Medicare is not comprehensive, it does provide some security against major medical setbacks.

Since there may be a combination of benefits under SSI and SSA, it is first necessary to elaborate on the former to understand the intra-agency discrepancies and how forces combine to pose work disincentives. Depending on his existing assets, the disabled person may be eligible for Supplemental Security Income within the first five months of injury (dependent on date of application). SSI in itself is a minimal amount, presently set at $238 per month, and it does not pose a major disincentive. However, entitlement to SSI may also ensure payment of benefits under Title XIX (Medicaid, Medicare, etc.). In addition to the indemnity amount from SSI, the individual may receive benefits from his county of residence as well as attendant fees. (In some states attendant fees approximate $600+). The greatest disincentive with this combination of benefits is the loss of medical and/or personal care attendant benefits in the event of employment. In many states, Title XIX provides coverage for hospitalization, physician fees, equipment, supplies, medications, and the like. With employment, these benefits are terminated unless a state provision for spend down and/or self-support plan is implemented. The purpose of spend down or a self-support plan is to allow an individual to earn income above the allowable amount if this additional income is needed to meet ongoing medical or attendant care costs.

Although these plans initially provide a financial incentive to return to work, when the trial work period is completed these benefits are lost. Unless the disabled individual has returned to work at a salary level which permits him to assume the ongoing expenses of medical and/or attendant care, he may be faced with the situation of being too poor to continue working. If he seeks employment, the disabled person may subscribe to a health and accident plan. In many instances, however, the plan does not cover pre-existing conditions or requires a lengthy waiting period before full entitlement for pre-existing conditions takes effect. It may also lack the inclusiveness of Title XIX coverage.

An additional deficit in the Social Security system as it exists today relates to the time period during which medical coverage is provided for disabled persons. If entitled to SSI benefits, the disabled begin receiving a monthly indemnity payment in addition to state medical coverage, and, if required and prescribed, aide and attendant fees. However, they may lose these benefits if they are entitled to SSA and if there is no spend down program in their state of residency. As soon as SSA benefits are in effect they often exceed the allowable maximum income from SSI. Thus not only will SSI be terminated, as well as any county supplement, but more importantly, there will no longer be entitlement to Title XIX and to aide and attendant fees. Two exceptions would be entitlement to an SSA amount less than the SSI indemnity amount, or a state spend down program which would continue entitlement to Title XIX and possibly aide and attendant fees. The individual is now without medical coverage until two years after entitlement to SSA, when Medicare takes effect. This benefit continues as long as the person receives SSA or for three years after a return to employment.

Suggestions for Remediation

Title XIX (Medicaid) should be extended as primary coverage for catastrophically disabled individuals not entitled to other medical sponsorship. Title XIX should be expanded in its scope to include prescribed equipment (we would include the term purchase, since many vendors hesitate to subscribe to payment on a monthly rental basis), drugs, and equipment repair. In addition, there should be provision for personal care attendant fees, for attendant costs alone can serve as a disincentive if the person sees a large portion of his monthly labor income allocated to attendant salaries. While full benefits may remain in effect during the trial work period, thereafter an offset formula should be applied to salaried income, including extraordinary expenses related to self-maintenance.

The disabled person should immediately be entitled to SSA benefits, eliminating the five-month waiting period and continuing for the longevity of the injury. The five months following injury is a period of financial crisis for most individuals and families, and income available through the social agencies is desperately needed during this period. Benefits for total and permanent disabilities need to begin immediately to help offset costs incurred in making necessary modifications in the environment.

Private Insurance Plans

Many people subscribe to mortgage insurance on their homes or property, disability insurance on loans or bank notes, or simply enroll in a plan offered through newspaper advertisements. They may also subscribe to private plans available through their place of employment which supplement disability compensation such as Social Security and Workers' Compensation. Still other plans pay a straight daily amount for the duration of the disability, which for most traumatic injuries covers a lifetime.

In most mortgage or loan insurance plans, payment is made only as long as the person is unemployed. Permanent and total disability is not recognized as cause to pay off the balance. Instead, payment is made in monthly installments. Though this is not actual cash in hand, it is a financial obligation the individual would have to meet should he return to employment.

Suggestions for Remediation

There is little expectation that insurance carriers will change their policies regarding private disability plans, mortgage insurance, and the like. Nevertheless, they, too, should give consideration to encouraging re-employment. Perhaps benefit to their concern would be realized by applying an offsetting principle to earned income. They could ultimately decrease their monetary involvement without jeopardizing the individual's total income. Consideration might also be given to settling such claims on an annuitized basis.

No-Fault Insurance

No-fault insurance laws were designed to expedite the assignment of responsibility for insurance benefits so injured persons could immediately receive appropriate treatment without first establishing fault of liability. Although it is no panacea, proponents believe it is far superior to the judicial system from the standpoint of fairness and speed in compensating the automobile accident victim on a first-party basis rather than a third-party basis (National Institute of Neurologic and Communicative Disorders and Stroke, 1975). No-fault provisions include coverage of medical expenses, rehabilitation expenses, work loss benefits, essential service benefits, and death benefits.

Lost wage benefits with a time or dollar amount limit are available in all states subscribing to a personal injury protection plan (PIP). Because the indemnity is in most cases paid within the first year of injury, it does not constitute a major life-long disincentive to employment. However, in such states as Michigan, New Jersey, and Pennsylvania, this is not the case, for there the amount paid is considerable, and payment of benefits may extend over a period of years. With return to employment these benefits may be discontinued. The possibility thereby exists wherein the individual may be covered by a plan providing lost wage benefits over an extended period which, in essence, presents a major disincentive to resuming employment.

Although most no-fault plans include medical coverage, this feature of the plan is limited to a dollar maximum or specific time period, and once met, the individual is forced to obtain such coverage through other sources.

Suggestions for Remediation

Though, in most instances, wage loss benefits are depleted before the individual is physically or psychologically ready for employment, it would seem prudent for insurance carriers to accelerate payments or agree to subsidize employment wages without monetary loss to injured individuals. This gesture is based on the presumption that an actively involved person is less likely to require excessive medical assistance.

Careful consideration should also be given to the necessity of attendant care, the number of hours required, and whether it should be paid to a family member, since this fee adds to total family income. Once fees have been established a penalty is felt if they are suddenly withdrawn when the individual becomes employed. If less care time is needed, fees should be withdrawn gradually until an economic balance is achieved. However, in cases in which family dynamics are disrupted as the result of the partner becoming the attendant, consideration should be given to paying someone other than a family member to provide attendant care.

Farsighted insurance carriers are endeavoring to work creatively within the limits of the no-fault law. Accelerating lost wage benefits may allow the individual to purchase a van or vehicle which is not an obligation of the carrier by law but essential to maintaining the disabled person's independence. They are also endeavoring to settle liability claims with greater expediency, a dual benefit to both carrier and claimant.

Liability or uninsured motorists claims should be here considered. Persons with total and permanent disabilities will in all likelihood be awarded policy limits under the responsible party's liability coverage. If the responsible party is uninsured, the individual will claim uninsured motorist coverage under his own plan.

Speedy settlement of claims can reassure the individual that he has received all benefits available and ensure his awareness of his financial status. The most positive approach to claims handling is to fully inform the individual of his rights under the law. This leaves no surprises which can upset the claimant and prompt him to seek legal counsel. It also relieves the psychological tension often observed in persons who must prove the extent of disability under tort action.

Finally, the advice of an attorney can be a contributing factor to unemployment since counsel may discourage employment as possibly jeopardizing the ultimate liability settlement. Unenlightened attorneys may discourage an injured employee from returning to work until the case comes to settlement, which often can take a number of years.

Coordinating Benefits

VA Service-connected Compensation

Little reference is made in this chapter to the Veterans Administration's system of compensation for service-connected injuries, since it is primarily a self-contained system. Benefits of entitlement as well as lifetime medical coverage continue regardless of employment status and should not pose a major disincentive to re-employment. The literature, however, indicates this method of compensation has not proven to be a great motivator to reemployment. One possible explanation is that the maximum allotment paid is substantial and service-connected veterans do not experience a financial need to seek employment.

Nonservice-connected Pensions

An individual receiving less than $6243 per year from the above-mentioned benefits (SSI, SSA, etc.) and who is in need of aide and attendant care may be eligible for VA benefits in the form of a monthly pension and aide and attendant fees. Although not given priority, they also have access to medical services for hospitalization, equipment, supplies, medication, and the like. With loss of pension through employment they are again relegated to a payment basis.

Eligibility for another type of compensation, G.I. benefits used for vocational and/or educational retraining, often include a monthly stipend based on number of dependents and number of credit hours taken.

Housing Subsidy

Subsidy may be available under Section 8 for a disabled individual living in rental property. The amount of subsidy is determined by adjusted gross annual income (after medical deductions) as well as the fair rental market in his area of residence. With increased income his contribution escalates until it exceeds the ceiling allowed.

Though other subsidy housing programs are available through HUD, including a low-interest rehabilitation loan for modifications to a home or apartment and a low-interest Farmer's Home Administration loan for constructing a new dwelling, the aforementioned Section 8 subsidy appears to provide the most direct benefits.

Following are case examples illustrating the interworkings of social benefit programs and how they work against the disabled's full employment.

Case Example 1

A 36-year-old man from Wyoming became paraplegic as the result of an oil field accident. His yearly salary as a rigger had ranged between $22,000 and $27,000. Following the accident, his benefits included indemnity under Workers' Compensation, Social Security Disability Benefits for a family of four, a private disability plan on a bank loan, as well as an additional disability policy that subsidized all other monthly income not to exceed $1,500. This gentleman was made aware that under Wyoming law he was entitled to all compensation benefits with lifetime medical coverage for his total and permanent disability, regardless of his employment status. The disincentive to employment, however, was created through Social Security benefits of approximately $928 per month tax free for himself and his family. With employment he would lose this amount on completion of his trial work period. In addition, he would again be responsible for meeting monthly payments on his loan.

Being a reasonable man, he was aware that he could not earn a comparable income, because he had limited educational and vocational skills. He simply did not feel that he could benefit financially by seeking employment. Certainly one can understand his reasoning. Though he does not equal his pre-injury income status, he is not willing to risk losing benefits at the cost of employment. Thus he stays at home. By his own admission, he has intractable pain, his spasticity has increased, and he feels that his family has little respect for him.

Case Example 2

A 40-year-old quadriplegic with two children was referred for marital counseling. The problem appeared to be that his wife had become his nurse/companion. She freely admitted that it greatly bothered her to have her husband underfoot as she tended to household chores.

The husband indicated that financial disincentives prevented his employment, though his former company had on several occasions offered him a position. Although his income did not meet pre-injury standards, it was tax free and he did not want to jeopardize his benefits which included a Social Security income of $974 per month, Workers' Compensation benefits of $130 per week, and attendant benefits of $650 per month paid to his wife, making for a total yearly income of over $20,000. He was aware that he had lifetime medical benefits under the Workers' Compensation law, in addition to Medicare.

Case Example 3

A 26-year-old unemployed oil field worker was rendered paraplegic as the result of a vehicular accident. He had no financial assets other than the camper truck in which he was living at the time of the accident. The truck was demolished in the accident, but at the time of purchase he had subscribed to a disability policy that would cover the monthly installments on the unpaid balance of the truck camper.

The young man had no medical insurance or income. Thus it was necessary for him to apply for Supplemental Security Income, Medicaid, and Social Security Disability Insurance to meet his ongoing medical maintenance, rehabilitation, and personal needs. Prior to discharge, application was also made for HUD subsidized housing since he had no residence or family support.

Because he was discharged from the hospital three months before entitlement from SSA, his only source of income was $208 per month from SSI and an additional $13 from the county in which he would reside (while hospitalized he was entitled to only $25). Because of a computer error his change of address information delayed payment of SSI until two months after his discharge. Though he obtained HUD subsidy housing and moved into a less-than-accessible apartment (the narrow bathroom door prohibited entrance in his wheelchair), he had no money for food, telephone, transportation, clothing, and the like. He could not draw on assets derived from selling the camper truck, for to do so would result in cessation of disability payments. He was supplied no Medicaid card at discharge and could not obtain necessary medications and supplies.

Through a local charitable organization he received a $300 automobile for which a vocational rehabilitation agency purchased hand controls. Through the auxiliary at the rehabilitation hospital he was given an allotment for installation of a telephone, initial rent and deposit, as well as a small supply of groceries. (He could not apply for food stamps until he had income with which to purchase them.)

Though he was not psychologically ready for employment at this early stage in the adjustment process, he indicated it was his only alternative. With employment, however, he would lose the much-needed medical assistance provided by Medicaid, SSI benefits (once they began), as well as potential income ($534) from SSA. Concurrently, his rental payment on the apartment would increase based on his salary. Fortunately he did not require personal care, though the hazardous bathroom accommodations would have warranted assistance.

The young man vascillated between total defeat and resignation that he would have to seek domiciliary care and extreme anger against the "system." Though his VA status was being reviewed, he had still received no determination of assistance from the VA at discharge. Consequently, he sought out legal assistance to review medical management during the emergency care period. In view of his financial straits he was literally clutching at every straw. The loss of pride he felt in having to battle the system and in accepting local charity has lead to threats to take his own life.

In conclusion, there are a variety of benefits available to the physically disabled through federal, state, and worker compensation systems and private insurance carriers. The combination of these direct and indirect benefits, including cash benefits, food stamps, rent subsidy, medical, educational, and social services, represent considerable cash value. Because the availability of many of these benefits is contingent on maintenance of an unemployed status, they in effect become major disincentives to re-employment. Although financial aids of this type are helpful and at times essential if survival is to be ensured, these compensatory systems can functionally prohibit the disabled from active vocational involvement, encourage invalidism, and reinforce a psychology of entitlement wherein the individual feels he has literally paid his premium for disability benefits and is entitled to reap the returns. Currently, there is a proliferation of proposed legislative changes which address the specific economic, social, vocational, and architectural barriers faced by the disabled. Although all these are necessary and no area of a person's functioning should be neglected, there are priorities that must be considered. Basic survival needs must first be addressed. Confusion over such priorities often results in contradictory and counterproductive laws. For example, recent legislation encouraging accessibility to the polling place is certainly desirable but meaningless to the disabled person who is uncertain if his attendant, whom he pays less than minimum wage, will arrive to assist with his personal care. Legislation on the federal level should be directed toward meeting the basic needs of all individuals suffering from catastrophic disabilities, such as spinal cord injury. If these needs are met with a minimum of confusion and dealt with in a unitary fashion, only then will the disabled population experience the freedom to seek outside involvement and be able to contribute productively to the national economy.

References

Carley, E. J. *Final report of the ad hoc committee: Ways to improve the trust fund and SSI program.* Providence, R.I.: Department of Vocational Rehabilitation, 1975.

El Ghatit, A. Z. Variables associated with obtaining and sustaining employment among spinal cord injured males: A follow-up of 760 veterans. *Journal of Chronic Disorders*, 1978, *31*(5), 363–369.

National Institute of Neurologic and Communicative Disorders and Stroke. Bulletin: Casualty and Surety, #1. DHEW Pub. No. (NIH) 76-729. Washington, D.C.: U.S. Dept. of HEW, January 1975.

Sims, B., & Manley, S. Disincentives to employment. Paper presented at the Annual Meeting of the American Spinal Cord Injury Association, New York, 1979.

State Workers' Compensation Laws, Bulletin #161. Washington, D.C.: U.S. Department of Labor, revised 1969.

11 Health Care Delivery

Problems for the Disabled

Judith Falconer

> We hold these truths to be self-evident: That all men are created equal;
> that they are endowed by their Creator with certain inalienable rights;
> that among these are life, liberty, and the pursuit of happiness.

Many disabled individuals find that only life is guaranteed. Liberty is conditional, and, though they are allowed to pursue happiness, political, economic, and social obstacles result in their achieving it far less frequently than the able-bodied. Many of the deficits in both liberty and happiness are direct and indirect consequences of decisions and decision-making processes in health care systems.

Obviously, health care decisions affect the able-bodied as well as the disabled. Because the disabled need more medical care, more often, health care problems become major obstacles rather than minor, infrequent inconveniences. When illness or injury occurs, most individuals are rapidly reduced to a childlike, dependent status. Those who fully recover return to adult status; the denigrating experience of disability soon becomes a distant nightmare. Those who fail to recover are forced to participate in a medical system which values health, beauty, and physical perfection. The disabled are the failures of medical care, to be hidden away, experimented on, kept alive, allowed to live in society only as second-class citizens.

The second-class citizenship the disabled experience is not a consequence of disability; it results from decisions that have been made, are being made, and will be made *for* and *about* the disabled, but seldom *by* the disabled. Decisions in health care systems are as much a consequence of the people who make them as the objective facts on which they are made. When substantive health care decisions are explored, one must also examine who makes the decisions and what criteria are used.

Decision Makers in Health Care for the Disabled

Our social system makes illness and disability individual and family responsibilities: parents are expected to meet the medical needs of minor children, spouses of their mates, adults of their aging parents. Adults are rarely forced to accept health care. (The contagious, the unconscious, and the mentally incompetent are, of course, exceptions.) If I choose to refuse medical care, extreme pressure may be applied to convince me to accept treatment, but I *can* refuse, both initially and at any point in the treatment process. We have perhaps made too much of the necessity for legal restraints against physicians keeping people alive. Such finger-pointing at physicians allows patients and their families to abdicate their responsibility. The ultimate decision maker in health care is the individual or that person's legal guardian (Schmale & Patterson, 1978). The disabled may refuse treatment. The problem is that they cannot demand, control, or pay for treatment; their decision-making power is limited: accept or refuse treatment. No other bargains are offered.

Traditionally, physicians have both the authority and responsibility to make health care decisions about individual patients, presumably using patient welfare as the sole criterion (Benoliel, 1978). They have, however, surrendered much of their decision-making power to the sociopolitical system. Especially for the disabled, health care is seldom a personal relationship between patient and physician. When disability occurs, others enter the role of decision maker and use criteria in addition to patient welfare to make decisions. It is the other people and other criteria that make the disabled second-class citizens, initially in health care settings, eventually in society.

Many of the decisions on health care for the disabled are made by politicians, using economic, social, and political criteria. Politicians decide what illnesses and disabilities will receive the lion's share of federal research dollars, how much individuals and families will pay for medical care, what drugs and procedures can legally be provided, where experimental treatments will be provided and who will receive them, and so on. Some disabling conditions, such as polio and smallpox, have been virtually eliminated because adequate research funds, facilities, and medical personnel were available to find cures and provide appropriate care to all potential victims. Other illnesses are rapidly being eliminated as a result of governmental decisions: for example, as all children are required to receive German measles vaccinations, the incidence of infant deafness and blindness secondary to maternal rubella declines.

Other political decisions have had negative consequences. The decision to approve the use of thalidomide resulted in the birth of a large number of children with severe birth defects; psychiatric patients suffer extrapyramidal complications of federally approved major tranquilizers. On the other side, disabled individuals may be forced to travel to other countries to obtain drugs and treatments not yet approved for use here.

Some political decisions have directly or indirectly led to severe disabilities. In states in which motorcycle helmet laws have been withdrawn, increased numbers of adolescents and young adults suffer brain damage and spinal cord injuries. Factory workers and miners are employed in OSHA-approved environments which directly cause lung and skin disorders. Federal subsidies support the tobacco industry after the Surgeon General labels cigarettes a leading cause of cancer and heart and lung diseases. Not all political decisions are rational!

The most important health care decision—who should live—is made by a variety of people, using moral, social, political, and economic criteria. Our ethical values and legal system lead us to abhor death regardless of cause: homicide, suicide, accident, disease, or disability. We declare suicide a violation of mental health laws as we gradually move toward the abolition of capital punishment. Even if liberty and the pursuit of happiness are severely compromised, life must be preserved. That decision has been made.

Sophisticated medical practices allow us to decide for life. Increasing numbers of individuals now defeat catastrophic diseases and injuries, to survive with severe disabilities. Physicians, assisted by respirators, monitors, pacemakers, and a supermarket of pills, capsules, and injections, can maintain vital functions even after meaningful brain activity has ceased. All of us are potential Karen Quinlans!

Historically, physicians, backed by the courts if necessary, have made the life-and-death decision. Recently, however, we have begun to move away from physicians as final arbiters of life-and-death decisions. States are providing legal guidelines that allow individuals and family members to decide whether to accept or continue heroic measures in the case of severe disability or terminal illness (Heifetz, 1978). We have not fully resolved some of the problems resulting from this change in who the decision maker is; lawyers, physicians, theologians, families, and individuals struggle daily to reach decisions about quality of life, on when to discontinue heroic measures, on when organs can be removed for transplantation (Rosenberg & Kaplan, 1979).

No matter who makes decisions or what criteria are used, patients must, in a very literal sense, live with the consequences of the decisions. For the disabled, more health care decisions are made by more people, the decisions have more severe and far-ranging consequences, and the disabled are less involved in the decision-making process.

Substantive Decisions in Health Care for the Disabled

The first and most important decision is whether and to what degree treatment will be available. Not all disabling conditions can be cured (e.g., renal failure) or even stabilized (e.g., diabetes). Some disabling conditions can only be cured by creating other disabilities: excising spinal tumors may result in paralysis; removing a cancerous larynx means speech will be lost. Some disabilities can be treated only experimentally. In certain types of cancer the cure may be worse than the original disease. Society decides what diseases and disabilities will receive the most attention. We, as individuals, respond to appeals for support from some disability groups and reject appeals from other disability groups.

The second decision is whether treatment will be sought. The poor frequently do not seek medical care: they have little medical knowledge; they cannot affort to pay; they have no medical facilities available to them (Mechanic, 1972). Consequently, they may become disabled from relatively mild conditions that were left untreated or were treated too late. Congenital or early childhood disabilities, especially retardation, may go unrecognized and therefore untreated. Unusual conditions may not be detected at an early stage by overworked public clinic doctors and nurses. So if you must be disabled, don't be poor!

If medical care is sought, the disabled must decide where to receive treatment. Consider, for example, the decision to enter a hospital. No matter how ill I feel, I cannot admit myself to a hospital; only doctors have that authority. Once admitted, I must comply with rules, accept suggested treatment, and generally give up my decision-making power. The physician decides when I should leave the hospital, whether I can return home or require placement in an extended-care facility, when I should return for followup care, what medications I should take, and so on. As a very healthy person, I would probably allow physicians to make these decisions. But how about the disabled? Does it work equally well for them to surrender this much decision-making power? Usually not.

The disabled may well know their own symptoms and warning signs better than most physicians, especially physicians who do not specialize in that particular disability. Disabled individuals may know hospitalization is required but be denied admission until symptoms worsen and their condition becomes critical. On the other hand, the disabled may be admitted solely for the convenience of physicians: it is easier to treat a patient who is available 24 hours a day, 7 days a week, even though treatment may require less than an hour a day. For the disabled person, however, hospitalization means time off work, extra expense, separation from family and friends, and no control over daily life. The decision to admit is more than a medical decision: it is also an economic, social, and political decision. Yet the disabled are not allowed to participate in the decision; they are only allowed to suffer the consequences.

Another important decision is what treatment will be provided. For most medical conditions there is more than one appropriate treatment (Barger, 1978). One may, for example, treat cancer by chemotherapy, radiation therapy, or surgery. Who decides? Physicians. For example, when possible, specialists treat laryngeal cancer surgically. I asked an otolaryngologist what happens when patients refuse surgery, insisting instead on radiation or chemotherapy. The response: no patient had ever refused surgery; all patients willingly surrendered their voiceboxes to the knife. How can this be true? Physicians can present the treatment alternatives in such a way that there is no decision to be made. The patient is co-opted.

When treatment will be provided is another important decision. Medical care is a five-days-a-week proposition. Hospitals and clinics are, for all practical purposes, closed on weekends. Physical therapy facilities darken at five each afternoon. Chemistry labs refuse to draw or analyze blood after the regular workday. Only emergency X–rays can be done after the day shift goes home. Because the disabled may need these services every week, or even daily, it is difficult for them to be employed and still get medical care.

Not all decisions which must be made are urgent, yet most are treated as if they were. For example, a friend who discovered a lump in her breast had difficulty finding a surgeon who would operate in two stages: biopsy the lump and, after the results were discussed with her, jointly decide whether to proceed to a radical mastectomy. Most physicians seem to have the motto "My way or the highway." If the disabled want treatment, they must accept physicians' timetables.

The decisions which have led to medical specialization in this country have a widespread impact on the disabled. Individuals with multi-system problems frequently feel as if they are dissected, defective parts whisked off to appropriate repair shops, and then only casually reassembled before return to the community. Specialists often find the medical problems of the disabled uninteresting or too challenging. Few plastic surgeons enjoy repairing the decubitus ulcer of the quadriplegic. Parents may find it impossible to locate a dentist to treat their retarded or emotionally disturbed child, much less one with special skills. Psychiatrists asked to treat psychotic dialysis patients hesitate to prescribe psychotropic medication because they lack knowledge of drug excretion routes in renal failure.

The primary physician may decide not to refer a disabled patient to a specialist. A deaf person may live with a badly scarred face because a physician decided that being attractive was not important to the deaf; quadriplegics may be celibate because they were not referred for sex counseling; the blind may show marginal psychological adjustment because they received no psychological support when blindness struck.

For the disabled, a major problem occurs when rehabilitation goals are decided by staff members and presented to patients as if engraved on tablets of stone. Patients have not been allowed to participate in the goal setting but, should they refuse to participate in the program, they are labeled as "unmotivated" and summarily discharged.

Some of the most important decisions are those involving payment for health care. Disability is outrageously expensive, with almost everything costing more. Yet we have decided that individuals must pay for their own care and that of family members.

The widely publicized problems of job discrimination and public transportation are addressed elsewhere in this text (Chapters 9 and 10), but hidden health care costs force the disabled into lives of economic slavery. Job discrimination creates both decreased ability to pay for medical care and increased personal cost of medical care. Most able-bodied workers participate in employer-subsidized health insurance plans. The unemployed disabled pay the total insurance bill, if they can obtain insurance at all. Some employers decide against hiring or retaining disabled workers because group insurance plans will not provide coverage.

Decisions about medication costs also cause severe problems for the disabled. Physicians, faced with hundreds of new medications each year, prescribe the product of the most recent salesman—by brand name. Only recently have consumers reduced drug costs by demanding prescriptions by generic name. For some disability groups, however, only one manufacturer produces the appropriate drug. The pharmaceutical company divides research and production costs by total units sold, and volume alone is not sufficient to reduce price. Similarly, minimal competition in production and sales inflates the cost of adaptive equipment. Special diets or food supplements may severely strain family budgets: the disabled pay extra for salt-free butter and vegetables, low-protein bread, and special formulas. In a population in which dietary compliance is a necessity for functioning more fully in society, proper nutrition unfortunately often becomes a luxury.

Those who schedule medical appointments sometimes act as if their goal is to have disabled patients in the hospital or clinic five days a week. Physical therapy is scheduled Monday, Wednesday, and Friday; speech therapy, however, is available Tuesday and Thursday. Someone decided on that schedule, and the disabled suffer the consequence. They eventually become unable to work and still receive medical care.

The disabled also find themselves paying for defensive medical practices. Test and procedures are prescribed to protect physicians from possible malpractice suits. If the disability is particularly interesting, additional procedures may be ordered solely to satisfy the curiosity of physicians or to settle academic arguments. We have not yet decided to restrain malpractice suits or to establish effective control, via lay review, of medical costs.

In some cases, diagnostic procedures or treatments are not prescribed because patients cannot afford to pay. Although many disabled individuals and their families would benefit from psychotherapy, they must weigh the cost of outpatient treatment against the cost of physical therapy. The disabled may volunteer for research projects solely to reduce the cost of their medical care. Obviously, we have not yet decided to pay for socialized medicine. And as health care becomes more specialized, the cost of adequate care rises astronomically.

Some of the decisions about health care for the disabled affect all disability groups, albeit differentially. All disabled individuals are affected by the expense; many are affected by architectural barriers; most are affected by medical practices specific to their disability group.

To fully understand the problems of health care for the disabled, one must focus on a single disability. Only then do generalities become painful specifics. Only then can one see the effect of health care decisions as they ripple out beyond medical care. Thus we now turn to the problems of end-stage renal disease (ESRD).

End-Stage Renal Disease as Prototype of Health Care Services for the Disabled

Because many readers may be unfamiliar with ESRD a brief medical review is needed. ESRD is nondiscriminatory: it strikes young and old, rich and poor, male and female. It may result from genetic conditions such as polycystic kidney disease, chronic medical conditions like diabetes or spinal cord injury, unwise acts like heroin or aspirin abuse, or its cause may never be determined. Onset may be gradual or acute.

The diagnosis of ESRD was a death sentence until the development of chronic hemodialysis in the early 1960s. With the reprieve came the multiple complications of this new treatment. The medical community reached into its bag of tricks and produced yet another miracle: kidney transplantation. Not one but two technologies were now available. Life can be guaranteed, at least temporarily, but the fact that liberty and happiness are compromised becomes obvious when the options are examined more closely.

Chronic Hemodialysis

In the early days of dialysis, the politics and economics of health care were such that the number of patients whose lives could be saved greatly exceeded available equipment. Those whom society valued less, those already disabled, the elderly, the crippled, the retarded, the emotionally disturbed, were denied treatment. No one felt comfortable making decisions that were, in effect, death sentences (Simmons, Klein, & Simmons, 1977). The health care system, or society in general, had to respond.

In 1972 the federal government agreed, through the Chronic Kidney Disease Amendment to the Social Security Act (Public Law 92-603) to pay for dialysis: equipment, space, personnel, medication, almost everything. Naturally, dialysis facilities expanded at a rapid rate. Now every patient who can benefit from dialysis is able to receive this life-saving treatment. Today more than 40,000 patients are dialyzed to maintain life; the numbers increase yearly (Chyatte, 1979). We decided to make available and even to pay for treatment of a single disability. The problems of health care for dialysis patients have been solved. Right? Wrong!

Although ESRD patients are frequently led to believe that dialysis will return them to a reasonable approximation of good health, few dialysis patients feel well (Chyatte, 1979; Czaczkes & DeNour,

1978). Most are chronically anemic, chronically depressed, have dry skin, itch unbearably, and are always thirsty. They take as many as 50 pills per day, some to counteract the side effects of others. Their diet rigidly limits protein, sodium, potassium, and fluid intake (my patients joke that, if it tastes good, spit it out, it's not on your diet). Some develop gastrointestinal complications, especially bleeding. Blood-access sites become infected or clot off. Some develop problems secondary to their kidney disease: brittle bones break easily; hearts become pathologically enlarged. Most experience decreased sensation in their extremities from peripheral neuropathy. Male dialysis patients are frequently impotent; few can father children. ESRD does not provide immunity from other diseases or disabilities; dialysis patients also contract cancer, arthritis, ulcers, and spinal cord injuries. Finally, dialysis patients die much sooner than their healthy peers.

The dialysis procedure, repeated two or three times a week for three to eight hours per session, takes place in a hospital, free-standing facility, or at home. If travel to a dialysis center is required, routine treatment may require 20 to 25 hours per week. For life. Liberty is severely curtailed. Vacations must be planned far in advance and scheduled near dialysis facilities that accept transient patients.

Before dialysis begins, one or two large needles (a colleague calls them sharpened pipes) are inserted into a surgically prepared access site, usually in the arm or thigh. The patient's blood flows, via clear tubing, to an artificial kidney, where waste products and water are removed; the cleansed blood is then returned to the patient's body. Dialysis patients who can't stand the sight of blood are in real trouble!

As they dialyze, patients may experience severe cramps throughout their bodies, become nauseated and vomit, and develop hypotension. They may have seizures or cardiac irregularities. Other patients in the room may also be experiencing these things. Imagine spending four hours watching your blood circulate outside your body while the person next to you vomits! Many patients feel extremely weak when they finish dialyzing; some have difficulty stopping bleeding from their access sites. It is difficult to pursue happiness when you feel rotten! Happiness becomes a smooth dialysis run (Chyatte, 1979).

Problems also exist for staff members on dialysis units (Kerr, 1977; Rustad, 1980). People enter clinical medicine to help people return to health. When a patient does not improve, the professional has failed. Yet dialysis is not a cure; it is palliation. Not only do patients fail to improve after the initial stabilization, they eventually die under your care. Staff members become frustrated, depressed, and angry.

The frustrations of staff are frequently directed toward patients, especially those who repeatedly abuse diet and fluid restrictions or medication schedules (Brown, 1979). The staff expects patients to be independent in their daily lives but dependent during the actual dialysis procedure: a classic double bind on both sides. And because they spend so much time with each other, patients and staff develop close relationships; they soon learn to hurt each other by attacking the most vulnerable spots.

Because the technology is so readily available, staff members may be obligated to dialyze patients who have a very slight chance of survival. Dialysis is an uncomfortable procedure at best, and nurses may feel they are inflicting futile and unnecessary torture. Only very special nurses can work in a dialysis unit. Even they burn out quite rapidly (Figgins, 1979a, 1979b).

Home dialysis is available to provide treatment more conveniently and economically and to avoid some of the problems of dealing with staff members and rigid schedules. Patients and their spouses learn to operate their own dialysis equipment. But many patients are ineligible because they have no partner to assist them, have medical complications during dialysis, or have other disabilities like blindness. If the spouse is employed outside the home, patients are requesting their mates to assume another half-time job, without pay of course. Landlords sometimes will not allow the plumbing and electrical modifications that must be made to set up the equipment at home. Only recently have dialysis patients been able to contract with nonfamily members to do the procedure in the home. Even when home dialysis works well, the spouse is under substantial stress (Abram, 1977; Czaczkes & DeNour, 1978); home dialysis is the only exception to the rule that medical personnel do not provide care for family members.

Many dialysis patients are physically unable to work. For others, especially those with limited education and few marketable skills, securing a job that will both pay more than disability income and allow the required time off work for dialysis and routine medical care is impossible. Dialysis patients are truly representative of the financial disincentives to work.

The restrictions of life on dialysis cause great stress for patients and their families (Chyatte, 1979; Reichsman & Levy, 1977). The dialysis regimen is particularly stressful for adolescents and young adults (Drotar & Ganofsky, 1976). At these life stages, social activity revolves around places that are off-bounds for dialysis patients: the local pizza and fast food places or discos. Others may interpret the multiple needle marks on a teenager's arm as evidence of drug use. Sexual functioning may be delayed or diminished.

ESRD has an unpredictable course: patients move rapidly from a state of chronic ill health to acute, life-threatening crises. It is difficult for patients to predict from one day to the next how they will feel. How then can they plan for the immediate, much less the long-range future? All dialysis patients treated at a particular facility know each other very well. They see fellow patients die and know their own death may occur at any time, without warning; the life-death continuum becomes distorted (Pattison, 1978).

Most of the cost of dialysis, $25,000 to $30,000 per patient year, is paid by Medicare and other governmental agencies. At some point in the near future it is highly likely that Americans will begin to question the return on their tax dollar (Simmons, Klein, and Simmons, 1977). Unless costs can be reduced, dialysis programs may be severely curtailed. Costs could be substantially reduced if the profits of those supplying equipment and service were controlled. Oil companies are not unique in needing windfall profits taxes!

By now it should be obvious that dialysis does not solve the problems of ESRD. It does keep patients alive, and it must be worthwhile, for patients are not forced to begin dialysis or to continue dialysis once they have begun (Oberley & Oberley, 1979). Most continue dialyzing until they die from causes beyond their control. However, some patients do not adapt to or succeed on dialysis (Levy, 1979). For them the only alternative to death is transplantation. But that transplantation has its own problems is easily demonstrated.

Kidney Transplantation

The 16,400 ESRD patients who had opted for kidney transplants by 1975 (Simmons, Klein, & Simmons, 1977), and those transplanted since, hoped to avoid the medical complications, the highly restrictive medical and dietary requirements, and the time and discomfort of chronic hemodialysis. Children and adolescents hoped to avoid the severely stunted growth of chronic renal failure. Adults hoped to regain sexual ability and to have children. All hoped to avoid the sick role, to become healthy once again.

Deciding to get a transplant is a stressful process, further complicated by different orientations among medical staff. Nephrologists who run dialysis programs strongly advocate their therapy; they see the transplant failures as they return to dialysis, sometimes in worse condition than when they left. Transplant surgeons, who tend to see only those patients who decide against dialysis, strongly advocate their therapy. Both specialists follow the medical progress of their own successes and see only the failures of the other. Patients must make their own decisions, often in the face of conflicting advice.

Obtaining kidneys for transplantation presents unique ethical and moral dilemmas for patients, their families, and society at large. Uniform criteria for determining death are not yet established, but families of the acutely ill are asked to donate organs before their injured spouse, parent, or child has ceased to breathe. This is a very difficult decision to make (Rosenberg & Kaplan, 1979).

Since grafts from living related donors are considerably more successful than those obtained from cadavers, family members may be under great pressure to donate their kidneys. The surgeon who removes a healthy kidney from a healthy patient is practicing very unique medicine. Some donors have developed complications from this surgery; a very small number have died. The psychological problems of kidney donation and transplantation have been thoroughly explored by Simmons, Klein, and Simmons (1977), a text which should be required reading for all concerned with problems in health care for the disabled.

After transplant surgery, the graft may fail to function, may function at marginal levels (chronic rejection), or may function well for a period of months to years before it rejects. When rejection occurs, patients must return to dialysis, perhaps awaiting another donor.

Even with successful transplants, patients are not completely healthy. The immunosuppressive drugs to prevent rejection of the foreign tissue increase susceptibility to infections, bloat the face, and may cause cataract formation and diabetes. Some of the problems of the original kidney disease are stopped but not reversed by transplantation. Although transplantation does not totally remove disability, research evidence indicates that patient satisfaction with the quality of life is quite high (Simmons, Klein, & Simmons, 1977; Sophie & Powers, 1979).

In many ways, ESRD patients are at the forefront of medical care for the disabled. They are unique in that their care is fully subsidized. Their treatment procedures are rapidly being improved and the quality of their lives is substantially better now than it was only 5 years ago. But they are still second-class citizens. They are still denied full lives, especially if they are on dialysis. They still have little happiness and little liberty. Many problems remain to be solved.

Conclusion

Solutions to the problems faced by the disabled in obtaining medical care require attack on at least three fronts: prevention and cure of disabling conditions, financing health care, and changing social systems and values.

The ideal solution would be to prevent or cure disabling conditions. Mandatory screening programs for early detection could significantly reduce the disabling consequences of conditions such as lead poisoning and glaucoma; they have already succeeded in reducing the severity of retardation from phenylketonuria. If the use of seat belts were mandatory, thousands of disabilities would be prevented at absolutely no cost.

Massive changes must occur in the allocation of our health care dollars. Socialized medicine, or at least insurance against catastrophic illnesses, seems inevitable. The legislation which covers ESRD patients may serve as a model for other disabilities. Disabilities must not automatically result in poverty. The disabled cannot continue in economic slavery while physicians live in luxury and drug companies show obscene profits. The families of the disabled must be paid for the health care they provide if we expect them to continue to provide service. If society decides to keep the disabled alive, it must also decide to allow them to live reasonable lives.

The puritan work ethic and our national obsession with beauty and health must fall before the disabled can participate fully in society. We must learn to value people for their abilities rather than pity them for their disabilities. Communities must become both physically and psychologically accessible.

Many high schools now have handicap days, when students attend classes and participate in school activities in wheelchairs, on crutches, or with blindfolds or hearing dampeners. Such activities sensitize them to the daily living problems of the disabled and allow schools to identify barriers to full participation by handicapped students. The mainstreaming movement, which requires children to be educated in the least restrictive environment, is rapidly making the handicapped visible in society. They are no longer hidden away in special schools and workshops. Soon they will ride our buses, work in our factories, and marry our sons and daughters. Are we ready?

Ultimately, the disabled must accept some limitations on their liberty and their happiness. The question is how much liberty and happiness can be made available, how soon, and at what cost.

References and Bibliography

Abram, H. S. Survival by machine: The psychological stress of chronic hemodialysis. In R. H. Moos (Ed.), *Coping with physical illness*. New York: Plenum, 1977.

Barger, S. L. Personal-professional support: From a patient's point of view. In C. A. Garfield (Ed.), *Psychosocial care of the dying patient*. New York: McGraw-Hill, 1978.

Benoliel, J. Q. Care, communication and human dignity. In C. A. Garfield (Ed.), *Psychosocial care of the dying patient*. New York: McGraw-Hill, 1978.

Brown, C. J. Chronic non-compliance in end-stage renal disease: Assessment and intervention. *Dialysis and Transplantation*, 1979, 8, 1210–1214.

Chyatte, S. B. *On borrowed time: Living with hemodialysis*. Oradell, N.J.: Medical Economics, 1979.

Czaczkes, J. W., & DeNour, A. K. *Chronic hemodialysis as a way of life*. New York: Brunner/Mazel, 1978.

Drotar, D., & Ganofsky, M. A. Mental health intervention with children and adolescents with end-stage renal disease. *International Journal of Psychiatry Medicine*, 1976, 7, 181.

Figgins, N. Burn out. *Dialysis & Transplantation* 1979, 8, 1011. (a)

Figgins, N. Prevention of burn out. *Dialysis & Transplantation* 1979, 8, 1222. (b)

Heifetz, M. D. Ethics in human biology. In C. A. Garfield (Ed.), *Psychosocial care of the dying patient*. New York: McGraw-Hill, 1978.

Kerr, N. Staff expectations for disabled persons: Helpful or harmful. In R. P. Marinelli and A. E. Dell Orto. (Eds.), *The Psychological and Social Impact of Physical Disability*. New York: Springer, 1977.

Levy, N. B. Psychological factors affecting long term survivorship on hemodialysis. *Dialysis & Transplantation* 1979, 8, 880–881.

Mechanic, D. *Public expectations and health care*. New York: Wiley-Interscience, 1972.

Oberley, E. T., & Oberley, T. D. *Understanding your new life with dialysis*, 2nd edition. Springfield, Ill. Charles C Thomas, 1979.

Pattison, E. M. The Living-dying process. In C. A. Garfield (Ed.), *Psychosocial care of the dying patient*. New York.: McGraw-Hill, 1978.

Reichsman, F., & Levy, N. B. Problems in adaptation to maintenance hemodialysis. In R. H. Moos (Ed.), *Coping with physical illness*. New York.: Plenum, 1977.

Rosenberg, J. C., & Kaplan, M. P. Evolving legal and ethical attitudes toward organ transplantation from cadaver donors. *Dialysis & Transplantation* 1979, 8, 906–907.

Rustad, L. C. Facilitating communication: An aid to effective treatment on the renal dialysis unit. In M. G. Eisenberg, J. Falconer, & L. C. Sutkin

(Eds.), *Communication in a health care setting.* Springfield, Ill.: Charles C Thomas, 1980.

Schmale, A. H., & Patterson, W. B. Comfort care only: Treatment guidelines for the terminal patient. In C. A. Garfield (Ed.), *Psychosocial care of the dying patient.* New York.: McGraw-Hill, 1978.

Simmons, R. G., Klein, S. D., & Simmons, R. L. *Gift of life: The social and psychological impact of organ transplantation.* New York.: Wiley-Interscience, 1977.

Sophie, L. R., & Powers, M. J. Life satisfaction and social function: Post-transplant self-evaluation. *Dialysis & Transplantation* 1979, *8*, 1198–1202.

12 Families of the Disabled

Sometimes Insiders in Rehabilitation, Always Outsiders in Policy Planning

Betty Goldiamond

The Patient's Family: At Risk, but Disenfranchised

This chapter is concerned with a category of people who have no identity as members of a group but who have in common the characteristic of close relationship to persons who have suffered a spinal cord injury. I have belonged to this category since 1970, when my husband was injured in an automobile accident. Persons like me do not often know each other, nor do others recognize us as individuals who share special interests and concerns. We have produced no spokesmen to describe our everyday lives, our sorrows, our hopes, our needs and efforts. Nor have we developed advocates, for we have no group organizational objectives and no programs. Though we have experienced similar personal and family disruptions and though we have social, psychological, and economic problems in common, we have yet to define these and to develop systems of mutual aid or self-help. If severely disabled people, like the spinal cord injured, are second-class citizens, we, their family members, are truly second-

The author wishes to express her gratitude to Julie Bulfer, Muriel Beadle, Mary Keenan, and Jeannette Taylor, who read and carefully criticized the original draft of this chapter. The continuing support and interest of my husband, Israel Goldiamond, and daughter, Shana Goldiamond, are much appreciated, as are the contributions made by all those other professionals, handicapped persons, and relatives of the disabled who have shared their thinking about their own experiences with rehabilitation with me during the years just past.

class citizens once removed. Even to ourselves we have been invisible and voiceless.

The implications of my lack of status as a person with legitimate interests in rehabilitation processes did not begin to become apparent to me until the summer of 1976. At that time, I requested and received an application form to attend the Illinois Conference on Handicapped Individuals. This conference was organized as part of the preparation for the first White House Conference on Handicapped Individuals, which occurred in May 1977. The publicity for the Illinois meeting announced discussion sessions and lectures that appeared to be of vital interest to me, as was the fact that state delegates to the White House Conference would be selected by those attending. To my surprise, I discovered as I filled out the application form that the conference planners did not have participants like me in mind. To apply for an admission card, I was required to categorize myself as being either (1) a handicapped person, (2) the parent of a handicapped child, or (3) a provider of services for the handicapped. Though I did not fit into any of the prescribed categories, I returned the application and was, indeed, allowed to attend the state conference. There I discovered that if I had wanted to go to the White House Conference as a delegate from Illinois, I failed to meet the qualifications established. Candidates had to be selected from the three categories listed above.

Illinois was not singularly perverse in this regard. I learned later that the official conference announcement booklet, *The White House Conference on Handicapped Individuals* (1976), stated that " . . . 50 percent of the 672 State delegates are to be disabled, 25 percent to be parents or guardians of handicapped individuals, with the remaining 25 percent to include others involved in research, labor, service delivery, medical, legal, advocacy and the broad variety of activities surrounding the needs and concerns of disabled persons." Invited nonvoting observers included representatives from national provider and consumer organizations, the fields of both business and labor, and directors of state programs in rehabilitation, developmental disabilities, education, and mental health. Governors, directors of significant federal programs and members of Congress also received special invitations (White House Conference on Handicapped Individuals, 1977). Everybody with a legitimate interest was represented there except those who share the bed or are the children, brothers, or sisters of the handicapped.

This same strange omission came through clearly in the *Implementation Plan,* published in June, 1978, as Volume Three of the Final Reports of the Conference (White House Conference on Handicapped Individuals, 1978). The report begins with a statement about priority action items identified by the National Planning and Advisory Council from among the 810 recommendations and 142 resolutions passed by the delegates to the White House Conference. The first priority action item calls on the Administration to move immediately to formulate and issue a strong statement of national policy to ensure that individuals with disabilities may participate fully in our society with full enjoyment of its benefits, and it urges that, in the formulation of policy, the Administration shall include *"Individuals with disabilities, their parents or guardians, and their organizations"* [italics added].

Following immediately after the above is priority action item two, recognition of the unique needs of individuals with disabilities. This recognition of needs is said to be " . . . a requisite for implementing the concept of *independent living* in the least restrictive environment . . . " [italics added]. Surely the people who prepared the implementation plan knew that the large majority of severely disabled persons, and, certainly, of those with spinal cord injuries, are not living independently but instead are living by their own choice with the families of which they are part. Why do the writers resort to the semantic camouflage provided by the phrase, "independent living," when the real goal for the disabled—as for the nondisabled—is a fulfilling and satisfying interdependence with others? Why the diversion of focus from the need for socially assisted living through the development of community support networks which buttress, supplement, and extend the care available from the families of the disabled?

To be sure, the White House Conference on Handicapped Individuals marked a significant advance in federal recognition of the needs and rights of the handicapped, a major step toward reorganization and coordination of programs affecting them, and a milestone on the way to increasing their options. It also widely publicized a shift in public policy which has been going on for almost two decades, that is, the change from emphasis on support of segregated institutionalization of the disabled to support of mainstreaming and community living for the majority of the handicapped. It is encouraging that the special problems of handicapped individuals are being recognized and addressed in a comprehensive manner at the federal level, with broad citizen participation in the planning process. But why does that citizen participation not include some input from those of us who live with handicapped persons? Why are we excluded from the process of public policy formulation? Our lives and futures are also on the line.

When did anyone ever ask the following questions? What effects will this policy—or procedure—or whatever, have on the handicapped person's family as a unit, as well as on the handicapped individual? What will be the consequences of the new tax law, or of the new Social Security, or Workers' Compensation, or SSI, or Medicaid regulation, with regard to the work, savings, or consumption decisions of those who share a household with the handicapped person and are intimately concerned? Will the approach strengthen or weaken family ties and, thereby, the preexisting primary supports for the disabled member?

Further, and in a different vein, is anyone who represents the handicapped's families monitoring the economic changes that are accompanying the shift from institutionalization to community living? Is it possible that a larger share of the cost burden is being shifted from the public to the private sector, and, most significantly for us, to the individual family? Is it conceivable that, though patient welfare is the avowed objective, limitation or reduction of the public debt is in fact the primary motivation for some of the current changes in policy toward the handicapped?

The answers to such questions are not readily available. It is clear, though, that some practices that have peculiar and, sometimes, destructive effects on the family life of the disabled have been set in place. For example, a few years ago the press gave some attention to the case of the young quadriplegic man who was living independently in his own apartment and who fell in love with and married his female attendant. The public aid program of the Midwestern state in which they resided promptly stopped paying her wages, since the relative responsibility laws of that state forbade that a spouse be paid for attendant care for which public aid *could* pay a nonrelative. The consequence for that couple was a financial impasse for which the solution was divorce.

In further illustration of the kinds of hardship families face under current regulations, consider the following case of two recent patients of the Rehabilitation Institute of Chicago. The circumstances are similar in the two families, except for the fact that one young disabled woman has a higher cervical injury than the other and, on occasion, requires respiratory assistance. Neither is fully independent with regard to eating and personal grooming, and each requires help with turning in bed at approximately two-hour intervals throughout the night. Neither is able to transfer from bed to chair without assistance. In both cases the disabled individual is living at home with both parents and several younger siblings, and in both cases, the mother of the individual is working outside the home as a registered nurse. One young woman is receiving Supplemental Security Income and some daytime attendant care, while the other receives Social Security Disability Insurance benefits. The mothers continue to work because the families need the income they earn and because they are acutely conscious of the importance of retaining the Social Security disability and retirement benefits that accompany their employment, as well as their own health insurance programs. But how long will those mothers, even with the occasional assistance of other family members, be able to endure the physical strain? How many years can a person work all day and then suffer interruption of sleep every night? Does it make sense in the long run that these mothers are forced to work outside the home rather than being eligible for compensation while working at home, where their skills are needed and they could take a nap now and then?

Our current sytems of health care and social security are set up in such a way that they create real *insecurity* for many family caregivers, and, in the long run, cannot be seen as assuring maintenance of the disabled member's welfare. Problems like the above, which in no way exhaust the range of difficulties families face, must be brought to public attention before our present "support" systems become more firmly established.

Research about Family Response to SCI

Effects of Trauma on Family Members

For the most part, the relatives of the spinal cord injured are silent, as are the victims themselves. I have found no autobiographical material written by family members, with the exception of a short piece called "Family Reactions to Quadness: Told by Two Families" (Brennan & Davis, 1973). Although there can be little doubt that the experience of having a spouse, a child, a sibling, or a parent suffer a severely disabling accident causes profound and far-reaching life discontinuities for most of us, it is necessary to search long and hard before locating material specifically devoted to SCI families and their responses to trauma. One startling exception is *Act of Love: The Killing of George Zygmanik* (Mitchell, 1976). This book tells the story of the trial of Lester Zygmanik for the intensive-care mercy killing of his newly quadriplegic brother, George. It describes most powerfully the initial disturbed behavior of a family member who, fortunately for other SCI victims, reacted to the shock of spinal cord injury in a manner more extreme than do most relatives.

Family Relationships as Factors in Adjustment to SCI

Spinal cord injury victims' families appear to be as infrequently targeted for research investigation as they are for the attention of action agencies. In her book *The Psychological, Social, and Vocational Adjustment in Spinal Cord Injury: A Strategy for Future Research* Trieschmann (1978) emphasizes the inadequate nature of existing information about family relationships as factors in the adjustment to cord injury. She says, "There is no article or research project which deals with the reactions of parents to their teenagers or young adults who suffer spinal injury. What little has been written deals with issues of satisfaction within marriage for disabled groups in general and statistics on marriage and divorce among veterans with spinal injury." Continuing, she notes that though there have been references to the role reversals which cord injury may impose on couples when the husband is injured, there is not at present any firm supporting data. With regard to marital adjustment in spinal cord injury, Trieschmann cites a study by Kerr and Thompson (1972) which found that the financial security of the couple was an important factor and that all the SCI in their sample who were rated as having made an excellent mental adjustment to injury had satisfactory lives prior to injury and most came from exceptionally warm and loving backgrounds.

Thus far, Trieschmann asserts, the major studies of marriage and divorce rates of the SCI are based on data collected on veteran populations and thus may not be representative of the civilian SCI population, since the relative financial security of service-connected veterans puts them into a special category. El Ghatit and Hanson (1975, 1976) found in a study of pre-injury marriages that 26.7% of the men who had been married at the time of injury were divorced at the time of the study, and of this group of divorced men slightly more than 75 percent reported that the injury had played an important part in their divorce. The divorce rate for those who married after onset of SCI was slightly but not significantly lower (24.6%), and of those divorced, only 41% thought that the spinal injury was a significant factor in the divorce. In both cases, that is, for both pre- and post-injury marriages, the divorce rate is lower than the base rate for the United States as a whole, which is 33%, and significantly lower than the current 50% rate in California, where most of the subjects of the study live.

Deyoe (1972), reporting similar data for veterans in the northeastern United States, found that marriages which followed injury were more stable than marriages which had occurred prior to the injury, but that for the sample as a whole, separation rates were lower than in the general population.

A Theoretical Framework for Evaluating Family Changes

Cogswell(1976), in a data-based longitudinal study of family changes in response to spinal cord injury, was alert to the fact that it is difficult to make generalizations about the impact of major illness or long-term disability on families, because most of the existing research is limited to the study of single types of disability or is cross-sectional, describing family reactions at one phase of patient care or rehabilitation, or is concerned with effects on behavior patterns within the family when the disabled member has a particular role within the group such as child, breadwinner, wife, or grandparent. In an effort to develop a conceptual approach of general applicability to the heterogeneous situations in which the family experiences the disability of one of its members, she proposed that the family be viewed as a group, a small social system in process of change. She developed a working analytic framework that permits longitudinal comparisons of a single-family system as it changes over time or cross-sectional comparisons of different families, and she applied it in the study of 12 households, seven of which had a cord-injured member, over a two-to-three year period.

She found that, with one exception, the families she studied as they adjusted to the disability of a member tended "to be adaptive, to take on group goals, to move toward more flexible role structures, to use antecedent and current experiences and future expectations as a basis for action, and to manifest changes over time in the permeability of their boundaries." In the process of adaptation, each family passed at its own pace through broad stages, which Cogswell defined as crisis, transition, temporary stabilization, and readaptation. At each of these stages, changes were occurring in family system properties, including general system characteristics, structures, goals, roles, and boundaries.

Commonly, family members initially responded to the occurrence of trauma with the assumption that the injured member would either die or make a complete recovery. Only in the later stages of adaptation did family members seriously consider the possibility of permanent disability. Acceptance of the family member as being disabled developed very gradually during the final adjustment periods.

Immediately after onset, family members tended to coalesce into a group focused on a single goal, the care and rehabilitation of the injured person. The group was highly permeable to outsiders, like professionals, members of the extended family, neighbors, and others who offered help. Family members put aside their individual pretrauma goals and eliminated many of their usual everyday activities. During the early convalescent period, almost all family members over the age of six contributed to the care of the disabled member, with little attention being paid to the traditional division of labor along sex and age role lines. Gradually, however, the performance of the necessary tasks involved in the care of the disabled person became better defined and routinized. Eventually, the diffuse family responsibilities were transferred to a single caretaker; if family composition made it possible, the caretaker was always a woman. Once the caretaker role was established, other family members were able to resume many of their precrisis outside roles, in addition to taking on some of the necessary responsibilities of the precrisis roles of the disabled person and the caretaker. Family concern slowly began to focus on handling financial problems and the social and psychological consequences of disability for themselves as well as the disabled individual and the usual problems of other individual members of the family. Nevertheless, the disabled member and the caretaker remained the hub around which other members of the family organized their own lives, with somewhat reduced openness to the presence and assistance of outsiders.

Cogswell found that regardless of the many variations between the families prior to the disability, most of the families showed evidence of residual change in role flexibility; group cohesiveness, direction, and goals; and more problem-solving and self-regulatory behavior. This study has provided a conceptual framework which may be useful to professionals who are trying to orient themselves to family clients, as well as factual information about the growth that many disabled persons and their families exhibit under stress. It should serve as an antidote to the more common emphasis on the psychological and social disturbances produced by trauma.

Family Members Talk about Things That Are on Their Minds

Organization of an SCI Family Group

The following is an impressionistic report on my observation of SCI family members who attended group meetings held for relatives of patients at the Rehabilitation Institute of Chicago between 1975 and

1978. Attendance at these meetings, held weekly, was entirely voluntary, and there was no charge to participants. The service, called "Families Helping Families," (Taylor & Keenan, 1978) was planned and carried out by a certified social worker and a registered nurse who, between them have about 30 years of experience in SCI rehabilitation. Planning of the purposes and activities of the group was done with the assistance of other professional staff. Such persons were occasionally invited to attend meetings, as were a few former patients who had acquired experience living in the community and several close relatives of former patients.

It was in the latter capacity that I was asked to attend the meetings and contribute to discussion. Sometimes I think that the main thing my presence accomplished was communication of the information that individuals who have spinal cord injuries can, and often do, live a long time. When I would be introduced as the wife of a very active, employed, former patient who was injured in 1970, there would always be some relative present who would stare at me in shocked disbelief. It takes weeks, or even months or years, for family members to be convinced that the injured may survive as long as, or perhaps longer, than they themselves do. And employed? Impossible. . . .

The main objective of the group was to provide a setting in which family members had the opportunity to meet and share ideas with others who were going through similar experiences and who had like concerns. Further objectives were the provision of information through the informal use of professional staff, referrals to appropriate agencies and individuals both within the Rehabilitation Institute and in the community, teaching materials of various kinds, and "models," that is, the family members and the former patients who had mastered some common problems.

Attendance at family group meetings, as at other events offered as supportive services for patients' relatives, was somewhat adversely affected by the fact that third party payers and public agencies do not provide reimbursement for family travel costs, baby sitters, or loss of salary. Nevertheless, over a period of 3 years, 227 family members related to 137 patients attended at least one group meeting. Some attended as many as eleven times. Parents were present four times more frequently than those having other relationships to the patient, and the attendance of mothers was twice that of fathers. Attendance by relatives of quadriplegics was more than double that of relatives of paraplegics. Family members were heterogeneous in race and social class, coming from occupations as varied as farming, heavy industry, and the professions, and from areas as diverse as Chicago's southside ghettoes, the elegant North Shore suburbs, and the flat Midwestern prairies. Almost all the relatives were taking their patients home for weekend visits and were trying to learn how care could best be carried out.

The sessions were held in a comfortable conference room, around a table. Most of the meetings were only loosely structured, a result of an unfortunate experience with a lecture meeting early in the history of the group. At that time, a resident was invited to speak on spinal cord injury. He arrived with models of the spinal column and slides in hand and for two hours presented an excellent description of the physical events characterizing cord injuries. Since there was no time left for questions that evening, discussion was postponed until the following week. When the group leader asked for reactions to the lecture, there was an ominous silence. Then someone said, "I went home and cried all night. I just could not get to sleep." Someone else affirmed that the same thing had happened to her, and then a third participant said, "Those things couldn't be true of my husband; he's getting so he can feel me touch his left foot." The final comment was, "I didn't need to hear all that about sex. My patient here is my 80-year-old mother, and the last thing in the world that we're concerned about is sexuality."

After that the group leaders decided that they would proceed without formal lectures, but, instead, would deal with questions raised by members of the group, allowing the family members to take the discussions in the directions they wished. This decision was based on the recognition that the relatives were at very different places in their understanding of, and response to, their patient's injury and rehabilitation, as well as on the conviction that the most effective teaching is that which is individualized.

The atmosphere of the meetings was usually relaxed. Possibly most of the family members in attendance felt that they were doing the best they could under conditions that all recognized as adverse. They had already proved their competence in many ways. Small achievements in the patient's progress toward recovery or in the preparations of the home for his return were always the occasion for celebration. And when participants looked around the table, they knew that they were not alone in either their rejoicing or their frustrations. In the group, it occasionally happened that family members who appeared to be apathetic or hopelessly immobilized found encouragement to voice a problem that turned out to be common: "I don't know what to ask." Once it was discovered that others felt equally at a loss, problems could be articulated and solutions considered.

Sometimes the mood of a session turned even cheerful. Strange as it may seem, with all the problems they were facing, family members in the group laughed a lot. Perhaps the easy laughter was a measure of the tensions aroused by discussion, but in any case, it helped people talk and exchange ideas and, occasionally, offer suggestions and criticisms. One meeting became positively jolly after a woman whose 15-year-old son was quadriplegic as the result of a fall out of a tree told about bringing her 90-year-old father-in-law to visit at the Rehabilitation Institute. The father-in-law, who had lived in her household since he had a leg amputated at the age of 80, had been complaining and fretting about his bad luck for the preceding 10 years. After his visit to RIC, she avowed, he had not said one single word about how bad off he was. . . . She was finally, and unexpectedly, freed from his constant litany of complaints! Though such a story would not seem funny to outsiders, the reaction to it demonstrated the kind of perverse joking that rehabilitation insiders can indulge in among themselves. That father-in-law finally had gotten the putdown he had long deserved. . . . But hadn't she gone a little too far to achieve quiet in the house? . . . Of course, everyone present felt a guilty recognition of the old man as a kindred spirit, for on occasion each of us had similarly fallen silent in recognition that somebody else was a lot worse off than we were.

Problems Expressed by Family Members

The kinds of concerns that were brought up in meetings fell into several major clusters. Perhaps the most commonly mentioned were those centering around the injured members' medical problems and their management. Parents of quadriplegics were worried about such things as whether their disabled child would be able to adjust to the extremes of heat and cold we experience in the Midwest and about how they should handle matters if he had difficulty breathing, choked on food, had hyperreflexia, or had severe spasms. Everybody worried about possibile urinary tract infections, decubitus ulcers, problems with bowel and bladder care, and how to handle accidents. Some were concerned about the possibility that whatever maintenance drugs their relative required would interfere with his performance at school or on a job. Others were upset because of the injured member's weight loss or continuing depression. Some reported that in spite of paralysis the patient experienced troublesome pain, either constantly or occasionally. In many instances, the patient had multiple injuries as a result of the accident that produced the spinal insult, and these always complicated recovery and produced much anxiety. Sometimes fusion or other surgery was anticipated, and family members would wonder how this would affect the patient's subsequent care. Some patients needed a body brace, special equipment, or prosthetic or orthotic devices others did not need, and this usually created requests for explanations and reassurance. In the same way, the differential progress of patients in their bowel and bladder management programs produced very real worries. Others, looking ahead into the future, wondered if they could rely on their usual family doctor for their patient's medical needs after the return home and what they should do in case unforeseen crises occurred.

Though the relatives usually seemed to have a good understanding of the medical problems surrounding the injury, many continued to be unwilling to accept the prognosis of lifelong paralysis and expressed in various ways their belief that there would be more return of function. A minority of relatives did not really grasp what had happened or understood or felt able to undertake some aspects of the continuing care. One woman from rural Mexico believed that the body has only a limited amount of blood that must last it forever, and that when blood was drawn from her son for diagnostic purposes, it should be replaced. Others were reluctant to learn techniques such as digital stimulation to cause movement of the bowels or the catheterization procedures that are essential to the maintenance of the quadriplegic in the home. Still others, who had back troubles themselves, feared the lifting tasks—with good reason.

Though most relatives felt that they had had satisfactory contact with the physicians, nurses, and other members of the professional staff, a few complained of difficulties in getting answers to questions that, to them at least, were urgent. An occasional relative complained of having been told brusquely, "too soon," that the patient would be paralyzed for life and a few others that they had not been able to get any firm prognosis at all. Another infrequent complaint, and this is of a most serious nature, was that the patient's vertebral injury had not been recognized in the emergency room of the hospital the patient had been taken to. Sometimes the cord injury itself might have been averted if the appropriate stabilization procedure had been carried out immediately.

Another cluster of concerns centered around the preparation of the home, whether the injured member planned to live with the family or out in the community on his own. Here the problems fell into two major groupings, the necessary alterations of the physical environment and the perceived difficulties in the social environment.

With regard to home modification, decisions were greatly affected by financial status and by the injured individual's prognosis and plans for the future. A few patients' homes were already virtually barrier-free, whereas other patients came from walkup apartments or lived in certain projects run by the Chicago Housing Authority, where visiting nurses associations and home health service providers will not allow their personnel to go for safety reasons. Others lived in split-level houses, in homes with all the bedrooms on the second floor, or in houses situated on a dune or on a steep hillside. The family members had to consider not only how extensive but also how permanent the home modifications needed to be. For example, some expected their injured sons or daughters to live with them for only a few months or a year, while they waited for college acceptance or found their own jobs and apartments. Of course, others postponed making changes because they were sure that the patient would be back on his feet and doing everything in a normal manner before the year was over.

Technology exists in abundance for building ramps, installing lifts, making bathrooms usable for the wheelchair-bound, and altering kitchens. So do remarkable assistive devices of various kinds. The problem is that all these things cost money, and most families have limited resources. Sometimes moving appears to be the simplest solution, but here family members must deal with the fact that barrier-free housing is in short supply and also tends to be expensive. In addition, there is usually some psychological resistance to undertaking the major task of moving and getting settled in a new community when the family yearns to retain their ties with old friends and familiar places. Each patient and his relatives must consider these decisions with care. The patient's weekend visits to his own home can be a real help in deciding what to do. On these occasions, the modifications which are absolutely necessary rapidly become apparent, and the whole family usually discovers that they are a lot more ingenious than they had ever realized they were.

Perceived problems in the social environment are of a different order altogether, in that there are only rarely any simple solutions available. In some cases there are simply not enough able-bodied persons present in the household to carry out the home care properly. For example, one mother whose 19-year-old son is quadriplegic found it nearly impossible to look after him on his weekend visits home, even though she had several other of her children living with her. It turned out that the older brother, who had been very close to the injured youth, "took off for Wisconsin" every weekend; he just could not bear to be around his brother now. The 17-year-old son was willing to help, but he was brain damaged and "had a plate in his head," and the mother feared that he was not capable of carrying out procedures correctly. He was allowed to turn his brother at two-hour intervals during the night, but afterward he always awakened his mother to ask her if he had done the turning correctly. The 14-year-old daughter was also cooperative and had gone to the Rehabilitation Institute to be instructed in bowel and catheter procedures, but the mother had reservations about allowing the daughter to carry out intimate care for her brother.

In other instances spouses were concerned about the already poor health of the one who was undertaking the primary care-giving duties, or about the possibility that the constant strain would simply wear the caregiver down.

In several cases family members discussed either the reluctance of the disabled individual to accept help from particular persons who were closely related and available or the reluctance of other family members, especially younger ones, to give assistance. Some were concerned that the children in the family appeared to be apathetic, either not caring about or not understanding the gravity of the patient's condition. On the other hand, others reported that the children were so distressed that they were bringing home poor marks in their schoolwork for the first time in their lives. Some said that college-age family members were afraid they would have to drop out of school to help out, and, of course, that fear was not always unfounded. In one extreme case, the father simply disappeared, abandoning his wife and three children, including a newly quadriplegic son.

It was not uncommon for a participant to bring up fears of social isolation, either for the injured one or for the family. Perhaps he had noticed that friends had stopped casual visiting, seemed to be avoiding the family, or were awkward in conversation with them. Perhaps the grandparents had not come to see the patient in the hospital and rarely telephoned, even though they were retired and had plenty of time and money to help out a bit. Several couples worried because they noticed that the person whom their injured child had been planning to marry before the accident was visiting less and less frequently or was going out with another person. Even restaurant dinners that family members shared with the patients could be the occasion for new concern, because they believed that strangers in such public places were trying to avoid them, or they felt that the disabled member was embarrassed and feared the reactions of others.

Another kind of worry was not that of isolation but of being overwhelmed. Sometimes the expressed concern was related to busybody neighbors, who insisted on watching from behind the curtains while family members tried, self-consciously, to transfer their quadriplegic youngster out of a station wagon and into the wheelchair.

Some resented neighbors and relatives who were sincerely trying to help but were getting in the way of the injured one's necessary care during the short visits home.

Problems in interpersonal relations between the newly disabled individual and the family caregivers were occasionally described. These often involved the caregivers' efforts to exert some kind of discipline over the disabled when they were not acting in what the relatives considered to be their own best interests. Some fathers brought up the fact that their adolescent sons' closest friends liked to come over and take them out drinking on the Saturday nights when they were home from RIC. If the group did not get in until 3 A.M., the parents endured hours of torture and were uncertain as to whether they should treat their sons as they would have prior to the accident or overlook their behavior. One woman said that her disabled son had been so "fresh" to her that she could hardly bear it, but she had hit him in retaliation only one time. Another said that her disabled spouse drank too much and then turned mean, and tried to run her down with his electric wheelchair; she did not know how to handle this. Others were concerned about the injured one's depression, as expressed in unwillingness to eat, to participate in family activities, or to do anything but lie in bed watching television. One husband complained because his wife, an incomplete quadriplegic, seemed to be more dependent on him than she had to be. If he refused to feed her when she was home on a visit, she threw the plate of food at him. Thus problems like alcoholism or intergenerational or marital conflict which existed within the family prior to the occurrence of the injury sometimes seemed to be exacerbated under the stresses of post-injury readjustment. Members of the group occasionally expressed the opinion that participation in the group had helped alert them to this possibility and prepared them to cope with incidents in a more understanding manner.

Another whole group of problems centered around resources in the community, what they are, where they are, and how access to them is gained. Family members often had only vague information about agencies active in their area or services that could be provided if they made their needs known. As in the case of the questions centered around modification of the physical environment, there are some straightforward answers to such questions. However, they are not always satisfactory in individual cases because of service gaps or eligibility requirements. Sometimes the conclusions that emerged from the group were like the following: "We really ought to get organized—we need a buyers' cooperative." "I'm going to talk to my alderman about curb cuts." "I know Ruth wants to keep up with the friends she's made here. Why don't we work out a transportation pool so the kids can attend courses at the community college together?"

These then are the kinds of things that relatives of SCI patients talk about when they are preparing for the patient's release from the hospital. In the report on their experience with the SCI family group, the two professionals who conducted it for several years summarized in the following words: "We have been impressed with the insight and innate sensitivity displayed by family members who have only life experiences and none of the professional credentials. The strength of human beings to cope and survive is repeatedly demonstrated in the group for others to take from for their own use." (Taylor and Keenan, 1978)

When the patient's transition to the home has been completed, the family moves into another phase, one in which it may assist the disabled individual's re-entry into the larger community. The various tasks family members undertake are essential to the rehabilitation process for the very severely injured, for without them, many more of the disabled would live out their days in nursing homes. However, it should be understood that the family members gain as well. They are facing their problems together, and that is what really matters.

Summary and Conclusions

The SCI constitute a special category among the disabled, a category that requires special study and perhaps differential treatment from that accorded the disabled in general. As a result of changes in medical and rehabilitation technology, the numbers of SCI survivors are increasing, and their life expectancy has been extended. It is their fate to be paralyzed for life, some from the neck down, others less extensively. Most are dependent on others in varying degrees for assistance with aspects of their everyday care. Nevertheless, with appropriate modification of the environment, many can and do work and otherwise carry on near-normal lives.

By custom and by law, the nuclear family has primary responsibility for the care of its disabled members, insofar as handicapped individuals need assistance of any kind. When a spinal cord injury occurs and the patient is necessarily immobilized for a lengthy period of time, the family generally serves a liaison function, helping the patient connect with the requirements of the unfamiliar new world within the hospital, as well as with people and events having significance for them on the outside. Though the disabled experience abrupt discontinuities in their customary social roles, their families often assist in their resocialization into whatever new roles they are able to assume, given the limitations imposed by their injuries and a generally unprepared environment.

Financial problems are frequently a source of major concern. The disabled individual and his family are responsible for paying for hospital and rehabilitation care. However, since the costs are high and other costs related to the injury will continue throughout the lifetime of the disabled, many families are forced to seek assistance from the public programs for which they can establish eligibility. At this point, if not before, they discover the inequities inherent in our current systems of health care and become familiar with the limits placed on rehabilitation by the inadequacies of the various public "support" systems.

After their discharge from the hospital or rehabilitation center, a relatively small number of the SCI choose to live alone in the community, and some few go into nursing homes, but the majority return to home and family. When they are unable to attend completely to their own needs, some member of the family, usually a woman, may assume the role of primary caregiver. Thus this person may be forced to withdraw from the labor force, with the result that the family's financial resources and provisions for Social Security undergo further reduction.

For those disabled persons who are able to and who wish to resume work, educational, and other activities outside the home, family members frequently act as ombudsmen, exploring the options available in the community and supporting the disabled as they venture out into what often appears to be an insensitive and frustrating world.

For both the disabled and their families, the tasks of adjusting to a spinal cord injury require prodigious expenditures of effort—physical, psychological, social, and economic. It is abundantly clear to those who are acquainted with the everyday problems of SCI care that the family itself is often at risk. Its current resources are usually strained to the limits, and the future of the entire family, particularly the well-being of the disabled and the primary caregiver, are sources of continuing concern.

Unfortunately, there has been very limited scientific investigation of either the effects of cord injury on the disabled individual's family or of the family's role in the rehabilitation of the disabled member. Nor has much research attention been devoted to assessing the impact on the family as a whole of current public policies toward the handicapped. By and large, the targeted outcomes of public interventions are the changes defined as desirable for handicapped individuals, and data collection and program evaluation are organized accordingly. Thus far, the additional consequences for others who are intimately concerned with the welfare of their disabled relatives are not being monitored. The little research that bears on this question seems to indicate that most families manage to stay together and to cope somehow, but that the price of coping under current conditions is very high.

Up to the present, families of the SCI have not organized extensively for purposes of defining and remedying their special common problems or trying to achieve public recognition of their needs, nor have they been formally represented in the councils where public policies are formulated. Recognition of the right of family members to participate at all levels in the planning of policies affecting not only the lives of handicapped individuals, but also their own, is a matter of first-order importance. Some basic issues, including the division of responsibility for assistance of all kinds to the severely disabled, deserve reconsideration. If, on careful study of the consequences of various care systems for all concerned, the encouragement of home- and community-based care remains a major objective of the rehabilitation system, the following questions must be faced squarely: Who cares for the family caregivers? In what ways can and should the larger society contribute to their welfare, both now and in the days to come?

References and Bibliography

Brennan, D., & Davis, D. Family reactions to quadness: Told by two families. *Rehabilitation Gazette*, 1973, *16*, 34–37.

Cogswell, B. E. Conceptual model of family as a group: Family response to disability. In G. L. Albrecht (Ed.), *The sociology of physical disability and rehabilitation*. Pittsburgh: University of Pittsburgh Press, 1976.

Deyoe, F. Marriage and family patterns with long-term spinal cord injury. *International Journal of Paraplegia*, 1972, *10*, 219–224.

El Ghatit, A., & Hanson, R. Outcome of marriage existing at the time of a male's spinal cord injury. *Journal of Chronic Disease*, 1975, *28*, 383–388.

El Ghatit, A., & Hanson, R. Marriage and divorce after spinal cord injury. *Archives of Physical Medicine and Rehabilitation*, 1976, *57*, 470–472.

Kerr, W., & Thompson, M. Acceptance of disability of sudden onset in paraplegia. *International Journal of Paraplegia*, 1972, *10*, 94–102.

Midwest Regional Spinal Cord Injury Care System. *Progress Report VII, 1978*. Chicago: Northwestern Memorial Hospital (Wesley Pavilion) and the Rehabilitation Institute of Chicago, 1979.

Mitchell, P. *Act of love: The killing of George Zygmanik*. New York: Knopf, 1976.

Taylor, J., & Keenan, M. *Families helping families.* Paper presented at the
    Annual Meeting of the American Congress of Rehabilitation Medicine,
    New Orleans, 1978.
The White House Conference on Handicapped Individuals. Washington,
    D.C.: U.S. Government Printing Office, 1976, 0-218-920.
The White House Conference on Handicapped Individuals. *The National
    Newsletter.* Washington, D. C.: U. S. Government Printing Office,
    1977, 0-228-502.
The White House Conference on Handicapped Individuals. *Volume Three:
    Implementation plan.* DHEW Publication No. (OHDS) 78-25512. Wash-
    ington, D. C.: U.S. Government Printing Office, 1978.
Trieschmann, R. B. *The psychological, social, and vocational adjustment in
    spinal cord injury: A strategy for future research.* Easter Seal Society
    for Crippled Children and Adults of Los Angeles County, Final Report,
    Rehabilitation Services Administration, 1978, 13-P-59011/9-01.

III

Coping with Physical Disability

Even with a complete analysis of society's responsibility for the second-class status of the physically disabled, our task is not complete. What remains is a very difficult, yet necessary, effort to understand disabled individuals so as to help them toward the most positive life-style possible. It is not enough that societal discrimination is lessened or even eliminated; if the individual remains fearful, depressed, or hopeless, additional efforts are required to make that person as fully functional a member of society as possible. No matter how well-prepared the social environment, disabled individuals must still make major readjustments in their feelings, thoughts, attitudes, and behavior. Thus, at some point, our focus must be on the particular person who is himself disabled. This shift in focus, from society to the individual, does not mean that social influences on the physically disabled person are ignored. Instead, it means that both social and individual factors are recognized as central determinants of how well or how poorly the disabled person will cope.

Viewing disability from an individual perspective brings the rehabilitation process into a position of importance in our discussion. Rehabilitation, by definition, concentrates on the individual's adjustment. This view is necessary, because the sociological perspective can minimize the contributions of the individual by focusing only on the social aspects of disability. The successfulness of adjustment any disabled individual makes is not solely a function of social-ecological factors. Coping and adjustment are fights that are individually fought, too. Because rehabilitation programs are efforts to promote individual coping, these programs must play a central role in any social-psychological approach to physical disability.

The purpose of this part is to examine how individuals cope with the physical, psychological, and social problems of physical disability. Suggestions are made to help disabled individuals in the adjustment process. In his chapter (13), Duval traces the development of psychological theories of disability and emphasizes the increasing recognition of social factors and therapeutic approaches in these theories. Slucki (Chapter 14) examines specific behavioral methods demonstrated to be effective in dealing with the individual psychological problems accompanying physical disability. In Chapter 15 on chronic pain and disability, Nehemkis and Cummings describe the complex interaction of individual and social influences in such problems. They make recommendations for decreasing the role that institutions play in creating and maintaining the problem of chronic pain.

Although this part is grounded in a behavioral orientation, we recognize the potential of other approaches to make significant new contributions to dealing with physically disabled individuals. Currently, however, the behaviorists are the only group taking both individual and social factors into account and translating this understanding into effective treatment modalities.

13 Psychological Theories of Physical Disability

New Perspectives

Richard J. Duval

In the past few decades the importance of psychological variables in the rehabilitation of the physically disabled has been increasingly recognized (Cruickshank, 1971; Wright, 1960). As a result, psychological theories of disability have come to play a unique and essential role in rehabilitation efforts. Understanding human behavior by means of psychological theories is essential " . . . to assure that the expense and effort of rehabilitation do not go to waste because of patients' poor psychological adjustments to their physical conditions" (Shontz, 1978, p. 251). Unfortunately, empirical data by which to directly evaluate the psychological theories of disability and rehabilitation remain scarce. Gathering the necessary data in methodologically sophisticated ways has begun only recently (Treischmann, 1978). Until the time that sufficient research is complete, the process of helping disabled individuals "to learn to live again" must be largely based on educated theoretical hunch rather than established psychological fact.

Despite this present dependence on theories, attempts to provide needed psychological services to the disabled must certainly continue. A proper course to take in such unsettled waters is a careful scrutiny of the theories used in rehabilitation planning. Part of this scutiny should include a judgment of each theory's adherence to formal criteria such as logical consistency, clarity of terms, deductive capacity, and parsimony. Another important yardstick in evaluating theories is the empirically proven utility of the treatments that each theory suggests. Clinical utility cannot prove the validity of a theory, of course, but it can act as evidential support for it. Thus both formal

The author wishes to express his appreciation to Don Weinstein and Jim Murray for their help in both conceptual and literary areas.

and empirical criteria are important in making comparisons among psychological theories of disability.

Unfortunately, a sort of "personality split" has become apparent within the field of rehabilitation psychology. This split is based on the fact that different people in the field have different needs they want filled by a theory. Theoretically oriented workers, who desire to explain how and why stable patterns of behavior occur in disabled people, usually prefer theories that emphasize unique individual variables. Mental processes and personality structures within the person have traditionally been the constructs these theories have used. Generally, the formal criteria mentioned above have been the only yardsticks by which these theories were evaluated. Those workers most interested in clinical treatments for the psychological problems of disabled people have focused on theories which speak more directly to rehabilitation. Rather than trying to explain how the person has come to act and feel a certain way, these clinically oriented theories emphasize the methods by which new and beneficial psychological changes can be brought about. In these theories, the individual's adjustment is usually explained in terms of social and environmental factors external to the person. Empirical demonstrations of the utility of treatment procedures are the most valuable criteria for judging theories from this point of view.

This difference in theoretical emphasis—explanation versus treatment—and the accompanying differences in the evaluative criteria thought most appropriate have led to much confusion in the field of rehabilitation regarding which psychological theories are best used. Some writers, like Shontz (1978), have tried to end this confusion by suggesting that both types of theories are necessary and useful. Though this is certainly true, it does not end the problem. Only a true integration of both explanatory and clinical treatment aspects in a single theory would be a satisfactory solution. This integration has not yet been achieved, but, as proposed later in this chapter, Bandura's social learning theory (1969, 1977) leads the way toward this goal. His theory allows explanations in terms of stable cognitive processes as well as suggesting powerful treatment techniques for inducing psychological change.

Before Bandura's theory is fully outlined, however, a careful analysis of other prominent psychological theories is in order. This analysis is meant to illustrate how the theories have changed their main emphasis from more explanation, to treatment considerations, and most recently toward an integration of both. To do this, each theory of disability is evaluated regarding its adherence to both empirical and formal criteria. Greater emphasis is necessarily given to the formal aspects of theories, since proper empirical data concerning the theories and therapies of disability are a recent phenomenon. Nevertheless, some mention is made of research investigations of the treatments each theory suggests.

An excellent survey of the trends in major psychological theories of disability proposed in this century has been provided by Shontz (1970, 1978). Shontz is a theoretical egalitarian, in the sense that he considers all theories equally valid, differing only in the proper sphere of application for each. This chapter is written from a different viewpoint: that all psychological theories are *not* equally valid, that one theory can have greater power and utility than another across a wide variety of applications. It is this writer's contention that certain theories do provide better explanatory and treatment perspectives for the field of rehabilitation than do others. The historical survey of the psychological theories of disability to be presented next provide evidence for this contention. Both formal and empirical criteria are used to judge the relative values of these theories for the rehabilitation professional.

Implicit Theories

The earliest theories of the psychology of disability were essentially implicit theories (not formally stated, but assumed). Almost all rehabilitation workers have been medical personnel, concerned with the overwhelming tasks of preserving life and health. In it the effects of physical problems on the individual's psychological status are taken at face value. Eliminating the physical problem is thought to end any possible psychological difficulty. If medical procedures are unsuccessful in ridding the individual of the disability, acceptance of physical limitations is considered a naturally occuring although difficult process.

Implicit theories of the psychology of disability are essentially drawn from common-sense notions about human behavior: widely shared beliefs about what "should be" rather than an explicit set of statements about actual events. As such, the formal criteria used to evaluate theories (e.g., parsimony, logical consistency) are not appropriate for evaluation of these ideas.

Not surprisingly, implicit theories have many difficulties in actual application. They were overly simplistic and narrow conceptions, unable to account for the wide variety of human behavior and experience. Essentially, implicit theories equate physical and psychological status in a naive mind-body parallelism. Good health is thought to mean a good frame of mind. Failure of individuals to return to normal functioning once their physical problems have been eliminated seems impossible. Yet many individuals continue to have psychological difficulties, even when physically restored. Furthermore, persons with continuing physical disability often function at a much lower level than their actual physical abilities would allow. Examples of such paradoxes for implicit theories include rejection of physical aids by amputees, poor skin care by paraplegics, and lack of return to work by recuperated surgical patients. What on first glance appears to be a perfect correlation between mind and body is in fact a mirage created by medicine's almost total focus on acute illness at that time (Bakal, 1979). Fairly direct mind-body correlations might adequately describe many of the acutely ill, but not the chronically ill or disabled. For them, a return to psychological good health would never occur simply by regaining physical health. Their physical problems must be faced for the rest of their lives; new ways of behaving and thinking must be learned. If psychological theories are adequately to explain the complexities of an adjustment to disability, they must improve on the sound body–sound mind theories. Such theories provide neither sufficient explanatory power nor powerful treatment techniques.

Motivational Theories

Other theories were obviously needed to account for the complexities of the psychology of disability. One approach which appeared to be appropriate was the use of motivational concepts. From this viewpoint, all behavior is assumed to be both directed toward some goal and energized by some internal motivational force or energy. Eating and sexual behavior are two prime examples of behavior explained by motives. Hunger and sexual drives are hypothesized to account for such behavior. In motivational theories of disability, poor rehabilitation is hypothesized to be due to a lack of motivational drive and/or lack of an appropriate goal.

Though the concept of motivation does allow a general description and explanation of the psychology of disability, it has many problems in its adherence to formal criteria. The logic of motivation is usually circular, in that the level of motivation is commonly inferred from the person's behavior and is later used to explain that very same behavior. For example, when a man with paraplegia due to spinal cord injury had frequently recurring pressure sores, a lack of motivation to take care of his skin was inferred. Poor motivation was then pointed to as the cause of the sores. The only justification for this inference is the behavior it was originally invoked to explain. Essentially, it is a renaming of the behavior in mentalistic terms and then using it as the "cause" of the behavior. Such renaming involves analytic "truths" (i.e., are true by definition) and are therefore tautologous. Certainly, it must be acknowledged that psychological events are involved in this situation; the question is whether motivational concepts best explain them.

Other formal problems in the motivational approach include the vagueness of motivational terminology (what would be an independent index of motivation, and how would it differ from any other type of motivation?) and the difficulty in making specific predictions about the individual's reaction to disability or treatment. In addition, it is difficult to understand how broad motivational concepts could properly account for complex emotional, intellectual, and social behavior. Recognition of the influence of both environmental and complex mental processes is lacking.

Also troublesome is the poor record motivational theories have had in suggesting effective psychological treatments for problem patients. Recommended treatments have included increasing the person's insight into the reasons for his or her improper level of motivation, as well as providing social encouragement in the hope that internal motivation could be re-established. Unfortunately, these approaches have been based on an incomplete understanding of the situation. As Shontz (1978, p. 252) notes, "In actual practice, few patients truly lacked motivation; the problem was not usually a deficiency of psychological energy, but a blocking or misdirection of it." The numerous instances of patients strongly motivated to engage in self-destructive or nontherapeutic activities forcefully underline this point. Thus methods to help patients learn how to use existing motivational sources seem to be the need, not methods based on the notion of increasing or decreasing motivational levels.

The problem with the utility of these therapies is motivational theory's emphasis on explanation, not intervention. Rather than suggesting specific treatment techniques, motivational theories more often than not provide post hoc explanations for the lack of rehabilitation progress among problem patients. Responsibility for such failure has been placed on the patient ("poorly motivated"), not on the rehabilitation workers or system.

Besides this assumption of an internal locus of causation, motivational theories also incorporate the idea that specific negative psychological effects necessarily follow disability. This has not been the case with the implicit theories; they have been quite vague as to the particular effects of disability. Now, physical disability is seen as inducing a specific result: a lowering of motivational energy for proper goals. How "proper" goals are defined is not questioned. At this early period in rehabilitation efforts, the disabled individual's competence to decide what was proper or desirable has not been considered. Many of the motivational problems could have been easily translated into problems of reconciling different viewpoints on what the appropriate goals of rehabilitation are. To workers at this time, the common assumption that serious psychological problems *necessarily* exist as a result of any physical loss make the motivational explanation appear to be the more plausible of the competing interpretations.

Once motivational theory formally incorporated this idea, a new way of looking at physical disability began. Previously, physical disability had been considered to be much like any other stressful event, such as the death of a loved one, a financial loss, an acute illness, or a divorce. A "normal" reaction to any of these involves sadness, anger, or frustration, followed by a period of recuperation. With the rise of explicit psychological theories, the psychological effects of physical disability were now considered unique, different than reactions to any other stress. Very specific negative psychological effects on the disabled person were theorized to set him apart from the able-bodied. The commonalities disabled individuals share with the able-bodied were no longer emphasized or investigated. One result of this emphasis on the uniqueness of disability was the proposal that specific personality types accompany specific physical disabilities (Wright, 1960). Thus not only were the disabled psychologically different than the able-bodied, but they were also seen as different according to their particular disability type. This view was widely shared by rehabilitation workers for many years; it was not until recently that mounting evidence (Shontz, 1970) led to an abandonment of this position.

Motivational theories were early, unsophisticated attempts to explain the psychological effects of disability. Since they had many difficulties in meeting both formal and empirical criteria, the emergence of new competing theories was not surprising.

Psychoanalytic Theory

Problems in the theory and clinical applications of simple motivational concepts led to a relative vacuum in the psychology of disability. Into that void quickly came psychoanalytic theory. Sigmund Freud, the originator of this theory, hypothesized that behavior is a result of a dynamic interplay of instinctual drives, defense mechanisms, and reality-based pressures. It is asserted that an understanding of this dynamic and the history of the person allows one to explain the often irrational aspects of human behavior.

The use of psychoanalytic theory in rehabilitation efforts becomes possible only with the translation of the previous motivational problems into mental health problems. This translation seems quite natural, as it appears that something must be wrong with the person's mind to account for such self-defeating behavior as noncompliance with rehabilitation efforts. Also fostering this translation is psychoanalytic theory's extensive reliance on motivational concepts such as drives and goals. In this way, the former problem—a depletion of motivation because of physical disability—is easily translated into a disease model of mental health. Problem patients become sick patients, that is, people with sick minds.

Once this recasting of the problem has been achieved, every disabled individual is by definition reacting to his disability with certain defense mechanisms. The individual's behavior is, therefore, best analyzed by reference to his or her personality structure (e.g., oral, phallic, narcissistic) and the accompanying defense strategies (e.g., projection, denial, reaction formation). The psychoanalytic orientation strongly asserts the necessity of the person's accepting the reality of disability. Good adjustment is possible only when built on the individual's recognition of his or her limitations. Given this proposition, any type of denial is viewed as a maladaptive defense mechanism. Any denial of the reality or permanence of the disability is thought to necessitate "working through" before the rehabilitation process can occur. This conception of denial as a maladaptive defense ignores the possible benefits it might have for the individual (Fordyce, 1976). It is also based on a view of disability as intrinsically and completely negative (Wright, 1960). Acceptance of disability is explicitly defined as acceptance of only the negative aspects of what is really a multifaceted experience.

Certainly, Freud's psychoanalytic theory is a powerful one. It is internally consistent, allows many strong deductions, and speaks to a broad range of human experience and activity. Psychoanalytic theory has spawned a wide range of newer theoretical positions and treatments. These newer approaches have the advantage of pushing individuals to explore potentials as well as limitations. Significant problems still exist, however, in its ability to meet such formal criteria as clarity of definitions, testability, and predictive capability. These difficulties are very similar to those of the motivational theories, another mentalistic approach.

Psychoanalytic theory largely ignores the role of environmental influences on behavior by concentrating on internal mental causes of behavior. Situational circumstances are of interest only insofar as they reveal the working and structures of internal defenses. Even more important than these formal difficulties, studies of actual changes in behavior of those persons who received psychoanalytically oriented treatments have had difficulty showing any more changes than that of individuals who have not undergone such treatments (Bandura, 1969; Rachman, 1971; Rachman & Wilson, 1980). Consequently, psychoanalytic therapy has seen great decline in use, a trend reinforced by the expense and length of such therapy.

Psychoanalytic theory was developed as an attempt to explain human behavior and experience. Its treatment techniques are secondary appendages to the primary theoretical orientation its originators had toward understanding human psychology. Given this emphasis, psychoanalytic theory's difficulty in suggesting powerful and efficient treatment techniques is not unexpected. The major decline in the use of psychoanalytic treatments reflects this empirical difficulty more than any formal theoretical weakness.

Body Image Theory

Body image theory (Schilder, 1950) is another theory that has had some penetration into the field of disability and rehabilitation. The basic notion in this theory is that thoughts, feelings, and attitudes about oneself are largely determined by the perception of one's own body. This body percept, or body image, is itself a result of the nonverbal cues (e.g., behavior and body language) of others and one's own physical status (size, beauty) and abilities. The body image is much like a self-concept; it is hypothesized to influence both internal mental processes and external social behavior.

From this orientation, the psychology of disability is explained by the effect of disability on the body image. Loss of physical ability is theorized to damage or lower the acceptability of the body image. As a result, both attitudes toward oneself and others are changed. Depression, denial, and anger are seen as the natural results of the loss of acceptability of body image. Body image theory is another mentalistic theory, in that it sees the primary causes of behavior residing within the mind of the individual. Change in physique can have its influence only secondarily, through its effect on the internal body image.

The body image construct does bear some relationship to other personality constructs and perceptual measures (Cleveland, 1960; Fisher & Cleveland, 1968). For instance, in an investigation of certain personality correlates of children's perceptions of human size, Beller and Turner (1964) found that autonomous achievement striving was significantly related to the accuracy of normal children's perception of their own and other people's sizes. Studies of the body image or self-concept of disabled people have also been conducted (Richardson, Hastrof, & Dornbuster, 1964; Simmel, 1966). Although it appears that changes in self-perception do occur following disability, the exact type or direction of these changes is difficult to specify with body image theories. Different people change their self-perceptions of their bodies in different ways after disablement. Also, it is difficult to know the cause-and-effect relationship in these changes: Which comes first, the changed body image or the other cognitive and affective changes following disability? And even if the exact order of events can be determined, this cannot be assurance that changes in body image caused other cognitive changes; both could be coeffects of a third event.

Some of these difficulties stem from the confusion over what a body image is. It has resisted attempts to arrive at clear and acceptable operational definition. Moreover, much confusion remains regarding its relation with self-concept (Wylie, 1961). Finally, it seems that body image theory has little predictive power or generality; it addresses only a small portion of the complexities of human behavior and experience. English (1971, p. 46) states that " . . . it is too oblique and lacks comprehensiveness to such an extent that it may not be a theory at all." This is best illustrated by the considerable difficulty body image theory has in predicting individual variations in reactions to disability. Not everyone loses appreciation or acceptance of his body due to disability. Many psychological and sociological variables besides just body image are involved in determining adjustment to disability (Kimball, 1969; Michael, 1970; Shontz, 1965).

Body image theory is another explanatory theory with secondary interest in suggesting remediation for problems in psychological functioning. Its usefulness for rehabilitation planning is questionable, therefore. In its present form this theory says little about possible therapeutic activities besides restoring the individual to predisability status.

The mentalistic theories already described—motivational, psychoanalytic, and body image—suffered major declines in popularity and influence during the 1950s. One reason that largely accounted for this dissatisfaction was the narrow focus of such theories on intrapsychic factors as the causes of behavior. Actual clinical practice made it clear that many other factors, external to the individual, also greatly affect both the experience and behavior of the disabled individual. Rehabilitation efforts seem to be as often hindered by negative social influences and physical and architectural barriers as by improper psychological adjustment. In addition, such narrow focus on mentalistic factors has made rehabilitation efforts very difficult. A combination of explaining human behavior with mentalistic constructs and providing little practical guidance for effective rehabilitation made the mentalistic theories difficult to use in a rehabilitation setting. Yet the decline in these theories' popularity has not been due to a widespread disregard for the role of internal processes; it has been a backlash against theories inappropriate for practical rehabilitation programs.

Sociological Theories

With growing awareness of the importance of social factors in rehabilitation efforts came a new trend in thinking about physical disability. Theorists began emphasizing the role of social influences in their accounts of the psychology of disability. Thus the pendulum had swung from the former extreme—sole reliance on mentalistic concepts—toward another extreme—sole reliance on social and environmental concepts. This position generally holds that illness and disability are not absolutes but are defined relative to present social norms of health and disease. According to this view, once an individual's physical problem has been socially defined and sanctioned via the medical profession, he or she begins to act in accordance with the expectations other people have for that specific "sick role" (Parsons, 1964). A role is defined as the enactment of a set of behaviors related to social status. Adjustment to disability is therefore seen as a role response to social attitudes and behavior rather than to the physical disability itself.

One well-known example of the explanatory power of social role theory is the "requirement for mourning" (Barker, Wright, & Gonick, 1953; Wright, 1960). In the social role of acquired disability, all individuals are expected to play a sad, frustrated, mournful role in reaction to their condition. When they do not exhibit these behaviors, pressure is often applied to make the disabled person acknowledge their loss in socially prescribed ways (Goldiamond, 1976; Wright, 1960). Much of the conflict in rehabilitation settings can be attributed to persons who do not exhibit this socially expected mourning.

Undoubtedly there is a general tendency toward increased depression and anxiety within the physically disabled group immediately after injury and during rehabilitation (Kemph, 1967; Warren & Weiss, 1969). Expectations of uniform psychological processes within all individuals of each disability type are nevertheless unrealistic. A very wide variety of individuals becomes disabled. Simply in terms of their diverse histories these individuals would be expected to have many different learned preferences for dealing with stress and loss. The evidence gathered concerning individual reactions to disability is clear (Shontz, 1978). Diversity not uniformity or even specificity by disability type is the rule. It is evidence of the power of social expectations rather than an indication of uniform adjustment following disability that the "requirement for mourning" should continue within rehabilitation settings.

With such sociological theories as Parsons' (1964) sick role theory and Mechanic's (1962) illness behavior concept, a significant change had occurred in the whole approach to disability. For the first time the environmental influences acting on the person and the overt behavior of the individual had become prime variables of interest. Attitudes and behavior of the able-bodied society were now being considered the central determinants of the psychological status of disabled persons. No longer did problems of adjustment exist solely within the person's mind.

Despite this change of focus, however, sociological theories have a number of deficits. From a formal criteria perspective they have great difficulty accounting for the wide variation among the individual reactions to disability. With the one-way direction of causality (i.e., social environment → behavior) that these theories posit, individual contributions to the adjustment process are ignored. External social forces are seen as blindly directing the fate of individuals as though they were pawns in a chess game. The possibility that persons can have reciprocal influence (Bandura, 1977) on their social environment, and thus on their own destiny, is not considered. As a result, the ways in which an individual's perception, evaluation, and behavior can themselves influence the social environment are simply ignored. Sociological theories are not useful, since they do not specify the processes by which social roles are learned or how such roles can be counteracted in the rehabilitation setting. Specific recommendations or predictions about individual cases are not made; instead, there is an emphasis on social programs to change widespread social attitudes and behavior. The possibility of treating individual psychological problems that result from disability is largely ignored.

Integrative Theories

Recognizing the limitations of psychological theories that utilized exclusively mental or environmental concepts, theorists have attempted to construct a single unified theory of disability that can incorporate both types of variables. Wright's (1960) somatopsychological theory is one such attempt. She recognized the great influence that social and interpersonal factors can have on both the behavior and experience of physically disabled persons. At the same time, she contends that external influences do not act directly on the person but through the mediation of internal mental processes. Wright posits a large number of such intervening processes, including expectation discrepancy, spread, and value, which would determine the meanings of external stimuli. Thus a person's perception of an environmental event is not simply a mechanical response to an impinging stimulus. What to one person might be a manageable problem—loss of hearing, for example—could to another person be an overwhelming trauma. Wright is proposing that the wide differences in reaction to the same physical event are the result of a uniquely individual interaction of external conditions and internal mental processes. This means that the individual's behavior can be understood only by including both environmental and intrapsychic variables. Despite this recognition, overt behavior itself is not the primary focus of Wright's theory. She considers subjective (mental) states such as self-esteem to be the critical tests of psychological adjustment.

Wright's work is truly integrative and far-reaching in scope, because it speaks to the widely divergent aspects of physical disability by its inclusion of both environmental and mentalistic variables. Moreover, Wright has a background in rehabilitation rather than in psychiatric or academic setting. Hers is the first major theory of the psychology of disability to arise from the rehabilitation setting. Wright's intimate knowledge of the complex issues of disability is obvious. She has been able to expose the biases characterizing most psychological theories of disability, including the common assumption of the totally negative character of all disability. Finally, Wright has provided an excellent analysis of the psychological research performed up until that time. The inadequacies of research performed based on simple notions of one-to-one relationships between physique and personality or behavior have been made quite apparent in her writings.

Despite these strengths, Wright's work cannot be considered a true theory. A theory is a congruent set of statements about the relationships among specific empirical events. Her work lacks the overall congruence or organization necessary for a theory defined in this manner. She has introduced a sophisticated psychological framework in which to deal with somatopsychological relationships, but the actual canvas has been left empty, remaining to be filled. Many intervening mental variables have been proposed by Wright to be important elements on that canvas, but in recognition of the tremendous amount of uncertainty in the field of disability she has not even attempted a complete organization of all the concepts she has reviewed.

Two points about Wright's work are central. First, environmental factors are viewed as necessary and important determinants in the psychology of disability. No incompatibility of environmental and mental variables as psychological causes is seen. This is the first time this integration has been accomplished in a major theory of the psychology of disability. Second, a major bias has carried over from the mentalistic theories—subjective states are considered better or more truthful criteria by which to judge psychological adjustment than is overt behavior. This mentalistic bias has remained, despite the acknowledgement that environmental factors are powerful determinants of both behavior and subjective experience. This notion of the primacy of subjective states isolates Wright's important work from the mainstream of experimental work in behavioral psychotherapy which was occurring at that time.

A similar all-encompassing theory of the psychology of disability was put forward by Meyerson (1971). Like Wright, he argued that physical status alone cannot account for the psychological adjustment of the individual. Individual reactions to the same physical disability vary widely. Some people completely withdraw into the safety of the world of disability, but others totally reject any involvement in such a community. Advantages and disadvantages exist for all the points along this continuum. To account for such widely differing adjustments, Meyerson has proposed that both internal and external variables interact to determine the disabled person's adjustment. Unlike Wright, however, Meyerson feels that social factors play a much greater role in determining adjustment to disability than do intrapsychic factors. In support of this view, he points to evidence that society first defines what will be considered a disability, then devalues the person for only those specific physical incapacities, and finally pressures the disabled individual to accept this devaluation. Intervening mental variables are acknowledged by Meyerson to be part of the adjustment process, but only in a secondary way. They are seen as entering into the adjustment process only after societal pressures have already "set up" the person. It is the individual's psychological inability to resist social pressure toward devaluation that allows him to fall prey to accepting this judgment. Thus Meyerson explains the way individuals adjust to disability primarily in terms of social factors and only secondarily in terms of individual mental variables.

Meyerson has done an abrupt about-face, however, when directing his attention to practical aspects of rehabilitation. He recognizes the difficulty of directly working with social attitudes and individual beliefs and so has turned to behavior modification as an essential rehabilitation tool. The particulars of this approach are discussed later in this survey; suffice it to say that behavioral techniques are not incompatible with the theory Meyerson proposed. His turnabout is simply a movement away from difficult-to-work-with social and mental variables toward working with the individual's observable behavior and its relation to the environment.

Both Wright and Meyerson shared the advantages of having two types of determinants in their theories: environmental and intrapsychic. This has enabled them to explain many diverse psychological phenomena, including both subjective and objective events. Yet this explanatory power is accompanied by similarly powerful treatment methods only in Meyerson's theory. He utilizes behavior modification techniques not derived from his explanatory theory to provide this treatment practicality. Thus in neither Wright's nor Meyerson's theory is there an integration of internal and external variables into both the explanatory and treatment sections of their work. It has remained for others, including Mahoney (1974) and Bandura (1969), to begin this type of integration.

Behavioral Theories

Behavioral theories are the most recent approaches to the psychology of disability. Though they are a widely divergent group, behavioral theories share a common heritage—the experimental learning laboratory. As a result, most have originated as attempts to explain animal learning. Although modern behavioral theories have been reformulated and extended to conform to human psychological processes, their background has left these theories with easily recognizable characteristics: (1) a heavy reliance on the measurement of observable psychological phenomena such as behavior, (2) a strong tendency toward examining environment-behavior relationships, rather than relations between attitudes and behavior or beliefs and behavior, (3) as little reliance as possible on inferred mental variables or hypothetical constructs, and (4) an emphasis on learning as the key explanatory concept in the development and regulation of behavior.

Underlying this emphasis on learning is the assumption that general laws governing the learning process can be discovered that have broad explanatory power. Thus adjustment to disability is seen as being governed by the same psychological principles that account for all other behavior; both normal and abnormal behavior are assumed to be similarly governed. This is not a new tact; other psychological theories have made this assumption, too. Yet, it has been only with the ascendence of behavioral theories that strong enough psychological principles (namely, those concerning the learning process) have been available to account convincingly for the wide variations in human behavior.

Behavioral theories do not propose special personality types to account for each type of behavioral adjustment. To explain reactions to disability, they apply the same general learning principles used to explain other psychological phenomena. As a result, there are no behavioral theories specific just to disability. Adjustment to disability is seen as only one type of psychological phenomenon explained within the behavioral approach. Given the assumption that learning is a principle explaining diverse phenomena, behavioral theories do not view disability as inherently different from other types of stress or loss. Though particular experience accompanying various stresses may differ in specific content or degree, the general processes governing psychological reactions to them are considered to be the same.

The general characteristics of behavioral theories outlined above vary, depending on the specific behavioral theory. Great diversity actually exists among behavioral theories. Strong evidence of this is seen in the diversity of thought concerning how behavior is learned. As mentioned, behavioral theorists consider learning to be the central explanatory principle for all psychological phenomena, yet each of three separate behavioral schools claim primacy for three different types of learning, each with a distinct procedure and process underlying it. The basic types of learning procedures distinguished are classical conditioning, operant conditioning, and observational learning. Each of these procedures uses systematic presentation of environmental stimuli to alter the individual's future responses. Despite this similarity, behavioral theorists point to the basic differences in procedures and processes involved in each type of conditioning as evidence for separate kinds of learning.

The behavioral theories all share in the significant advantages of being rooted in the experimental learning laboratory. By necessity, they are operationally clear in terminology, quite parsimonious because of their closeness to experimental data, and fairly consistent.

Deductions from the theories have a good degree of testability. In addition, two of the three behavioral "schools"—Pavlovian theories and observational learning theories—acknowledge the role of internal psychological processes in human learning. These internal processes, moreover, are not vaguely defined as in most mentalistic theories of disability. Instead, these behavioral schools make use of information-processing language, such as encoding, retrieval, and storage, to describe the cognitive aspects of learning.

Empirical evidence demonstrating the utility of many behavioral treatments for disabled persons is already at hand (Fordyce, 1974, 1976; Ince, 1976; Katz & Zlutnic, 1975; Wooley, Blackwell, & Winget, 1978). The types of physical disability to which behavioral techniques have been applied run the gamut—asthma, chronic pain, quadriplegia, blindness, arthritis, brain damage, hypertension, deafness. The goals of these treatments have also varied tremendously, from modifying specific physiological functions such as muscle tension to improving the quality of complex behaviors such as assertiveness, medication usage, and self-control. These interventions also have a number of methodological advantages over the nonbehavioral approaches. Techniques are clearly defined in operational terms, goals are likewise explicit, and measures of therapeutic success are continuous throughout treatment to ensure that modifications are made as needed.

The weaknesses of behavioral approaches lie in their lack of emphasis on the internal psychological processes that influence each person's perception and organization of his own personal world (Neisser, 1967). A less than complete understanding of these factors can lead to an alienation of rehabilitation professionals from the disabled in a classic "insider-outsider" split (Dembo, Leviton, & Wright, 1956). Ultimately, this split can block any constructive behavioral or cognitive change. An integrative approach is needed in which both internal and external variables can be properly placed in a more comprehensive understanding of disability and rehabilitation.

Providing the most recent and comprehensive of all behavioral theories is Bandura's social learning theory (1969, 1977). As its name implies, this theory shares the behavioral emphasis on learning as its central explanatory concept. Yet this social learning theory is unique in its emphasis on mediation in human learning. All behavioral change is viewed as involving cognitive mediation, that is, symbolic and information-processing abilities. Furthermore, Bandura asserts that almost all complex human behavior is a result of observational learning or modeling. In this process, information about new ways of acting, thinking, and feeling is obtained (learned) via observation of others or from symbolic information describing new responses. Thus no overt behavior actually has to occur in this type of learning. Learning by means of direct behavioral experience, as in classical and operant conditioning, is considered too slow and inefficient to be able to account for complex human learning. Of course, Bandura recognizes that both these learning procedures can have significant effects, but he argues that any learning which occurs in them is due to the same congitive processes that acocunt for observational learning.

In Bandura's social learning theory neither environmental nor internal cognitive variables are singled out as the primary determinant of behavior. A reciprocal interaction between external and internal influences is instead hypothesized. The individual's characteristics—cognitive and self-reactive abilities, physiology, and present behavioral repertoire—are seen as continually influencing and being influenced by both antecedent and consequent environmental events. Thus behavioral, cognitive, and environmental influences are all considered to be equal sources of influence.

Bandura's social learning theory shares all the advantages of the behavioral approach—clearly defined terms, logically consistent principles, and strong deductive capacity. Experimental research concerning both theoretical concepts and suggested therapies is relatively easy to accomplish. Social learning theory is not, however, as simple as other behavioral theories. Many cognitive variables, such as attention, encoding, and imaging abilities, are included as important and necessary explanations to account for complex human psychology. This increased complexity is not a liability, however; it allows Bandura's theory increased predictive power and utility.

Empirically, social learning theory has received strong support. It is based on a broad base of experimental findings regarding both human and animal behavior. A very large range of complex human behavior has been shown to be consistent with and amenable to observational influences (Bandura, 1977). Such diverse areas as moral reasoning, self-control, language development, vicarious reinforcement, and control of physiological functions can all be powerfully addressed from this perspective.

Conclusion

A thorough integration of both explanatory and treatment perspectives is required before the wide chasm between the clinician and theoretician can be bridged. Some movement toward such an integrated theory can be seen in the inclusion of both cognitive and behavioral variables in the theories of Wright and Meyerson and in the recognition (Parsons, 1964; Skinner 1953; Wright, 1960) of the role that the environment plays in psychological adjustment to disability. Most important, however, has been the development of theories which incorporate these assets within a system that deals equally with explanation and treatment. Bandura's (1977) social learning theory is one such integrative attempt. Although a thorough extension of social learning theory to the field of physical disability and rehabilitation remains unwritten at this time, such an application offers great promise for the future. This theory can accommodate the need for an overall explanation of human stability and development, while simultaneously providing therapeutic methods by which to deal with the practical, everyday problems in the rehabilitation setting.

References and Bibliography

Alexander, F., French, T. M., & Pollack, G. H. (Eds.). *Psychosomatic specificity* (Vol. 1). Chicago: University of Chicago Press, 1968.

Anderson, T., & Andberg, M. Psychosocial factors associated with pressure sores. *Archives of Physical Medicine and Rehabilitation*, 1979, *60*, 341–346.

Bakal, D. *Psychology and medicine: Psychobiological dimensions of health and illness.* New York: Springer, 1979.

Bandura, A. *Principles of behavior modification.* New York: Holt, Rinehart, & Winston, 1969.

Bandura, A. *Social learning theory.* Englewood Cliffs, N. J.: Prentice-Hall, 1977.

Barker, R. G., Wright, B. A., & Gonick, M. R. *Adjustment to physical handicap and illness: A survey of the social psychology of physique and disability* (rev. ed.). New York: Social Science Research Council, Bulletin 55, 1953.

Beller, E., & Turner, J. Personality correlates of children's perception of human size. *Child Development*, 1964, *35*, 441–449.

Brewer, W. F. There is no convincing evidence for operant or classical conditioning in adult humans. In W. B. Werner, & D. S. Palermo (Eds.), *Cognition and the symbolic processes.* Hillside, N. J.: Lawrence Erlbaum Associates, 1974.

Chomsky, N. A review of B. F. Skinner's verbal behavior. *Language*, 1959, *35*, 26–58.

Cleveland, S. E. Body image changes associated with personality reorganization. *Journal of Consulting Psychology*, 1960, *24*, 256–261.

Cruickshank, W. (Ed.) *Psychology of exceptional children and youth.* Englewood Cliffs, N. J.: Prentice-Hall, 1971.

Dembo, T., Leviton, G., & Wright, B. Adjustment to misfortune: A problem of social-psychological rehabilitation. *Artificial Limbs,* 1956, *3,* 4–62.

English, R. The application of personality theory to explain psychological reactions to physical disability. *Rehabilitation Research and Practice Review,* 1971, *3,* 35–47.

Fisher, S., & Cleveland, S. E. *Body image and personality.* New York: Dover, 1968.

Fordyce, W. Treating chronic pain by contingency management. In J. Bonica (Ed.), *Advances in neurology (Vol. IV), International Symposium on Pain.* New York: Raven Press, 1974.

Fordyce, W. *Behavioral methods for chronic pain and illness.* St. Louis: C. V. Mosby, 1976.

Fordyce, W., Fowler, R., Lehman, Delateur, B., & Treischmann, R. B. Operant conditioning in the treatment of chronic clinical pain. *Archives of Physical Medicine and Rehabilitation,* 1973, *54,* 399–408.

Goldiamond, I. Coping and adaptive behaviors of the disabled. In G. L. Albrecht (Ed.), *The sociology of physical disability and rehabilitation.* Pittsburgh: University of Pittsburgh Press, 1976.

Ince, L. *Behavior modification in rehabilitation medicine.* Springfield, Ill.: Charles C Thomas, 1976.

Katz, R., & Zlutnik, S. (Eds.). *Behavior therapy and health care: Principles and applications.* New York: Pergammon Press, 1975.

Kemph, J. Psychotherapy with patients receiving kidney transplants. *American Journal of Psychiatry,* 1967, *124,* 623–629.

Kimball, C. Psychological responses to experience of open heart surgery: I. *American Journal of Psychiatry,* 1969, *126,* 348–359.

Luborsky, L., Docherty, J., & Penick, S. Onset conditions for psychosomatic symptoms: A comparative review of immediate observation with retrospective research. *Psychosomatic Medicine,* 1973, *35,* 187–203.

Mahoney, M. *Cognition and human behavior.* Cambridge, Mass.: Ballinger, 1974.

McGlynn, F. Graded imagination and relaxation as components of experimental desensitization. *Journal of Nervous and Mental Disease,* 1973, *157,* 377–385.

Mechanic, D. Concept of illness behavior. *Journal of Chronic Diseases,* 1962, *15,* 189–194.

Meyerson, L. Somatopsychology of physical disability. In W. Cruickshank (Ed.), *Psychology of exceptional children and youth* (3rd ed.). Englewood Cliffs, N. J.: Prentice-Hall, 1971.

Michael, J. Rehabilitation. In C. Neuringer, & J. Michael (Eds.) *Behavior modification in clinical psychology.* New York: Appleton-Century-Crofts, 1970.

Neisser, U. *Cognitive psychology.* New York: Appleton-Century-Crofts, 1967.

Parsons, T. *Social structure and personality.* Glencoe, Ill.: Free Press, 1964.

Rachman, S. *The effects of psychological therapy.* Oxford: Pergamon, 1971.

Rachman, S., & Wilson, G. T. *The effects of psychological therapy* (2nd ed.). Oxford: Pergamon, 1980.

Richardson, S., Hastrof, A., & Dornbuster, S. Effects of physical disability on a child's description of himself. *Child Development,* 1964, *35,* 893–894.

Schilder, P. *The image and appearance of the human body.* New York: International Universities Press, 1950.

Shontz, F. Reaction to crisis. *Volta Review,* 1965, *67,* 364–370.

Shontz, F. Physical disability and personality: Theory and recent research. *Rehabilitation Psychology,* 1970, *17,* 51–69.

Shontz, F. Psychological adjustment to physical disability: Trends in theories. *Archives of Physical Medicine and Rehabilitation,* 1978, *59,* 251–254.

Simmel, M. Developmental aspects of the body schema. *Child Development,* 1966, *37,* 83–95.

Skinner, B. F. *Science and human behavior.* New York: Free Press, 1953.

Skinner, B. F. *Verbal behavior.* New York: Appleton-Century-Crofts, 1957.

Treischmann, R. B. *The psychological, social, and vocational adjustment in spinal cord injury: A strategy for future research.* Los Angeles: Easter Seal Society of Los Angeles, 1978.

Warren, L. W., & Weiss, D. J. Relationship between disability type and measured personality characteristics. *Proceedings of the 77th Annual Convention of the American Psychological Association,* 1969, 773–774.

Waters, W., McDonald, D., & Koresko, R. Psychological responses during analogue systematic desensitization and nonrelaxation control procedures. *Behavior Research and Therapy,* 1972, *10,* 381–393.

Wolpe, J. *Psychotherapy by reciprocal inhibition.* Stanford, Calif.: Stanford University Press, 1958.

Wooley, S., Blackwell, B., & Winget, C. A learning theory model of chronic illness behavior: Theory, treatment, and research. *Psychosomatic Medicine,* 1978, *40*(5), 379–401.

Wright, B. A. *Physical disability—A psychological approach.* New York: Harper & Row, 1960.

Wylie, R. C. *The self concept: A critical survey of pertinent research literature.* Lincoln, Neb.: University of Nebraska Press, 1961.

14 Behavioral Rehabilitation

The Promise of Things to Come

Henry Slucki

Too often, the advent of technology engenders a paradox: *progress*—
with its promise of an improved quality of life—is accompanied by
retrogression with its undesirable side effects, such as pollution, disease, disability, and even death. Thus the implementation of new
discoveries may occasion negative consequences, unforeseen but
nonetheless injurious to the unsuspecting consumer. So a disability,
such as paralysis, may be the unfortunate product of advanced human engineering on our environment, with the sources of injury to
be found within an industrial, home, or recreational setting (including a vehicular accident). The effects may include behavioral disabilities—especially in the activities of daily living, self-care, mobility, and communication—loss of employment, and psychological
disabilities, especially depression. To reverse these effects the field
of rehabilitation medicine (with its allied health professions) is devoted to maximizing the handicapped person's return to the behaviorally functional ("normal") repertoire that was present prior to the
disability, or, if congenital or permanent, to some optimal or compensatory capacity. For those circumstances in which total loss of function has resulted from limb amputation or complete neuroanatomical
lesion, the goal of therapy is to restore or reinstate the behavioral
equivalent through artificial means such as prosthetic devices or substitute manipulations from other parts of the body to compensate for
the nonexistent or diminished function.

It is the central argument of this chapter that it is the rehabilitation professionals who reap the credit for returning the injured and
disabled persons to the ranks of the self-sufficient, functioning, and
gainfully employed members of the society, therefore, it is they who

must also be assigned a major share of the responsibility for misdirecting the disabled into a second-class status, one that is inferior or in some manner inadequate. It will be shown that rehabilitation professionals can contribute significantly to the disabled person's continuing inability to progress beyond some limited level, largely through mismanagement of the therapeutic process, primarily because these professionals lack behavioral knowledge and skills to apply them appropriately. Additionally, behavioral research in rehabilitation medicine has been woefully lacking or of questionable value for helping the therapists with improved methods of intervention.

In the final analysis the field of rehabilitation has been dominated by medicine, with its biases and shortcomings, especially in its dependence on the medical model as an explanatory framework for behavior. Aside from its obvious deficiencies on theoretical grounds, it also fails empirically as a system (Ullmann & Krasner, 1965).

Because patient management is a behavioral problem within a medical/rehabilitation context, it is from the behavior analyst, in cooperation with the physician that the impetus for its solution must come, and be elaborated and encouraged by the rehabilitation therapist in collaboration with the disabled person. Only when these four elements contribute their respective shares will the rehabilitation process succeed.

Rehabilitation Medicine

Within a rehabilitation setting conventional methods of intervention have evolved that are rich in clinical wisdom and practical experience. However, they may suffer from serious shortcomings they share with other areas of clinical medicine, namely, the lack of experimental rigor for both validity and reliability. Thus too often it is impossible to distinguish between fact and fiction, observation and inference, good practice and good luck, knowledge and superstition—in short, technological evidence and ephemeral allusion all seem to have an equal status of acceptability.

It became apparent to me after visiting the exercise gyms in physical and occupational therapy services that gross errors in behavioral management are being committed every day because of ignorance of the scientific principles of behavior analysis.

Therapists' attention as a potent social reinforcer is often made contingent on maladaptive behaviors exhibited by patients, such as complaining of pain, inactivity or lack of exercising, or other similar supplicative behaviors; or such social reinforcement may be delivered noncontingently, that is, in a more-or-less random fashion rather than contingent on appropriate behaviors (such as exercising correctly). It is noteworthy that too often it is the perennial "squeaky wheel that gets the oil," namely, the quarrelsome and uncooperative patients, the ones who complain and do not exercise, who get the therapists to respond to them; whereas the ones who are carrying out the prescribed exercises by being busy constantly and involved in their therapy will rarely get more than a "Keep it up!" or "That's good work!" comment. The instructions by the therapists to the patients often specify the mismanaged contingency in this fashion: "When you have completed the prescribed exercise, just sit and rest. *I'll come to check you when I see you are not working*" (emphasis added). Thus, from a behavioral point of view, the cessation of exercising—whether from completion of the regimen or because the patient hasn't even begun to exercise—is reinforced by the therapists' attention. When a therapist returns and says to the patient, "I see you are resting. Did you finish the exercises?" the reply is usually "Yes," which the therapist reinforces by saying "That's good! I'm glad you did," or some such statement. Not only is the appropriate behavior (exercising) not reinforced while an incompatible behavior is, but the "credibility gap" widens, with the patient becoming convinced that the therapy is of no value, and, if on out-patient service, this person is neither likely to do the exercises at home nor to continue to come in for therapy.

In addition, there are numerous factors operating against a patient's adherence or compliance to the exercise regimen. When, for example, an injured limb is moved, there is usually pain, a consequence that reduces the likelihood of doing the exercises. Also, for most but the highly motivated patients, there is a good deal of boredom in the repetitive patterns which characterize physical and occupational therapy rehabilitation programs. Assuming that the patient has been convinced that there is validity to the exercise program, namely, that lifting a weight, for example, will affect the recovery of the use of that limb for everyday tasks, the patient may still become discouraged rapidly in the absence of meaningful recovery of function which, unfortunately, usually takes a relatively long time.

From the patient's point of view, the immediate effects of exercising are: (1) pain, (2) boredom, and (3) no improvement in the recovery of function—at least none that the patient can yet observe. The immediate feedback to the patient from the therapist may be (1)aversive, ranging from nagging and admonition to reprimand and reproach or

(2) mismanaged, that is, either contingent on maladaptive behaviors or noncontingent on appropriate behavior emitted by the patient or (3) systematic, that is, differential and contingent according to the principles of behavior analysis (to be discussed below).

On the other hand, the therapists' behaviors are also controlled by their respective consequences, often originating from the patients' behaviors themselves. Thus a nonproductive and poorly motivated patient, one who does not show a high output, may produce for the therapist a diminution in the therapist's support for that patient (which, in turn, may contribute further to depress the patient's behavior even more). The resulting lack of success in the patient's progress will tend to influence the therapist into shifting away from that patient and putting more effort into working with a more "productive" patient.

This descending spiral—in all probability—will eventually result in termination of therapy either from the patient's "dropping out" or the rehabilitation team's concluding that the therapy program is no longer effective in producing results, since the patient has apparently reached a plateau. By contrast, a productive and energetic patient who continues to be motivated and to show progress in therapy will tend to receive more support from the rehabilitation team.

In addition to the above analysis of factors contributing to a pessimistic and grim portrayal of rehabilitation, there is the profound and sometimes overriding influence of the disability payment. "The behavioral psychologist looks at the grant of disability benefits as a potential secondary gain which, in chronic cases, 'teaches' the individual to be sick in order to obtain financial rewards." (Grossman, 1979, p. 41). Although this inference establishes purpose in the recipient, a conclusion that goes beyond the data, it is a fact that when viewed in this manner, "the grant is a reinforcer of idleness" and "the law thus provides for built-in resistance to any return to gainful activity" (Grossman, 1979, p. 47). "Similarly, the rehabilitation counselor is frustrated by the fact that many beneficiaries believe their disability checks to be permanent income which they have earned, which belief causes them to view rehabilitation as a threat to financial security rather than a preparation for return to productive activity" (Grossman, 1979, p. 41).

Consider the following excerpt from the Ways and Means Committee of the U.S. House of Representatives (96th Congress, First Session), during a hearing before its Subcommittee on Social Security. The testimony is that of Mr. John H. Miller, consulting actuary to the Committee (1976):

> Under present law, disability benefits are awarded only if (i) the disability is judged to be permanent or (ii) is not permanent but is expected to last for a long time and at least twelve months in any case. In effect (i) is a life sentence to dependency and uselessness and (ii) is an indeterminate sentence with a possibility of "parole" via recovery or rehabilitation but no definite timetable or program for re-evaluation although certain cases are diaried for future medical re-evaluation. Both beneficiaries and administrators are therefore left with the inference that a disability pension has been granted. The very sorry showing of rehabilitation efforts and the low and declining rate of recoveries seem to support this conclusion. The psychological impact on the disabled individual of the judgment that his disability is permanent or of long and indefinite duration certainly does not set the stage for early recovery or for a serious attempt at rehabilitation. (p. 124)

With all these combined factors added to the medical fact that recovery often will occur simply because of the passage of time, it is a miracle that patients continue to participate in physical and occupational therapy rehabilitation programs!

Physical and occupational therapists are behavioral engineers in the full meaning of this term. Many consider their task to be more than that of "merely" repairing and reshaping the use of limbs and neuromuscular units that have been damaged. These professionals express concern for the "whole" person and not merely a damaged limb. Viewing their roles in these broad terms, these well-meaning and well-trained therapists engage in activities that may be, in fact, antitherapeutic. Michael (1970) details some of these practices and their behavioral effects on the patients. In reviewing the therapeutic aims of rehabilitation, one is always faced with the question of whether the patient improved because of, regardless of, or in spite of the staff's intervention. Mismanagement in many medical areas, such as an error in clinical practice or judgment, may result in death or very obvious worsening in the patient's condition. By and large, physical medicine and rehabilitation do not fall into this category: this realm of practice results in nonlethal effects, for rarely, if ever, does one of its patients die because of an error, a miscalculation, or incorrect procedure. More often, the effect is that of delaying or hampering the rehabilitation process. As is true in other applied areas of medicine and therapy, lack of progress can be blamed on the physical limitations of the patient, the state of the art, or limited knowledge accumulated by that area or discipline, or, in the last analysis, on the patient who lacks motivation. The erring rehabilitation professional escapes blame free!

In general-medicine wards a nurse administers therapy in the form of medication or specific procedures very carefully and supervises the patient at all times (even if the monitoring is carried out from a distance). Too often, the physical medicine therapist, by contrast, supervises the patient minimally, giving the patient some general statements about the purpose of the particular intervention (e.g., to strengthen a given muscle group), followed by a more-or-less specific instruction (e.g., "Do this exercise 10 times or until you get too tired, and then take a rest.") Because most exercises are routine, the therapist moves on to a second patient and returns to the first one at a later time. The patient is blamed for any lack of motivation because he or she understands the disability as well as the rehabilitation process, "wants" to get well, should, therefore, perform as instructed, and because the therapist, who is *not* a babysitter, should not be given the task of overseeing patients as they carry out routine exercises. Hence, one major behavioral management problem too often avoided or overlooked by therapists is whether the patient is, in fact, doing the exercises and whether these are being carried out correctly as prescribed. A second question is whether the prescribed program of rehabilitation has been designed to produce the behavioral end product most effectively. A third question deals with the changes that may be needed in the therapeutic program as the patient improves, namely, what new interventions are indicated and what are the criteria for determining when and how these should be implemented.

By contrast, until recently the role of a psychologist within a physical-medicine ward setting has been limited to counseling the patient and anyone immediately concerned with his or her rehabilitation (family members, ward personnel, etc.) and thus oriented toward assisting the patient "adjust realistically to and better understand" the particular disability. Rarely, if ever, was a psychologist called in to aid in the development of strategies for more usual therapeutic interventions—this task was seen to be exclusively within the purview of the physical and occupational therapists.

In the rapidly growing discipline of the experimental analysis of behavior as it pertains to medicine—behavioral medicine—and by analogy, to rehabilitation—behavioral rehabilitation—the elimination of certain behaviors and the maintenance of others, the establishment of specific stimulus control conditions that affect these changes, and the alteration of response emission rates by means of schedules of reinforcement are all topics within the realm and expertise of applied behavior analysis or behavioral engineering.

Experimental Analysis of Behavior

The experimental analysis of behavior has a long history, with its philosophical origins reaching back to the earliest roots of scientific thought, through the Greeks, the French Encyclopedists, the British Empiricists and Associationists, Darwin, John B. Watson (the American behaviorist), Pavlov (the Russian physiologist), culminating in B. F. Skinner. Its significance is its ability to systematize behavioral knowledge, that is, to generate and collect data through experimentation resulting in the formulation of behavior principles, which, in turn, can be applied systematically to produce reliable effects. It is not within the scope of this chapter to discuss behavioristic philosophy or to justify the existence of a science of human behavior. Others, especially Skinner, have done so articulately and extensively.

What are the principles of the experimental analysis of behavior and how may they be applied to rehabilitation? What lessons may we learn from such an analysis? For a more thorough and much broader discussion of applied behavior analysis in medicine—behavioral medicine—the reader is referred to Davidson and Davidson (1980), Ferguson and Taylor (1980), Ince (1980), Katz and Zlutnick (1975), and Pomerleau and Brady (1979). Also of special importance are the following articles: Fordyce (1971), Meyerson, Kerr, and Michael (1967), Meyerson, Michael, Mowrer, Osgood, and Staats (1960), Michael (1970), and Pomerleau (1979).

Principles of Operant Behavior

The following account, intended only to highlight some principles, gives samples of our research into their applications to the rehabilitation of patients who, having suffered from brain injuries, manifest sensory losses, communication handicaps, brain dysfunctions, behavior management problems, and impairment of behavioral self-control repertoires. Our research data demonstrate both accelerated recovery and the extent to which the functions have been regained by the patients who served voluntarily as subjects in our experiments. These persons, for whom all other efforts including excellent but conventional rehabilitation had failed, had had their injury at least a year or two earlier. In fact, as a prerequisite for eligibility to participate in our studies, these individuals documented the extent of neurological damage by medical charts (including its source—head trauma, stroke, or other—immediate and chronic effects, dates, and full particulars) and evidence of rehabilitation efforts elsewhere, their results, and eventual discharge because of lack of progress.

A most basic observation that has been formalized into what is often called the empirical law of effect is that of *positive reinforcement*, namely, the operation of presenting a positive consequence (reinforcer) contingent on the emission of a given behavior, effecting an increase in its probability of occurrence on a future occasion. Thus the delivery of praise by a therapist or obtaining the knowledge that the extension of an arm is improving (positive reinforcers) will produce an increase in the range of motion, the rate of movement, or some other measurable change. This phenomenon is elementary, endorsed by professionals, and well-documented in the laboratory and the clinic. Its universality is recognized in all avenues of human behavior. But there are several important guidelines to be followed if a positive reinforcement procedure is to be effective. First, the positive reinforcer to be used must *in fact* be a positive reinforcer. That is, it is essential to demonstrate empirically that for this person, in this setting, under these conditions, at this time, *this* stimulus is positively reinforcing. Food, for example, may be a positive reinforcer for a hungry person but probably not for one who has just eaten. Additionally, attention from one therapist may in fact be very reinforcing, while from another it may not. Second, the delivery of positive reinforcement must be immediate; if delayed, it may be delivered simultaneously with the occurrence of a segment of behavior that may, in fact, be undesirable or incompatible with the desired one. Thus if a patient is lifting a weight [the desirable behavior] and as he or she puts it down with a complaint that "I can't do it" [the undesirable behavior], the praise by the therapist is delivered, that moment's delay will likely result in the inadvertent reinforcement of the undesirable behavior. Another guideline for the use of positive reinforcement is to maintain a consistency in the criterion for reinforcement if the response rate is to be sustained.

A closely related phenomenon, *extinction*, is simply the manner in which a learned bit of behavior may be eliminated: the operation of withholding a positive reinforcer previously contingent on the behavior, with the observed decrease in the rate of its occurrence on future occasions. A common mode for incorporating an extinction procedure within a ward setting is simply to ignore the behavior to be extinguished, that is, pretend that it didn't occur. It is relatively easy to do if one simply does something else at that time. In other words, go about your business as if you were blind or deaf vis-à-vis the patient's undesirable behavior: pick up a telephone and make a call, open a book, turn to talk to another person, leave the room—in short do anything but pay attention to the person who emitted the behavior to be extinguished. The effects of such a procedure will be the disappearance of the behavior on which it is contingent.

There are some important facts that must be recognized by anyone using extinction as an intervention mode in therapy. First, because most reinforced behaviors take longer to extinguish than to condition, a therapist using this behavior modification method should be aware that if extinction is to be effective there must be a *total* withholding of actual and potential reinforcers for that behavior. If there is the slightest reoccurrence of reinforcement, the behavior will return. This inadvertent reintroduction of reinforcement by the therapist has several and far more severe fallout effects, namely the introduction of intermittency in the pattern or schedule of reinforcement. This phenomenon, studied extensively by Skinner and his students, is a very technical and complex aspect of behavior analysis, far beyond the scope of this chapter. However, it is of unique importance that behavior emission may be maintained more efficiently through intermittent reinforcement, that is, for extensive periods of time with fewer reinforcers during acquisition and with greater persistence during extinction. Knowledge of the intricacies of schedules enables behavior managers to regulate the performance of those in their care far better. What began as a fortuitous discovery (Skinner, 1956) has developed into a most significant technology for behavioral control. For the interested reader, Ferster and Skinner (1957), Morse (1966), and the *Journal of the Experimental Analysis of Behavior* are strongly recommended.

Second, because it is always a particular behavior that is being extinguished, the applied behavior analyst must remember to reinforce positively those behaviors that are appropriate and desirable. Thus although therapist attention may be withheld from a given patient to eliminate or extinguish a specific behavior, the therapist must be attentive, watching for the occurrence of an appropriate behavior which may then be reinforced positively. This form of intervention will ensure good motivation and a positive attitude on the part of the patient, both of which, it is well-recognized, are critical for success in the therapeutic process.

From time to time we are asked to consult with the staff of our burn ward and assist them in managing the oppositional behavior of some children, ranging from crying and screaming excessively and refusing to follow directions to picking off skin grafts prematurely—in short, behaviors often arising from pain which interfere with proper medical treatment and delay the recovery process significantly. The first step in applying behavior analysis is to observe the behavior in question and its environment, that is, the conditions under which it occurs—which events in the immediate vicinity were setting the occasion for the child to "misbehave" and which ones were reinforcing this pattern of oppositional behaviors. As is often the case, this behavior occurs during a session with the physical therapist, during which time the affected limbs, the legs, for example, are moved passively to prevent joint contractures and to facilitate normal muscle functioning; they are wrapped with Ace bandages to provide support for the lower leg capillary circulation; and the child is required to walk with the assistance of a walker-aide. Our baseline observations suggested that the oppositional behavior occurred in the presence of the physical therapist and was being reinforced intermittently by this person's attention and verbal statements—both positive and negative, such as encouraging, cajoling, and finally threatening the patient to cooperate. The intervention program we recommended, after these initial baseline determinations were completed, was designed to extinguish the crying behavior, that is, to allow the child to cry and be oppositional but receive no reinforcement for it. Thus the therapist continued to work with the child (e.g., moving his legs—since stopping the treatment is often the result that is most reinforcing to the child!) but withheld all attention including eye contact, until he ceased to be oppositional, whereupon she praised him for not crying, for being cooperative, and so forth. Whereas before he was getting a great deal of attention for his tyrannical behavior, now he was getting it *only* when that behavior was absent. The results of this procedure were evident almost immediately and by the second day, his oppositional behavior had virtually disappeared completely—a pattern which had been in his repertoire for several months!

What is being suggested by the above-cited illustration is that the simultaneous application of positive reinforcement for one behavior and extinction for another is a more effective intervention than either one separately. This process, called *differential reinforcement,* is central to all behavior modification procedures—whether educational or therapeutic. What is Skinner's greatest contribution to the science of human behavior is his understanding of the power of differential reinforcement, especially as it is applied to a process of gradual behavior change. This process, called *shaping,* is the systematic application of differential reinforcement to successive approximations of the target behavior, the goal that is to be brought about. As the final behavior is approached, the criterion for reinforcement is raised gradually, with a twofold effect: a decrease in the undesirable behavior (extinction) and an increase in the designated one (positive reinforcement). Shaping is an essential process to establish behaviors that are not in the current repertoire of a given person or to refine those that are not adequately developed, as in skills, for example. The level to which behavior is emitted at any given moment by the individual may be expressed as a statistical mean, that is, average performance: some behavior will be above and some below that value. The process of shaping through differential reinforcement eliminates the poor performance and enhances the desired one.

From the "subject's" point of view, to behave or not to behave, *that* is the question! From the point of view of the experimenter/therapist, however, when the behavior of a patient/client/subject is emitted, to reinforce or not to reinforce, *that* is the question! The answers to these questions, of course, depend on the point in the shaping process at which that behavior is occuring. More specifically, in applying behavior analysis, the strategy must be based on a three-element formulation: (1) What is the *target behavior* or desired end product, that is, what will this person be doing as a result of the intervention that he or she is not doing now? (2) What is the *current baseline* of that behavior? (3) What will function as a *positive reinforcer* for this person? What follows is the formulation of a blueprint or detailed, step-by-step prescription of what the behavioral engineer is to do to bring about a change in that person's behavior.

VM

VM, a 55-year-old woman who had suffered a stroke resulting in a left hemiparesis, was hospitalized and underwent physical therapy for the ensuing 2½ years. As a result, there was a partial recovery of her ability to walk with the help of a quad cane and a short leg brace, but there was no evidence of movement in her left forearm. Her goal was to improve her walking, if possible. Because there was electromyographic (EMG) evidence of some intact motor units in her left leg, it was decided to attempt modifying the range of motion for knee extension and foot dorsiflexion, both maneuvers having been impervious to physical therapy for months (just prior to our intervention). The knee extension was programmed for shaping in the following manner. VM was seated in a chair while one of our technicians was next to her, on the floor so as to view closely and record accurately the distance between the rear tip of VM's heel and the floor (by means of a meter placed vertically in a plane parallel to the arc prescribed by her heel). Baseline data were recorded by instructing VM to raise her lower leg as high as possible several times without giving her any feedback information about her performance. Next, another technician raised VM's leg (passively) to its full extension several times to obtain a reliable target-behavior recording.

The intervention consisted of asking VM to raise her lower leg as high as possible, reading the height accurately and giving her the information immediately. If a given trial produced an increase in the height, she was given praise in addition; otherwise, nothing else was said and, after a brief time, as designated in the research protocol, the next trial took place. In this manner only the positive (improvement) was accentuated. Marked improvement was achieved almost at once, and she continued to show progress; within a very short time she was extending her leg to its full limit. The dorsiflexion exercise was modified through EMG biofeedback which also proved to be very effective in producing rapid and notable results. As a result of these two interventions, after 9 weeks and a total of about 12 hours, she was able to walk with only a simple (single-stem) cane and no leg brace. Some arm pronation was also brought about with only the aid of EMG biofeedback intervention.

Biofeedback is a special instance of behavior modification in which the behavior being modified is observed on a physiological level by means of a special voltage monitor. Thus rather than shaping a change in the angle of ankle rotation or the height a leg has been lifted, it is the bioelectrical voltage intensity that is increased (or decreased) through differential reinforcement for covert (physiological) behaviors. This procedure has obvious advantages when the overt behavior, such as either the movement of a limb or muscle contraction, is not of sufficient magnitude to be observed visually.

It is noteworthy that EMG biofeedback has been used efficaciously during rehabilitation for reconditioning the use of disabled limbs. If there is any meaningful criticism of applying EMG biofeedback to rehabilitation, it is simply that if the behavior—however small—may be readily observed, the need for recording the bioelectrical potential is greatly reduced. In the case of VM, that the knee extension was an easily measured response made the use of EMG biofeedback unwarranted and superfluous. The face validity of shaping overt behavior is of much greater value than monitoring individual muscle changes electronically and then assembling these into coordinated gross movements.

There is, however, a major advantage in utilizing EMG biofeedback procedures as adjuncts to shaping overt behaviors, especially for modifying limb movement when spasticity may interfere with the desired coordination. In such instances monitoring the antagonistic muscle groups enables the therapist and the disabled to observe and dissect the complex behavior patterns and through differential reinforcement simultaneously shape changes on both the overt and the physiological levels.

BB

BB, a 24-year-old, left-handed man "lost" the use of his left hand (including elbow, wrist, and fingers) as a result of brain damage sustained from a head injury he received when a car collided with his motorcycle. He was hospitalized, underwent therapy at a leading outpatient rehabilitation center, and, after about a year-and-a-half, was discharged from the facility, because he had shown no progress for some time. Because some very minimal movements at the several joints of the upper limb were observable during baseline determinations, shaping procedures were put into effect at once. Knowledge of results showing small but measurable gains in the range of motion of the left-hand index finger, for example, was an extremely effective reinforcer. Thus, in retraining this response, great progress was achieved rapidly: finger extension evolved into a flicking response (measured by the distance the checker traveled on our vinyl corridor floors) and eventually writing in a very legible manner (and to our mutual delight, finger snapping!). The gains were recorded in minute millimeters, vertical travel from a flat table-top surface; next, the rate of finger extension repetitions was increased by shaping a reduction in the number of seconds (to the nearest tenth) it took to do ten repetitions of the exercise.

It is noteworthy that the therapist who asked for the referral to our laboratory suggested that perhaps we could do something about his "depression." After the first few minutes of our initial interview, it became obvious to us that his "depression" was simply a realistic appraisal of his current state of affairs and that the "depression" would be "lifted" when his "real" problems were eliminated. This hypothesis was verified as he regained the normal functions in his left hand.

A similar process of shaping was observed to operate efficaciously for DL, a 24-year-old woman who, because of cerebral palsy, had never produced forearm pronation nor supination (baseline 0°–5°) and who was shaped to exceed 150 and for MO, a 48-year-old woman who had suffered an ideopathic facial nerve hemiparesis (Bell's palsy) from unknown origin and whose right eyelid's closure was shaped in less than one hour.

MW

MW, a 52-year-old woman, developed a form of spasmodic torticollis in which her head was deviated to her left with a slight upward tilt obliquely to the right. The effect was to restrict the range of motion and her posture when sitting, standing, and walking. In addition, she reported pain at all times that was especially intense when rotating her head to either side beyond a small degree. To assess the behavior and determine her range of motion, we fitted her with a football helmet and restricted all compensatory movements of her trunk and shoulders by strapping her into a chair by means of football shoulder pads. (I wish to thank the Department of Physical Education at the University of Southern California, Dr. Richard Perry, the athletic director, and John Robinson, the coach of the football team, for their kindness and cooperation in giving us access to this equipment.) A 25-centimeter pointer was attached onto the face mask and an arc of plastic placed on the table in front of her enabled the experimenter/therapist to read the exact degree of angular rotation as the range of motion directly. Reinforcement consisted of praise and verbal feedback of performance. The shaping procedure consisted of differentially reinforcing greater travel to the right and the left and resulted in an increment from a baseline range of motion of approximately 35° (from extreme right to extreme left) to 170° and still improving at this time.

In addition to the simultaneous reinforcement and extinction of behavior, the process of differential reinforcement may be made contingent on the occurrence of behavior in the presence or absence of a stimulus. Thus one stimulus signals that reinforcement is available, contingent on a response, while another stimulus serves as an environmental event to indicate that behavior emitted in its presence will be extinguished; that is, reinforcement will not be delivered. What is learned is that behavior may be emitted (and reinforced) in the presence of one stimulus and extinguished during another. The process of applying differential reinforcement to the stimulus is called *discrimination* or *stimulus control*.

JL

JL, a 35-year-old woman who had suffered a stroke in the midbrain region, was hospitalized and underwent conventional rehabilitation as an outpatient for about 1½ years. Much motor activity had returned during this time, but she continued to experience a pronounced sensory loss accompanied by paresthesia only on the right side of her body. This tingling sensation appeared to vary with the intensity of any sensory input. Neurological examination confirmed the absence of sensitivity to pain, temperature, touch, and proprioception on the right side of the body only. She sought help from our laboratory because she had burned herself badly on repeated occasions while attempting to conduct activities of daily living (washing with hot water, cooking, etc.), since she felt no pain in her affected right hand.

An intervention program was designated to capitalize on the intact but modest modality for discerning stimulus changes, namely, paresthesia. The results indicate that with a simple discrimination paradigm she learned—using her right hand only—to recognize the difference between 37° C (body temperature) and 50° C (hot enough but neither painful nor injurious) in less than 60 discrimination training trials. She reported a qualitative difference in the subjective tingling sensations when her hand was in hot or body temperature water. In effect, the training enabled her to translate changes in the tingling sensations' characteristics of frequency and intensity into a correlated temperature discrimination, even though she did not regain the thermal sensitivity, nor did she lose the paresthesia itself.

JL presented us with another one of the many problems that resulted from her stroke, namely, the loss of balance whenever she raised her nonaffected left arm above a certain height—in reaching for something on a shelf, for example. This loss of equilibrium is a very common result of stroke and other brain injuries. A behavioral analysis indicated that she did not bring to bear the necessary righting responses in sufficient time to compensate for balancing in a coordinated fashion. By the time she realized she needed to activate the contralateral side (the one affected by the stroke) to maintain herself in a stable posture, she was already falling, because her reaction time was too slow. For this coordinated chain of behavior segments we used the arm raising response in which she climbed the wall using her index and middle fingers of her (nonaffected) left hand alternately. This climbing was done on a large wall mirror with a centimeter scale in the center to measure the height accurately. Baseline data were collected for just a few trials since she started to fall each time (only to be caught and supported by two technicians standing on either side to avert her getting hurt). An arc of 5° to each side of the scale was marked on the mirror just above her eye level, and a headband held a 20-centimeter pointer vertically at the center of her forehead (between her eyes). When she stood perfectly straight, she had the pointer lined up with the centimeter scale on the mirror. She was instructed to climb the wall on the centimeter scale and continue climbing as long as she kept the pointer within the prescribed arc; she was to stop as soon as the pointer deviated beyond the arc and start climbing again a few centimeters below the point at which she had veered. A technician stood behind her to confirm when she was "on course" and "off course." The results showed clearly that she was able to learn to balance well. She has never fallen since. The righting responses were not really in need of retraining; rather JL had to learn to discriminate proprioceptive control, that is, under what internal stimulus conditions certain righting responses had to be called in, when, and of what magnitude.

A third problem area that JL presented for us to help solve concerned a more serious ramification of the loss of proprioception: unless she continued to look at her hand, she reported not being aware of its location in space nor of its motion. For example, if at the supermarket she keeps both hands on the handlebar of the shopping cart and continues to look at them, she will be able to control her right hand almost as well as her left one. If she turns her head and looks away, her right hand may remain on the cart's handlebar, or it may wander off and knock over a display of canned goods or a stack of jars nearby (within an arm's reach). In neither of these conditions is she aware of the location of her hand!

It is a common observation of most rehabilitation therapists that stroke patients and those individuals who have had a brain injury and who have learned to move their hands, fingers, and so on, correctly in spite of deficiencies in proprioception, have done so through visual discrimination and feedback training. In most cases, they continued to depend on visual feedback, even though it was only utilized as a training method by occupational therapists. If these former patients are asked to shut their eyes and go through the appropriate movement, they may, in fact, make quite a few mistakes; that is, for the vast majority since the proprioceptive discrimination has not been re-established, removing the visual stimuli on which these individuals are dependent may also result in no movement whatsoever, one of the opposite movements (flexion instead of extension, for example), or some other movement that is quite bizarre.

We have established a program designed to assist brain-injured individuals (JL, for example) to shift from complete visual dependence to total visual independence and to rely more appropriately on proprioception as the controlling agent for neuromuscular movements. The systematic change of stimulus control is based on the research paradigm of *errorless discrimination* (Terrace, 1966) which weans the individual systematically while maximizing success in maintaining the correct behavior. As the stimulus dimension is faded gradually, a more difficult discrimination is required once the easier one has been successfully implemented. Progress is made very rapidly, and retraining is accomplished with little effort.

Methodologically, the problem is one of engineering the fading process across some stimulus dimension. For our program, the visual dimension was faded using a video monitor in the following manner. A video camera equipped with a large zoom lens is positioned directly over the patient's shoulder, thereby blocking direct viewing access to the hand and showing the hand in the video monitor in front of the patient. The transfer of viewing the hand indirectly through the monitor instead of seeing it directly is achieved with very little difficulty. The patient is given tasks to perform and as he or she does so appropriately, the intensity on the video monitor is faded very gradually over trials. This engineering process is continued, until eventually the patient is performing the hand (neuromuscular) coordination tasks in front of a totally darkened screen *without errors*. This accomplishment is easily transferred to other laboratory tasks and to nonlaboratory settings as well. Throughout the sessions, a video tape recorder is available for continuous or time-sampled recordings for data storage and feedback to the patient. Also, even though the monitor is faded, the video tape recorder and the monitor for the camera are not faded, nor are they affected by the fading procedure whatsoever. This technical fact is important, otherwise it would not be possible to record and intervene at the same time.

For JL, learning proprioceptive discrimination errorlessly was a relatively rapid intervention. Many others have also benefitted from this straightforward, mechanical intervention and they are free to activate a hand or finger movement and are no longer dependent on looking at the hand to produce the appropriate behavior.

The foregoing is but a brief introduction into the behavioral principles utilizing positive reinforcers, with examples from our laboratory of their applications to rehabilitation interventions. The reader is referred to other sources cited above (especially the introductory chapter from Katz and Zlutnick, 1975) for more extensive elaborations of the principles—for both positive and negative reinforcers—especially as they pertain to more complex human behavior.

What is of greatest value in the application of these principles to medicine is the effect it will have on the philosophy and practice of medicine itself. Rarely is the doctor-patient relation seen as an active partnership in which both have clearly delineated and egalitarian roles. The patient is usually viewed as a passive recipient of the disease entity and, likewise, of the curative powers of the physician. There are many interventions including, but not limited to, surgery when this is not only an accurate but proper perspective. Rather than simply issuing an order, the doctor must alter the tactics to motivate the patient to function either as a passive recipient of the health care team's actions or as an active agent in the rehabilitation itself. In fact, it is precisely in rehabilitation medicine, where the patient is required to collaborate actively with the health professional in the therapeutic process itself, that behavior modification has been of the greatest value.

Important Lessons to be Learned

By appropriate control of reinforcement contingencies, health practitioners may profoundly reduce or completely eliminate behavioral disabilities or undesirable sick-role behaviors, thus facilitating rehabilitation, eliminating suffering, or curtailing illness. From a behavioral standpoint, therapists in rehabilitation medicine will be effective in bringing about behavioral improvement and recovery only if the intervention corresponds to the behavioral principles known to be controlling those functions.

Our research probes into behavioral rehabilitation have produced some very important lessons for those working in this area. By learning from our past errors we may improve our techniques, thereby influencing the recovery of function and helping the disabled to fulfill their potential more fully, while enabling us to meet our professional obligations and our pledge to the patient/client—a promise of things to come.

First, we must reassess the current attitudes and practices in physical medicine and rehabilitation. By adhering to the medical model, health practitioners are being handicapped either because they are set in the ways of the traditional, psychodynamic approach or because they are ignorant of behavioral principles (or both). What is much more desirable, of course, is the open and pragmatic expedient and the willingness to examine new approaches.

Second, it is necessary for therapists to differentiate between what a patient is or is not doing from what he or she can or cannot do. The latter must be determined empirically and independently of the former—otherwise, the therapeutic process is necessarily aborted.

Consider the following situation: a 24-year-old male is a victim of a vehicular accident resulting in a head injury which leaves his preferred hand paralyzed. The occupational therapist assesses the paralysis and, although pessimistic about the results, attempts to retrain the hand. After some time, no improvement is effected, and the patient is depressed: he has a paralyzed hand and he must be cared for by others for his every need. The occupational therapist—after consultation with the rehabilitation team members, including a neurologist, a neurosurgeon, a physiatrist, a psychiatrist, a social worker, a nurse, and several therapists (physical, occupational and recreational, etc.)—decided to retrain the nonpreferred hand, that is, to take on the functions previously carried out by the preferred hand, so as to enable him to become more self-reliant. This decision, based on a complex of issues, is significant because (1) it gives him the means for a more independent functioning since training the nonpreferred hand to take on new tasks (e.g., writing) is relatively easy but (2) it brings a finality to the disabled, preferred hand, namely, there will be no further attempts to retrain it for recovery of function. This young man is asked to accept this reality and to adjust to a "partial" disability, while the therapist works with his other hand. What is an obviously ethical question is: at what point in time is this decision reached and how overwhelming does the medical/neurological evidence need to be for therapy to be terminated (for the preferred, paralyzed hand)? This case is that described above (BB), and it is obvious—at least in BB's situation—that the "wrong" decision was made by the therapist and the rehabilitation team members. Of course, they were functioning within their level of competence, skill and knowledge, and felt justified in making that decision. But there is more to consider: the empirical distinction between *is not* and *cannot*. When an injury results in total amputation of an arm, for example, there is, of course, no recourse to "retrain" that nonexistent arm. Rather, the tactic is one of working toward accepting the loss and establishing compensatory means of coping, such as an artificial limb. However, as long as there is evidence of function at some level of observation, there must be a steadfast commitment to rehabilitate, that is, to restore or reinstate the normal function or an approximation to it. The same conclusion must hold true for neural damage, whether in the brain or the spinal cord or peripherally.

It might be a good idea to re-examine, in the light of these comments, the designing, manufacturing, and dispensing of the many prosthetic devices, accessories, and compensatory "gadgets." These aids, which must be considered of great value in making the individual more self-sufficient, may have been prescribed primarily *not* because of therapeutic indications, but rather because they make life easier for family members (a consideration not to be eliminated in a precipitate manner).

Third, rather than to blame the patients/clients or their neural pathologies for the lack of improvement, therapists must recognize that the burden is on them to find appropriate ways to bring about the needed behavioral changes.

It is clear that the patient's sick-role behavior is directly attributable to the reinforcement contingencies controlled in large part by others (relatives, friends, and even health and helping professionals). Too often, well-meaning persons hamper the progress of rehabilitation by indiscriminately dispensing the universal medication: tender loving care (TLC). Displaying sympathy, empathy, or concern for a suffering or disabled human being is a very normal, understandable, and humane reaction. However, when these social behaviors function as reinforcers for behavior patterns that are incompatible with therapy, the patient/client will display poor or marginal motivation. Michael (1970) asserts that "from a behavioral point of view, . . . such marginal motivation seems merely to be a case of insufficient or poorly arranged reinforcement. The basic question that should be asked is what does the patient get out of this activity? The problem of motivation is essentially a simple one. One must merely arrange the environment so that its desirable features are only available contingent upon participation and accomplishment in the rehabilitation training activity. It is in this area that the behavior modifier is making and will probably continue to make the greatest impact on the field of rehabilitation" (p. 65). Thus, from this orientation, "the problems of the disabled person require the acquisition of some new behaviors, the maintenance of adequate behaviors, and the extinction of inadequate or deficient behaviors." (Meyerson et al., 1960, p. 70)

Fourth, the fields of physical and occupational therapy are replete with instrumentation designed to assess behaviors—both deficits and strengths—accurately. Because baseline determination is the first step in a behavior modification intervention, we were able to incorporate the existing equipment with only a few changes centering on increased precision. The important lesson we learned is that all measuring instruments may function as training devices through contingency management.

The history of scientific research and clinical practice has shown that progress is greatly dependent on the development of the appropriate apparatus for both experimental manipulations and data recording. Furthermore, with greater precision in behavioral monitoring, greater skill in behavior modification is possible. Thus, the quicker a small change—increase or decrease—in the behavior is noticed and the shorter the delay between that behavioral change and the delivery of reinforcement, the more effective will be the therapeutic or experimental intervention.

A few examples from our laboratory which have been applied to the clinic will suffice.

Stationary Exercise Bicycle or Ergometer. Widely used in physical therapy, this apparatus is admirably equipped with an adjustable resistance, a speedometer, and an odometer or mileage indicator. To generate one-tenth of a mile requires 35 to 45 revolutions of the pedal, more work output than a patient recovering from a leg injury or disability may be able to produce. A patient who is in the early stages of rehabilitation will not achieve any reinforcement on the odometer, even though he or she may have managed, with great effort, to produce two or three or even 20 revolutions on the pedal. To ameliorate this situation, we attach a permanent magnet to the spokes of the wheel and place a reed switch on the bicycle frame, thereby allowing us to record each revolution of the wheel. (If it is desirable, more than one magnet may be placed on the wheel or more than one reed switch may be attached to the frame of the bicycle to record partial revolutions of the wheel).

Quadriceps (Knee) Board. This apparatus is for progressive resistance exercises in which the patient may have minimal, intermit-

tent, or no supervision at all. The exercise may call for repeated raising or straightening out of the lower leg and holding that position for a
short time. With pain, fatigue, or boredom, the patient who is unsupervised may either cease the exercise or perform it incorrectly, for example, by lifting his or her leg and putting it down immediately without the brief or extended pause, or by not lifting it high enough—
especially when a weighted cuff is attached to the ankle. To monitor
patients on this apparatus, we designed an adjustable, limiting (electrical) switch attached to an adjustable ring-stand, thus maximizing
flexibility. Analysis of an event record may assist in the diagnosis/
prognosis of the case and also aid in prescribing the exercise program.

Pulleys.   These may be used frequently in physical and occupational therapy with little or no supervision. We designed an arrangement of microswitches whose actuators are contacted by attachments
on the ropes or the weights themselves. The exact location, electrical
and mechanical characteristics will vary from institution to institution and require only a little ingenuity to instrument properly.

Parallel Bars and Rubber Runner.   These are probably the most
common walking-assistance apparatus in a physical therapy exercise
gym. The distance, velocity, and pattern of walking can all be monitored by a pressure-activated switch (in or under the runner) or a more
expensive and versatile system with photoelectric cells, either of
which is activated immediately by the physical presence of the leg.
Feedback may be supplied via a display of several lights, each activated by a different switch, with the sequence reflecting the progress.

Walker-aid.   An apparatus modification we are currently developing is designed to assist the evolution of reestablishing unassisted
walking behavior which begins with the walker-aid and proceeds—
as does physical therapy—through a quad cane and single stem cane.
The process utilizes an errorless discrimination training paradigm
described above and the dependent variable—the one whose change
is being monitored—is the decrease in pressure placed on the appliance measured electromechanically—the less pressure being an indication of the patient's readiness to shift to the next appliance and,
therefore, greater independence.

In conclusion, automation of the exercise equipment is significant because it (*a*) aids both the patient and the therapist by defining
precisely the behavioral criterion, by recording the behavioral occurrence and by measuring and assessing its parameters objectively, (*b*)
monitors and controls the behavior of the unsupervised patient—

especially at home with microcomputers or via telephone lines to a central facility, and (c) programs rehabilitation or instruction for change by reinforcing the patient's exercise behaviors in what would otherwise be a nonreinforcing or perhaps aversive situation.

Fifth, what must be *the* most important lesson we have learned from our extensive research in behavioral rehabilitation is that behavioral intervention may transcend neural tissue damage and, in spite of it, retrieve lost functions to some degree greater than with conventional procedures. For some strange reason, psychologists have been more reticent than rehabilitation therapists to intervene behaviorally when they learn that there is a neuroanatomical lesion or damage responsible for the "behavioral deficit." This attitude of pessimism is reflected even in the school personnel who will abandon hope when a child is classified minimally brain damaged. Perhaps it is because of the importance placed on the central nervous system that, given real evidence of neural damage, psychologists consider remediation or rehabilitation—that is, returning or restoring the disability to its previous level of functioning (or to some approximation of it)—as totally insuperable. (That a behavioral intervention may override physiology is also implicated in biofeedback and respondent [Pavlovian] conditioning—both phenomena that startled the medical profession. The time is long overdue for the medical community to have recognized this principle.)

Sixth, as a unifying principle, therapy must adhere to behavioral laws if it is to be efficacious. This statement holds equally true for the general practice of medicine and for rehabilitation as a specialty. As such, it becomes essential for physicians and rehabilitation therapists to have more than just a passing acquaintance with the principles of behavior. It is the least they can do for their patients.

Epilogue

It is of more than a passing interest that the area of rehabilitation for neurological or brain-injured persons has been increasingly attracting public attention. This trend, of course, is related to the fact that in our technological society, with an increase in industrial, home, vehicular, and recreational accidents, strokes, and other degenerative diseases of the central nervous system, more people have come to the realization that, although they are in good health at this moment, they may become victims of brain damage without warning. Additionally, the population of disabled persons continues to grow larger and they, along with other handicapped individuals, are raising their levels of consciousness and are becoming more aware of their long history of privations, asserting their rights to medical care, custodial care, and rehabilitation.

The disabled have fewer rights because they are handicapped, that is, they have lost certain motoric behaviors. If they should reverse their disability and magically regain their motor function, their rights would be restored automatically. This "Catch-22" predicament exists because—obviously—since their lost functions cannot be reestablished, neither can their rights be regained. The advocate rights' groups argue convincingly that although functions have been lost permanently, the disabled persons' rights must be asserted and safeguarded on humanitarian, political, and rational principles. As a complement, the behavioristic position presented here simply adds that some functions may be regained. It is worth considering.

One final word of advice to anyone considering the application of the principles of the experimental analysis of behavior to rehabilitation: although it is very rewarding to therapists, teachers, parents, and others who apply them systematically because they are so effective— to achieve that level of competence requires a great deal of patience! One needs patience to learn the many subtleties of a deceivingly simple methodology, patience to become a keen observer of behavior and notice minute changes along some identified dimension, patience to effect a behavioral analysis, ferreting out the variables and their functional relations, and patience to apply the techniques proficiently and appropriately, that is, altering the intervention as necessary. In rehabilitation, small behavioral changes often take hours to produce (after hours of planning)—at that, under the best of conditions! Much of the work is similar to that of a detective—identifying the functions and planning the engineering strategy—the rest is similar to a laboratory scientist: applying the procedures, recording the effects, and deciding on the basis of the data what the next step should be. But, in the final analysis, a good clinician is a scientist— with each intervention a mini-experiment—and a humanitarian in the full meaning of the word!

References and Bibliography

Davidson, P. O., & Davidson, S. M. (Eds.). *Behavioral medicine: Changing health lifestyles.* New York: Brunner/Mazel, 1980.

Ferguson, J. M., & Taylor, C. B. (Eds.). *The comprehensive handbook of behavioral medicine.* New York: SP Medical and Scientific Books, 1980.

Ferster, C. B., & Skinner, B. F. *Schedules of reinforcement.* New York: Appleton-Century-Crofts, 1957.

Fordyce, W. Psychological assessment and management. In F. H. Krusen (Ed.), *Handbook of physical medicine and rehabilitation* (2nd ed.). Philadelphia: W. B. Saunders, 1971.

Grossman. H. I. A new concept of disability. *Journal of Rehabilitation,* 1979, *45,* 41–71.

Ince, L. P. *Behavior psychology in rehabilitation medicine: Clinical applications.* Baltimore, Md.: Williams & Wilkins, 1980.

Katz, R. C., & Zlutnick, S. (Eds.). *Behavior therapy and health care: Principles and applications.* New York: Pergamon, 1975.

Meyerson, L., Kerr, N., & Michael, J. Behavior modification in rehabilitation. In S. W. Bijou, & D. M. Baer (Eds.), *Child development: Readings in experimental analysis.* New York: Appleton-Century-Crofts, 1967.

Meyerson, L., Michael, J. L., Mowrer, O. H., Osgood, C. E., & Staats, A. W. Learning, behavior and rehabilitation. In L. H. Lofquist (Ed.), *Psychological research and rehabilitation.* Washington, D.C.: American Psychological Association, 1960.

Michael, J. L. Rehabilitation. In C. Neuringer, & J. L. Michael (Eds.), *Behavior modification in clinical psychology.* New York: Appleton-Century-Crofts, 1970.

Miller, J. H. Preliminary report on disability insurance. In *Disability insurance program, public hearing before the subcommittee on ways and means.* 94th Congress, 2nd Session, May 17, 21, 24; June 4, 11, 1976.

Morse, W. H. Intermittent reinforcement. In W. K. Honig (Ed.), *Operant behavior: Areas of research and application.* New York: Appleton-Century-Crofts, 1966.

Pomerleau, O. F. Behavioral medicine: The contribution of the experimental analysis of behavior to medical care. *American Psychologist,* 1979, *34* (8), 654–663.

Pomerleau, O. F., & Brady, J. P. (Eds.). *Behavioral medicine: Theory and Practice.* Baltimore, Md.: Williams & Wilkins, 1979.

Skinner, B. F. A case history in scientific method. *American Psychologist,* 1956, *11,* 221–233.

Terrace, H. S. Stimulus control. In W. K. Honig (Ed.), *Operant behavior: Areas of research and application.* New York: Appleton-Century-Crofts, 1966.

Ullmann, L. P., & Krasner, L. (Eds.). *Case studies in behavior modification.* New York: Holt, Rinehart & Winston, 1965.

15 The Chronic Pain Syndrome

Killing with Kindness

Alexis M. Nehemkis and Carol Cummings

Description of the Problem

Chronic pain is one of the most disabling and expensive disorders in the United States. The debilitation resulting from chronic pain is widespread; it is long-lasting and frequently lifelong. An estimated 75 million Americans suffer from chronic pain, with 50 million of those classified as partially or totally disabled. The annual cost of chronic pain, in treatment and workdays lost, is estimated at a staggering $57 billion. Twenty-three million people with back pain account for nearly one-third of these expenditures. The cost in terms of human suffering is incalculable.

Although acute pain is usually a communication that the body is not functioning properly, chronic intractable nonmalignant pain serves no such useful warning purpose. Moreover, chronic pain inflicts physical, emotional, and economic stresses on the patient, his family, and society as a whole.

The nature of pain is elusive; it is a sensation, a perception, and an emotion. It is influenced by heredity, past learning, economic and cultural traditions, as well as underlying physical impairment. To date, no single therapeutic modality has proven completely safe and effective in alleviating chronic pain.

To study and treat this complex disorder, in recent years numerous pain clinics have been established in medical centers. These clinics provide multidisciplinary programs, utilizing the expertise of various specialities to treat the physical and psychological problems of patients who suffer from chronic pain.

We are greatly indebted to our colleagues Paul S. Alm, M.S.W., who suggested the concept of "dysynchronous retirement," and Mary J. Lukin, Ph.D. for having illuminated the concept of the working span in Gaussian terms.

The amount of disability experienced from chronic nonmalignant pain is not correlated closely with the objective physical findings. Patients who are referred to pain clinics may have no seriously abnormal physical condition, or they may have had several unsuccessful operations for pain relief. The majority have suffered job loss, medication abuse, marital stress, and a history of many treatments for pain, including drugs, injections, heat, massage, and other physical therapies. They share a downward spiral of increasing disability to which they themselves contribute in ways that can be described as self-destructive. We shall demonstrate that this pattern fits the description of indirect self-destructive behavior.

Indirect Self-Destructive Behavior and the Chronic Pain Patient

The 1970s have witnessed a resurgence of research interest in indirect self-destructive behavior. Indirect self-destructive behavior had been identified in the writings of Durkheim in the last century and by Menninger as early as 1938. However, it remained for Norman Farberow to provide the impetus for systematic study of this pattern of self-limiting behavior—behavior that included unconscious suicidal tendencies of which the individual seemed unaware or denied that the actions were intended to destroy or injure self. In addition, such behavior did not appear to have any immediate impact detrimental to the person. Whatever harmful effects ensued tended to be long-term and cumulative. This pattern has recently been recognized as a significant aspect of suicidal behavior, distinguishable from the more familiar overt and direct forms of suicide.

In an effort to classify the situations that give rise to the concept of indirect self-destructive behavior, Farberow (1980) has proposed a four-fold taxonomy, based upon the interaction of the impact of the self-destructive activity (on body or personality) and the source of that activity (personality or preexisting physical condition).

As may be seen from Table 1, the intersection of the rows and columns yields four main groups.

The first consists of those potential patterns of indirect self-destructive behavior in which a physical illness is present and is used self-destructively, with resulting serious injury or damage to the body. The examples Farberow suggests include the exacerbation of psychosomatic conditions, metabolic and cardiovascular diseases, invalidism, and polysurgery patients. A second group includes those cases in which an underlying physical condition is present, but the main destructive impact is directed against the person or self. Included in this second group are those conditions which reflect a

Table 1 Indirect Self-Destructive Behavior

Prior physical condition	Primary effect on: Body	Primary effect on: Person
Present: Prior physical condition exists: individual's activity increases actual or potential damage.	Psychosomatic: Asthma, ulcer, colitis, dermatitis, etc. Diabetes Buerger's, Raynaud's diseases Cardiorespiratory diseases Hypertension Physical debilities of elderly Neurasthenia Hypochondria Invalidism Polysurgery Malingering	Loss of body part or function: Limb (accident) Mobility (stroke; aging) Mastectomy sequelae Sense
	Actual	
Absent: No prior physical condition exists; actual or potential damage may result from activity.	Hyperobesity Smoking Drug addiction Alcoholism Self-mutilation Disregard of adequate, appropriate diet	Severe sexual disorders Asceticism
	Potential	
	Violent crime; rioting Assassination Repeated accidents; traffic, industrial	Nonviolent crime, delinquency Compulsive gambling Workaholic
	Stress-seeking, risk-taking	
	Mountain climbing Sports parachuting or skydiving Scuba diving Circus artists; trapeze performers Stuntmen Motorcycle, boat and auto racing	Stock market speculation

From *The Many Faces of Suicide* by Norman L. Farberow. Copyright © 1980 McGraw-Hill Book Company. Used with permission of McGraw-Hill Book Company.

functional or anatomic loss of some part of the body. This development results in an extensive change in self-image or self-concept,
such as loss of limb, mobility, sensory loss.

A state of chronic nonmalignant pain is another condition which
readily lends itself to self-destructive management and can exemplify
either one or both of the first two groups in Farberow's schema. There
is a voluminous literature on pain and a growing body of literature on
indirect self-destructive behavior, including a delineation of the characteristics of various populations in which a chronic disease process
may be used self-destructively (e.g., Farberow & Nehemkis, 1979;
Nehemkis & Groot, 1980). However, despite the richness of this literature, very little research even touches on indirect self-destructive
behavior patterns and the chronic pain syndrome.

From our experience at a large Veterans Administration (VA)
medical center, a pattern of indirect self-destructive behavior emerges
in patients applying for treatment for their chronic nonmalignant pain
problems. This pattern appears in rather characteristic fashion and
typically includes increasing disability without progression of the
"disease," diminished activity disproportionate to the physical findings, resistance to a prescribed medical regimen, overuse of analgesics and sedatives, disregard of dietary guidelines, doctor-shopping
and doctor-antipathy, the undergoing of increasingly frequent medical treatments, and impaired family relationships, sometimes with
role-reversal. Typically, the patient does not consider himself to be
suicidal; his behavior is not intentionally directed toward self-injury
or a premature demise.

Suicide in the Chronic Pain Population

A striking finding from our review of the work of others was the
absence of evidence for suicidal behavior in the chronic pain population (Farberow, Schneidman, & Leonard, 1963). Moreover, in our
own experience with pain patients, we did not find increased evidence of suicidal history, communication of suicidal ideas, or increased suicidal risk.

The low incidence of overt suicide, both completed and attempted, among chronic pain patients in the VA system is all the
more surprising when compared to the trend for male veterans of
comparable age who have a fairly high rate of suicide: 37 and 143
(per hundred thousand) for the 45–54 and 55–64 age groups, respec-
tively. One possible explanation for this difference in suicide rates is
that a wide range of indirect self-destructive behavior is being sub-
stituted for the expected overt self-destructive activity.

The chronic pain syndrome provides the means and opportunity to employ indirect self-destructive behavior as a suicide substitute, avoiding the stigma of overt suicide. Moreover, the extent to which indirect self-destructive behavior frustrates health care personnel may explain its adoption by some patients as a vehicle for expressing dissatisfaction with the health care system and their own lack of mastery over it. Or, alternatively, a second explanation is that pain per se is simply not a significant predisposing factor in the decision to commit suicide.

Killing with Kindness

The "career" of a chronic pain patient is not ordinarily regarded as self-destructive, either directly or indirectly. The pain patient does not take illegal medications; he does not engage in activities known to be injurious; he does not fail to take the medicine or wear the brace prescribed by his physician. In fact, he seems to be taking good care of himself. He gets plenty of rest; he does not overexert; he has enough to eat.

As we will demonstrate, it is his very effort to take good care of himself that is, in fact, self-destructive. He is killing himself with kindness, with the help of society, family, and the medical establishment. In contrast to the diabetic who fails to take insulin, or the patient with Buerger's disease who continues to smoke, the pain patient's self-destructive behavior is even more indirect.

One of the manifestations of this self-destructive behavior by the pain patient is that he rests too much. Many spend most of their day reclining, even though bedrest has no curative or restorative function in the treatment of chronic pain. This behavior is only appropriate for acute pain, when rest gives the body a chance to heal and prevents reinjury during that period of time. In the case of chronic pain, rest only furthers the loss of muscle tone and strength and leads to compounding effects of overweight if the dietary intake remains constant.

The chronic pain patient typically is overmedicated with narcotic analgesics and tranquilizers. Narcotics have no proper role in the treatment of nonmalignant chronic pain. Their use over time leads inevitably to the development of tolerance and physical and psychological dependence, in addition to the clouding of consciousness, constipation, and sedation, which are their active effects. Longtime use of minor tranquilizers is not indicated for muscle spasms and may increase depression as well as produce unwanted sedation. It should be noted that the chronic pain patient rarely uses street drugs; his overuse is of prescribed medications, although he may obtain them from more than one physician.

A third notable aspect of the behavior of the chronic pain patient is his overutilization of the health care system. For example, low back pain typically has exacerbations and remissions. These are to be expected, and an increase in back pain—which has been present for years—is not an emergency. Yet, many back pain patients will report to the nearest emergency room when they have one of these to-be-expected exacerbations. Their overuse of medications is part of this pattern. When a patient returns again and again to a physician who has exhausted the rational methods of back pain treatment, it is a temptation to give the patient what he wants: a new analgesic or tranquilizer prescription.

What motivates the chronic pain patient to indulge in overrest and overmedication, when such activities contribute to the worsening of his condition? Our experience suggests that the motivating factor is fear—fear of suffering additional pain. The patient's various manifestations of self-destructive behavior are in reality attempts to escape from pain. He reacts as if he were in acute pain, for which rest and medication are legitimate short-term therapies. On a conscious level, he is afraid of causing harm to himself if he is physically active. On another level, he is afraid of pain and governs all his actions to avoid that event.

The MMPI and Chronic Pain

Previous reports of the psychological assessment of chronic pain patients have made frequent use of the Minnesota Multiphasic Personality Inventory (MMPI). The typical MMPI profile for patients with chronic pain has been described as an elevation of the scores on the three scales which make up the neurotic triad (Scale 1—hypochondriasis, Scale 2—depression, and Scale 3—hysteria) in the so-called "Conversion V" profile, with hypochondriasis and hysteria more elevated than depression.

This profile is more elevated in patients who are considered to have a functional overlay to their pain as opposed to those patients with strong organic evidence for pain and little evidence of psychological problems. Patients with chronic pain have a more elevated 1–3 profile than patients with acute pain.

Caldwell and Chase (1977) recast the interpretation of the 1–3 profile of the MMPI in such a way as to shed additional light on the indirect self-destructive behavior of the chronic pain patient. They do this through a novel analysis of the characteristic chronic pain MMPI profile.

Caldwell and Chase reinterpret Scale 3 (hysteria) as measuring the patient's current level of fear of pain. As pain persists and becomes chronic, the progressive elevation of Scales 1, 2, and 3 reflects a progressive increase in fear of pain and suffering as well as vulnerability of the body. Scale 3 (hysteria) appears to be most directly reflective of the fear of pain. Scale 1 (hypochondriasis) reflects the rise in fears of body vulnerability, including the feeling of damage, the experience that "something awful is going wrong in my body," and the need for immobilization of the body so as not to aggravate its already precarious condition.

The hypothesis by Caldwell and Chase of an underlying fear of pain fits in well with the behaviors predicted by an elevation of Scale 3: those who score high are seen as overly protective of their bodies, highly sensitive to even minor pains and dysfunctions, and peculiarly addictive to pain medications, sedatives, and tranquilizers. Paradoxically, the patient's tendency to protect himself excessively against pain impedes his recovery. He inflicts invalidism upon himself: the body is held with great care, movement is slow and cautious, long periods are spent in almost total immobility, and exercises are done with great pain-protective inhibition.

The chronic pain patient is internally rewarded again and again for becoming increasingly constricted in his sphere of activities, for placating others, and grasping at any sort of medical or surgical care that will provide immediate reduction of his underlying fear of pain and insulate him from future pain.

Society's Contribution to the Validation of Self-Destructive Pain

The Role of the Family

From a systems perspective, the disability of the pain patient cannot be viewed in isolation from its effect on the rest of the family, which has been forced to relate to him in new ways. As the husband becomes increasingly disabled, loses his job and withdraws, a vacuum is created within the family. The wife, in her need to maintain the family equilibrium, attempts to fill some of the roles the husband has abandoned. A new pattern becomes established, and henceforth she is resistant to further change and becomes invested in maintaining the status quo.

A 65-year-old retired engineer had not worked in 10 years because of chronic low back pain. He spent much of his time either sitting in a wheelchair or walking behind it in case he should "collapse" and have to sit down in a hurry. In the course of six weeks of aggressive hospital treatment, he was eventually weaned from the chair to a walker and then to a single cane.

His wife never came to any of the weekly group meetings for families, nor would she make individual appointments with her husband's therapists. She cited her own ill health, visiting relatives, the long distance to the hospital, and her belief that she was already well-informed about her husband's health problems.

The patient was discharged in good spirits and walked without the aid of a cane. Two months later, he was seen in the wheelchair once more, pushed by his wife. She explained that it was much too dangerous for him to walk unaided and that he had almost fallen on several occasions. (He had never fallen during his six weeks in the hospital.) Two years after his discharge, the patient is still confined to a wheelchair and making regular visits to the hospital for examination and prescription of pain medications.

Should the family balk at accepting a pain patient in their midst, the husband-patient may resort to a more explicit way of communicating his impairment. One patient, who had been unemployed for 11 years because of back pain, posted a framed certificate (his Social Security Disability Award) in his living room and pointed to it righteously whenever his children questioned his inactivity or reluctance to participate in the household chores.

If the wife is unable to tolerate the added stress, marital conflict may ensue. She becomes resentful and irritable and ceases to be sympathetic and supportive. Divorce is not infrequent. Separation from his wife costs the patient his only ally in his whole pain career. He is left alone—helpless and hopeless.

In another variant, rather than becoming disgusted and abandoning the marital relationship (i.e., obtaining a divorce), the wife may redouble her efforts, thereby maintaining and strengthening the cycle of indirect self-destructive behavior. She may adopt a maternal role toward the patient, treating him as a sick offspring. "He's just like one of the children," as one wife said, indulgently. Why this reaction? The answer may lie in the common tendency, even among professionals, to confuse irritability, crankiness, and whining with pain and depression. The wife, according to this formulation, is easily persuaded that her husband is not unpleasant but is actually suffering. She interprets his irritability as increased pain. Thus, the needs of both parties are fulfilled. He is rewarded for "taking it easy," and she can maintain a picture of herself as nurturing a sick and therefore deserving person. For example, Sternbach (1974) states that neurotic depression is the most common diagnosis among pain patients. The MMPI findings with chronic pain patients do not support this position, unless one views the pain behavior itself as a depressive equivalent. In 74 chronic pain patients, the mean MMPI profile showed hypochondriasis and hysteria scales significantly elevated, whereas the depression scale was near normal limits (Cummings, Evanski, DeBenedetti, Anderson, & Waugh, 1979). In fact, these chronic pain patients rarely appeared clinically depressed.

How the Health Care System Perpetuates
Indirect Self-Destructive Behavior

By Polypharmacy. As suggested in an earlier section, the chronic pain patient not infrequently is overmedicated with narcotic analgesics and tranquilizers—the overuse of medications being part of his self-destructive overutilization of the health care system. The problem of chronic pain in nonmalignant disease complicated by iatrogenic polypharmacy is illustrated in the following case.

A 47-year-old former department store executive came to a Veterans Administration medical center because he could no longer afford private medical care. He had undergone three operations on his back between 1955 and 1971. He was confined to a wheelchair and was obviously sedated; his speech was slurred and slow, and his affect was flat. He reported that he spent most of his time in bed. He had been taking large amounts of medication for many years, all obtained by prescription from his private physician. Included in his prescriptions were: Percodan, 2 tablets every 4 hours around the clock; Tuinal, 2 capsules at bedtime; Etrafon Forte, 1 tablet 4 times a day; Valium, 10 mg 5 times a day. Before he could be admitted to the pain program it was necessary to admit him to the medical service partially to detoxify him. Gradual tapering of his narcotic and barbiturate intake continued while he was in the pain program. He became progressively more alert, was able to discontinue the use of his wheelchair, and resumed sexual relations with his wife for the first time in two years.

Not only may withdrawal from narcotic analgesics produce significant relief of the general symptoms related to addiction, it may markedly lessen the pain itself. Brodner and Taub (1978) describe the sequence whereby long-term narcotic use, with resultant tolerance and withdrawal, may be associated with the exacerbation of a pain syndrome, indistinguishable from the original pain complaint for which narcotics were initially prescribed. If the clinician mistakes this exacerbation of pain, which is a complication of long-term narcotic therapy, for a progression of organic disease, an escalating, cyclic pattern of higher narcotic dosage, followed by increased pain, treated with more narcotics, inducing greater pain often ensues. At this point, surgery may be recommended and performed.

By Polysurgery. The following cases illustrate the role of the health care system in perpetuating self-destructive patterns through polysurgical procedures:

A 33-year-old former heavy equipment operator was admitted to the hospital for evaluation of recurrent abdominal pain. Four years earlier, while he was in the army, a vagotomy and pyloroplasty had been performed because of symptoms suggestive of peptic ulcer. No evidence of ulcer was found at surgery, but the patient continued to have abdominal complaints. He was discharged with the diagnosis of psychophysiologic gastrointestinal reaction. His symptoms continued, and three years later, a splenectomy and partial pancreatectomy were performed. As his health did not improve after this procedure, he was declared 100% disabled by his physician and never worked again.

He had had many operations and illnesses prior to his Army service. He had four operations for umbilical hernia and associated problems (extruding metal stitches, etc.) between the ages of five and 16 years. When his wife was pregnant, he suffered "morning sickness" while she did not. At the time of his preinduction Army physical examination, he gave a history of headaches and cervical pain as sequellae to a head injury, recurrent back pain for which he wore a brace, peptic ulcer disease, mumps, pancreatitis, and a history of taking "nerve medications." Letters from two physicians documented his treatment for cervical pain and for peptic ulcer.

Years later, when the patient was trying to obtain a government pension for service-connected disabilities, he said that his preinduction history was inaccurate, and he had exaggerated it in an effort to avoid the draft. He was granted only 10% disability.

The patient's MMPI profile was consistent with his long history of expressing emotional conflicts via physical complaints. The pattern began in childhood and was exacerbated by three unhappy marriages, the stresses of combat service, and by his abdominal operations. He was encouraged to seek outpatient psychotherapy to help him cooperate with his medical regimen and diet, to avoid invalidism, and to deal constructively with his chaotic home life.

Three years later, he was referred to a pain management program. He said that his health had continued to deteriorate and he now complained of constant and severe headaches, "passing out without warning" once or twice a week, abdominal pain from "11 pieces of loose wire" from previous operations, and severe "shakes." He was taking large amounts of tranquilizers and codeine. He never had had the previously recommended psychotherapy.

A 55-year-old married housewife was admitted to the hospital because of severe "knifelike" abdominal pain. She had undergone 17 operations, of which 10 were abdominal or pelvic procedures. Despite her report of constant nausea and vomiting, she gained 20 pounds in the three weeks prior to admission. Exploratory surgery was being considered, and the patient said she would do anything to get rid of her pain.

In the course of her illnesses, her husband (who worked 12 hours a day) and her 20-year-old daughter had assumed all the housework. The patient complained that her daughter "doesn't understand me being sick"; she was withdrawn and did not communicate with her mother. The patient said, "I just suffer it out" rather than ask her family to give up any of their activities on her account.

The patient was a plump talkative lady who recited her long medical and surgical history in cheerful detail. Although she minimized any psychological problems, her illness had a negative impact on the family; they did all the household chores, but both the daughter and the husband were withdrawing from interaction with her, and her husband refused to participate in marital counseling which had been recommended. For this patient, ill health and repeated surgeries had become a way of life.

These two cases illustrate the tragic sequence that can ensue from the chronic pain patient's proclivity for overutilization of the health care system. In particular, they highlight the uncanny ability of the pain patient to anticipate the medical institution's expectations of an acutely ill patient. The incongruity between the patient's presenting himself with chronic pain and emotional problems and his manipulating the physician to legitimize the problem as an acute medical illness illuminates the clinical progression of the polysurgery career (Devaul, Hall, & Faillace, 1978). Once the attending physician accepts the patient's complaints of pain as an acute medical problem, clearly within his area of responsibility and meriting vigorous attempts at relief, interventions designed to relieve acute organic pain escalate but are bound to fail.

Unwittingly, the physician's inquiries help to shape the patient's description of his own symptoms. Eager for relief, the patient contributes the "existence" of pain to conform with the physician's inquiries. It is axiomatic that the more frequently a patient is presented at case conferences, the more accurately his symptoms will begin to mirror a classical clinical syndrome—pure operant conditioning.

In his analysis of "l'homme douloureux," Szasz (1968) offers the following characterization, which helps to explain how the "painful person" sets forth on the road to polysurgery:

> Patient and physician play complementary roles in this situation. The patient insists that his problem is physical, not mental; the physician insists that he is a medical doctor (neurologist, internist, etc.), not a psychological healer (psychotherapist). Just as pain authenticates the patient's illness as physical (in a way that anxiety, for example, does

not), so it also authenticates the healer's role as medical (in a way that a marital problem, for example, does not). Patient and physician thus engage in a kind of tacit collusion to accept pain, and pain alone, as proof of the "reality" of bodily illness, and hence as sufficient grounds for the patient's adoption of the sick role. (p. 103)

Chronic Pain as Dysynchronous Retirement

Societally-induced pain on which the health care system is required to focus may be far more prevalent and the victims more numerous than is generally realized.

It may be assumed that the number of years spent in gainful employment, like so many other sociopsychological characteristics, follows a bell-shaped curve. Thus there are a great many individuals who are employed for approximately 35 years during a lifetime but only a few with an employment span as short as 15 years or as long as 50 years. Let us suppose that on the average this bell-shaped working span extends for 35 years from the time of entry into the stream of employment. Take the case of a typical day laborer. He begins his working life at an early age. By his fiftieth birthday—give or take a few years—he has completed his working span. At age 50, more or less, he is too young to be decently considered a retiree. He is not eligible for a comfortable corporate pension, and he is too young to claim his Social Security retirement benefit. A substantial proportion of any adult population, a day laborer no less than a lawyer or physician, will have bony abnormalities and diseases of the lumbosacral spine that are detectable on X-ray (Hadler, 1978). Moreover, the onset of low back pain is not necessarily associated with any extraordinary pattern of use (e.g., external force, stress, posturing). Thus a relatively minor injury or the flairing up of an old pain may provide the basis via Social Security Disability or VA pension for a rational and socially acceptable means of effecting the final exit from the labor force. The complaint of pain and discomfort becomes chronic because it is the ticket to a graceful transition. Pain becomes a necessity in order to validate middle-age retirement—a "retirement" that is out of synchrony with that time-span prescribed by social custom.

Here we see how the health care system is loaded with a *social* problem that is not within its competence. Plainly, the "medicalization of social problems" is extraneous to their solution. As we have seen in the case of chronic pain as dysynchronous retirement, the roots of the problem are embedded in the societal structure. Consequently, a strictly biomedical approach fails to come to grips with the real problem.

When It Pays to Have Pain

A humane society is faced with the dilemma of caring for the genu-
inely needy while not removing the incentive for the speedy recovery of its citizens from their acute illnesses. A well-intentioned network of support for the disabled seems inevitably to remove the
motivation to return to work for some persons who would be forced
to do so in a less benevolent society. Both governmental and private
insurance systems face this problem.

Consider the case of a 54-year-old married former retail clerk who was
medically retired because of low back pain. He spent six weeks in the Long
Beach VA Medical Center Pain Program and was significantly improved in
that he had increased strength and endurance, reduced pain, a marked decrease in weight, and improved relationships with his family. He was seen
by a rehabilitation counselor, but expressed no interest in job seeking, since
he had adequate retirement pay and no financial incentive to work. It was,
therefore, a surprise to the staff when the patient announced his intention to
pursue vocational rehabilitation through a state program. This would involve
interviews, testing, job retraining, and an attempt to work in some capacity.
The patient admitted that he had no intention of returning to work. However, he explained, if he went through the vocational rehabilitation program
and demonstrated that he was unable to hold down a job, he would then be
entitled to receive $10 per month from a private insurance policy.

Inflexible Work Rules: The Contribution of Industry

In the unlikely circumstance that the chronic pain patient is not
rendered dysfunctional by polypharmaceutical prescriptions or polysurgical procedures, he will, on occasion, become the victim of the
industrial "system"—a system whose inflexibility can be detrimental
to the employee-patient, and the employer's own self-interest. A case
in point:

A 55-year-old crane operator had been unable to work for five months
because of increasingly disabling low back pain. He had an excellent work
record, having been employed for 23 years by the same firm. At the time
he was admitted to the Long Beach VA Medical Center Pain Program, he
expressed fear of returning to work since he needed strength and a fine
touch to operate the controls. He was worried that he might cause an
accident. Later, after six weeks of treatment, his pain had markedly decreased, he was less depressed, and he was once again physically fit. He
still planned to file for Workman's Compensation, however, feeling that his
back precluded future work. With much encouragement from the vocational
counselor and the rest of the program staff, he was persuaded to return to

work. He did so and was initially able to work without difficulty. Three months later, he reported that his firm was short of staff and he was now being required to work 10 to 12 hours a day, seven days a week, to retain his job with the company.

Conclusion

Most persons with low back pain or similar acutely painful conditions make an uneventful recovery within weeks or months. Some vulnerable individuals, whose organic impairment may be no greater, progress into long-term disability. The vast majority of patients with chronic nonmalignant pain have musculoskeletal disorders which are not incompatible with an active and useful life and even employment in some capacity. Society bears the major responsibility for maintaining their disability by indiscriminate monetary awards, by a health system peculiarly responsive to the treatment of acute illness, and by an industrial complex which is not interested in employing individuals whose physical condition is imperfect.

The dynamics of a vulnerable personality cannot be changed on a mass basis, and the larger societal contributions are not amenable to immediate solution. However, aggressive rehabilitation, instituted the moment the disability has stabilized, can and should be the goal of the health care system in this country.

References and Bibliography

Brodner, R. A., & Taub, A. Chronic pain exacerbated by long-term narcotic use in patients with nonmalignant disease: Clinical syndrome and treatment. *Mount Sinai Journal of Medicine,* 1978, *45*(2), 233–237.

Caldwell, A. B., & Chase, C. Diagnosis and treatment of personality factors in chronic low back pain. *Clinical Orthopaedics and Related Research,* 1977, *129,* 141–149.

Cummings, C., Evanski, P. M., DeBenedetti, M. J., Anderson, E. E., & Waugh, T. R. Use of the MMPI to predict outcome of treatment for chronic pain. In J. J. Bonica, J. C. Liebeskind, & D. G. Albe-Fessard (Eds.), *Advances in pain research and therapy,* Vol. 3. New York: Raven Press, 1979.

Devaul, R. A., Hall, R. C. W., & Faillace, L. A. Drug use by the polysurgical patient. *American Journal of Psychiatry,* 1978, *135*(6), 682–685.

Durkheim, E. *Suicide.* New York: Free Press, 1951.

Farberow, N. L., Schneidman, E. S., & Leonard, C. V. *Suicide among general medical and surgical hospital patients with malignant neoplasms*

(Medical Bulletin 9). Washington, D.C.: Veterans Administration Department of Medicine and Surgery, February, 1963.

Farberow, N. L., Stein, K., Darbonne, A. R., & Hirsch, S. Indirect self-destructive behavior in diabetic patients. *Hospital Medicine,* 1970, *6*(5), 123–135.

Farberow, N. L., & Nehemkis, A. M. Indirect self-destructive behavior in patients with Buerger's disease. *Journal of Personality Assessment,* 1979, *43*(1), 86–96.

Farberow, N. L. Indirect self-destructive behavior: Classification and characteristics. In N. L. Farberow (Ed.), *The many faces of suicide: Indirect self-destructive behavior.* New York: McGraw-Hill, 1980.

Hadler, N. M. Legal ramifications of the medical definition of back disease. *Annals of Internal Medicine,* 1978, *89,* 992–999.

Menninger, K. *Man against himself.* New York: Harcourt Brace, 1938.

Nehemkis, A. M., & Groot, H. Indirect self-destructive behavior in spinal cord injury. In N. L. Farberow (Ed.), *The many faces of suicide: Indirect self-destructive behavior.* New York: McGraw-Hill, 1980.

Rogers, D. E., & Blendon, R. J. The academic medical center: A stressed American institution. *The New England Journal of Medicine,* 1978, *298*(17), 940–950.

Sternbach, R. A. *Pain patients: Traits and treatment.* New York: Academic Press, 1974.

Szasz, T. S. The psychology of persistent pain: A portrait of l'homme douloureux. In A. Soulairac, J. Cahn, & J. Charpentier (Eds.), *Pain.* New York: Academic Press, 1968.

IV
A Call to Action

The preceding chapters in this text have dealt with ways in which society and its bureaucratically rigid institutions have contributed to the second-class status of disabled people in our country. Although most of the authors have included in their discussion descriptions of how these discriminatory practices can be combated, the reader's attention must be focused on the issue of remediation. Many of the contributors have underscored the need for the disabled themselves to become involved in this process, to become political, and to organize themselves into a cohesive consumer group advocating, indeed demanding, the equality promised to them by law. As long as the disabled leave their future in the hands of others, they will remain second-class citizens. It is only by committing themselves to this struggle, by lending their expertise and energy to this fight, and by assuming leadership roles in the consumer rights movement, that their rights will in fact be secured. It was, for example, only after blacks and women organized that meaningful progress in the civil rights and the women's movements was made. Prior to this occurrence, they were patronizingly provided crumbs from the table, so to speak—society's attempt to prevent them from becoming too vocal in their demands for full equality. This part considers how the disabled have made and can continue to make progress in their quest for equal treatment under law.

Russell Bruch (Chapter 16) offers ideas on career/life planning from outside the rehabilitation world. He maintains that the same basic problems face all job seekers, disabled and able-bodied alike. Using the method developed by Richard Bolles and published in What Color is Your Parachute?, he shows how all job seekers can exercise more control in the job search; how they can inventory their skills, research organizations, and find a job without being at the mercy of the job market. Staff members from the Berkeley Center for Independent Living (Chapter 17) describe the philosophy of the independent living movement, which best represents the disabled minority's efforts to become political and regain control over *their own lives. They discuss independent living centers, in which the disabled themselves control the delivery of survival services, and describe in depth their own housing assistance program to illustrate how such a center operates. Bruch (Chapter 18) urges the disabled to become consumer activists in the area of goods and services. She describes, with numerous anecdotes and examples, how private businesses, from banks to supermarkets, have ignored America's largest minority and discusses how the disabled can use their shopping dollars to make the private business sector more responsive to their needs.*

In the final chapter of the text, Krause, coming from a slightly different perspective, examines the economic and political climate of the country and capitalistic values which contribute to the problems faced by the disabled.

16 Creative Vocational Planning for the Disabled

Russell Bruch

This chapter begins with a puzzle.

O.T..T . . . ; the reader is to determine what comes next in the sequence.

Examining this array of letters and dots and anticipating the next letter in the sequence exemplifies the degree to which one's perspective has become functionally fixed. The next letter in the sequence is "F." One arrives at this answer by abandoning preconceived notions regarding sequential patterning tasks. Most individuals tend to perceive this sequence as a series of dots and letters, when in essence it is a series of dots. These dots, however, have been duplicated by the first letter of the word for the position of that particular dot. There is the "1" dot, hence "O," then the "2" dot and the T, then the "3" dot and a "T," and so on.

The chapter starts in this way because it illustrates what often happens when the issue of vocational planning is addressed: all too often we lock ourselves into a fixed perspective that is not particularly true or may even be false. The problem of defining problems in their narrowest terms is one experienced by *everyone* who is job hunting. Although this chapter is written for a text presenting the special problems and discrimination faced by the disabled, this point can not be stressed strongly enough. Everybody, disabled or not, becomes locked into the same boxes when they become job seekers—the same limiting, discouraging constraints and unidimensional thinking which can keep them unemployed or underemployed. The disabled certainly have additional problems when seeking employment and are often put into their own special box, usually marked "seconds," but the basic problems and issues involved in job hunting are the same, regardless of the disability. Therefore, everyone searching for a job must gain a broadened perspective when approaching the issue of locating suitable employment. This chapter presents new concepts and approaches which can be effectively utilized in formulating meaningful and satisfying vocational goals and identifying vocational alternatives.

It is necessary to assume a new perspective to acquire meaningful and satisfying vocations because of two radical changes in thought: first, so that the job seeker can be in control instead of remaining vulnerable and at the mercy of potential employers, and second, that the abilities or skills the job seeker possesses are more important than his particular disability or the skills which he lacks. Because employers have the same tendency as that of the general public of focusing on functional deficits, this is an especially important factor to recognize when the job seeker is a so-called "disabled" person. These employers focus on what the disabled cannot do as opposed to the able-bodied majority. Such thinking, however, severely curtails the employer's ability to critically appraise the disabled applicant's special skills and aptitudes.

Special Aptitudes of the Disabled

An appropriate term to use in describing the "normal" segment of our population is "temporarily able-bodied." This term is appropriate to use because everyone has some physical capabilities he may not always have and the disabled do not possess. On the other hand, the disabled, *because* of their disability, have some special skills and capabilities that most able-bodied individuals do not have. At least one author (Bolles, 1981) has considered this issue and compiled a list of possible special strengths and skills which might arise from disabilities of various kinds.

Broadening the Vocational Search

As inferred from Table 2, what is necessary in obtaining meaningful and rewarding work is the ability to focus one's attention on strengths rather than on limitations the individual might possess. Essential in securing a suitable position is the ability to discover what the job applicants have to offer, who they really are, and what combination of likes, dislikes, knowledge, and talents make them unique. One should not concentrate on only what the job seeker has to offer the world of work, for that is only one part of one's life. Also to be considered is what the applicants have to offer the world of education and the world of leisure, elements of life that are just as important to explore as the skills these persons might possess. In essence, what is being suggested is an approach to job hunting as life planning, which is not the same as career planning. Life planning takes career, that is, work, into account but also includes likes and dislikes in use of leisure time and ongoing learning in order to obtain a comprehensive picture of the individual. Bolles (1977) discusses the importance of these three areas. He points out that job seekers often are unable to integrate them in any meaningful way. People see themselves as either playing or working or going to school. Usually these three activities are kept separate, and quite often they are even seen as being in conflict with one another.

Identifying Potential Job Markets

Most people do not realize that 80 percent of the available jobs are not listed. Saying that another way, if a person seeking employment were to use all the traditional methods of job hunting—going to a job counselor, looking at the want ads, submitting a resume, and so on—they would at best locate only about 20 percent of the jobs that are actually available at a given time. This means that most jobs available are not publicly advertised. If one is creatively to assist people in locating employment, ways must be found to tap into that hidden job market. Following are some ideas as to how this can be done.

Although the statistics vary a bit on the average length of a job hunt, the important fact to realize is that finding a job—especially a good job—usually takes a long time, sometimes up to 9 months! The job applicant should, therefore, be prepared for some months of hard work to find the right position.

One reason people have difficulty finding a job is that they do not have a clear picture of that for which they are looking. They have no concept of what kind of job they would most enjoy. The job seeker can be assured that if he or she does not know what type of job to look for, he or she will find almost everything but that—and take it! Unfortunately, many people let the job market control them rather than determining what is important to them and actively seeking that. Figure 1 is a diagram of what a job could look like.

At the core of this flower-like figure are the transferable skills we each have. In essence, there are three kinds of skills: transferable, adaptive (how we adapt to change), and work-content (those rooted to a specific area of work). Regardless of the many kinds of skills one might have, what must be first identified are skills one

Table 2 A Holistic View of Specific Disabilities[1ab]

The so-called handicap	The Normal rehabilitation compensations external to the disability	The strengths developed internally by the handicapped, compensatorily, under optimal conditions	Samples of some of the environments where these strengths can be utilized
Blindness Visual impairment	Strong glasses, low-vision aids, electronic devices, cane, guide dog	Highly developed hearing, sense of space, memory capacity, verbal skills	Not disturbed by surrounding sights; able to work confidently in the dark
Deafness Hearing impairment	Electronic hearing devices, pencil and paper, lip reading, sign language	Awareness of visual cues, highly observant, manual dexterity, ability to read facial and body language	Can work without interruption from conversation, can dismiss distracting environmental noises
Mute Speaking impairment	Typewriter, picture-point, talking board, manual communications module, sign language	Writing skills, manual dexterity, facial and body expressiveness highly developed	Not distracted by conversations, able to write uninterruptedly for long periods
Amputation hand impairment	Orthotic devices, teaching to use other muscles, assistive/adaptive devices, prosthesis	Highly developed use of the other limbs (sometimes), ability to use one-handed typewriter, if has a hook: can do new things the hand can't	Places where a visible handicap is an asset (as in organizations under the gun about Affirmative Action)

238

Condition	Treatment	Skills	Environments
Quadriplegic Polio-paralyzed Spinal cord injured	Assistive devices, wheelchairs that operate on voice command, specialized pain centers, physical and occupational therapies, teaching of survival and independent living skills	Highly developed problem-solving skills, highly developed expressive skills, good at careful planning and long-range forethought, highly creative and adaptive, high intuition tolerance for frustration, sensitive to non-verbal communication	Jobs requiring thorough mental concentration, problem solving, long-range planning in highly organized or structured situations
Orthopedic Congenital deformity	Braces, adaptive lifting techniques, surgery	Highly-developed verbal skills, manual dexterity (sometimes), ability to lift, inventiveness	Environments where longevity is an asset, plus high tolerance for sitting
Diabetes	Diet and weight control, exercise and regular routine, insulin	Self-discipline, highly developed awareness of emotional balance needs, alert to nutritional aspects of living	In environments where pacing of oneself is important, self-regulation or self-management
Seizure disorders Epilepsy	Therapies dealing with seizure patterns, biofeedback, lowering of stress, medication, good routine, rest	Highly developed life-regulating skills, empathy, self-discipline, alert to nutritional aspects of living	Good in environments where there is community, need for empathy, and so on
Drug abusers Alcoholism (arrested) Alcoholism (nonarrested)	Structured support-communities (Synanon, A.A., Delancey Street, Discovery House), therapies, other drugs	Strong self-discipline (sometimes), high-energy level, highly developed verbal, assertive, persuasive skills (hustling)	Environments where high drive, high energy is needed (sometimes), continual improvement is needed, or ability to perceive other peoples' "cons"

(continued)

(continued)

Learning disorders Neurological impairment Brain damage Aphasia (handicapped in receptive/intake, and/or processing, and/or expressive/output)	Learning clinics, speech therapies, sensory-motor therapies, alternative communication devices/assistive devices: pictures, boards, sign language	*When left hemisphere of brain is damaged:* highly developed pictorial sense, recognition and memory of facial and spatial cues (often), use of colors, music, dance *When right hemisphere of brain is damaged:* high verbal skills (sometimes), highly-organized (sometimes), keeps lots of notes	Meticulous about detail, writing down, and excellent in environments where spatial or facial memory is an asset
Psychiatric limitations (Low stress tolerance)	Drugs, therapies, structured environments	More adept at asking for help (sometimes), means of alternative expression greater (sometimes), extremely sensitive to appropriate environments	In jobs where high sensitivity to environments is needed, and/or greater insight into self or others
Mental retardation	Special education programs, structured environments	Highly developed in the right hemisphere of the brain (sometimes), capable of following orders (sometimes), demonstrates consistency of behavior (sometimes)	Environments where there are routine, repetitive situations

[a]This chart does not cover multi-handicapped persons, e.g., blind *and* deaf. It does not distinguish between congenital handicaps, where the person may have had longer time to develop compensatory strengths, and adventitious (more recent) handicaps. Attitude and motivation are crucial throughout.

[b]*Source:* Richard Bolles, Director of the National Career Development Project. It was published in his Newsletter on Life/Work Planning.

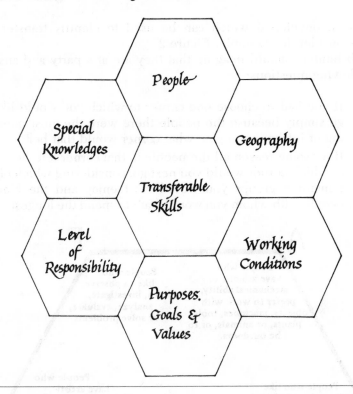

Figure 1. Diagrammatic representation of a job. (From *The Quick Job-Hunting Map, Beginning Version,* by Richard N. Bolles and Victoria B. Zenoff. © Copyright 1979 by Richard N. Bolles and the National Career Development Project.)

currently possesses. In considering this, the job seeker must think of skills as being more than those things in which he was formally trained, like typing or aircraft maintenance. Skills include negotiating and peacemaking, motivating and energizing, organizing, decorating, knowing your city, and so on. To assess the breadth of skills possessed totally, one must broaden the perspective to include all one's capabilities.

One method of focusing on the problem of identifying personal skills has been suggested by Crystal and Bolles (1974). Their approach maintains that to focus on the center portion of the flower, the transferable skills, one needs to write an autobiography. From that autobiography, sentence by sentence, paragraph by paragraph, talents and skills are extracted. Because that is a difficult task, alternative models have been developed which can be used to identify transferable skills. Consider, for example, Figure 2.

Job hunters should imagine that they are at a party and answer the following questions:

1.   If you had to choose one corner to which you would like to go simply because the people there were the most interesting or intriguing to you, what corner would that be?
2.   If for some reason all the people in that corner left the party, to which corner would you next go, considering which of the remaining groups you would most enjoy and the kind of people with whom you would want to spend the longest time.

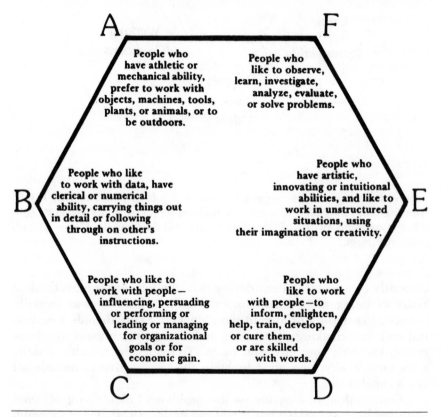

A

People who have athletic or mechanical ability, prefer to work with objects, machines, tools, plants, or animals, or to be outdoors.

F

People who like to observe, learn, investigate, analyze, evaluate, or solve problems.

B

People who like to work with data, have clerical or numerical ability, carrying things out in detail or following through on other's instructions.

E

People who have artistic, innovating or intuitional abilities, and like to work in unstructured situations, using their imagination or creativity.

People who like to work with people— influencing, persuading or performing or leading or managing for organizational goals or for economic gain.

People who like to work with people—to inform, enlighten, help, train, develop, or cure them, or are skilled with words.

C   **D**

Figure 2. Identifying transferable skills. (From *The Quick Job-Hunting Map, Beginning Version,* by Richard N. Bolles and Victoria B. Zenoff. © Copyright 1979 by Richard N. Bolles and the National Career Development Project.)

3. Finally, if *those* people left the party, to which corner would
    you go?

Answering these questions can provide much valuable information
about an individual's sense of personality, identity, talents, and
skills. This exercise, based on the work of Holland (1973), suggests
that jobs are basically people environments. Prior to seeking employment, one must be able to recognize preferred people environments.
Returning to the job picture (Figure 1), examine the top petal. A
portion of Holland's theory suggests that people are not only attracted to others who have similar kinds of interests, but these preferences provide a reliable picture of their own interests. For readers
who are familiar with interest testing, the Strong-Campbell Interest
Inventory now includes these same six people environments. Holland continues by saying that we are not only attracted to people
with similar kinds of *interests* but also to those whose *skills* are
similar to our own. Skills are here defined in a very encompassing
way, including all those talents, abilities, and competencies an individual possesses. If professional counselors are to assist clients with
the problem of job finding, they must first help them focus on their
abilities. An efficient way of obtaining this information has been
suggested by Bolles (1979) in *The Quick Job-Hunting Map, Advanced Version.*

Next, it is important that the job searcher be helped to identify
the geographical area in which he or she would like to live. For
many that might seem to be predetermined: Most people find that
they must continue to live fairly close to where they currently reside.
If, however, there are no constraints placed on individuals, allowing
them to live anyplace, how would they describe those places? What
factors would be important to them? Some might be the physical
characteristics and the kinds of people mentioned earlier.

The next petal deals with working conditions. What factors allow
people to do their best work? We all thrive in unique environments
just as plants are made to exist in certain environments. The factors
one usually needs to examine are the physical characteristics of the
work area.

The next petal of the job flower consists of purposes, goals, and
values. There are several ways to determine purposes, goals, and
values. One method, developed at the Lawrence Livermore Laboratory, involves use of a value card sort. It is a quick way to examine
approximately 40 different values. Each value is printed with its
definition on a separate card. As one goes through the cards, a decision must be made whether that particular item is valued always,

sometimes, or not at all. After the cards have been divided into categories, the person is asked to examine his or her present job and determine if it meets his or her value structure or if the job being considered meets those values identified.

A second method one could employ to clarify goals is to ask the job seeker: "If you had all the money you would ever need or want for the rest of your life, what would you do with your time?" And, "If you had to give away a large sum of money, to whom or for what would you contribute it?" Before answering these questions, the individual must consider what kinds of concerns or issues, causes, or programs he or she would like to support. The answer to these questions can help in selecting work that is truly consistent with the person's values and goals in life.

The next petal of the job flower, level of responsibility, refers to the nature of the working relationship wanted with coworkers. To determine this the following questions should be asked: "Would you rather work alone or with others?" "How many others?" "Do you want to give directions or are you more comfortable taking them?" The answer to this last question is usually related closely with money. In general, the more responsibility one assumes in a job, the higher the salary associated with that job. This becomes critical if making money is especially important. If so, one must be prepared to assume more responsibility than perhaps wanted.

The last petal on the job flower contains the special knowledges that the job seeker possesses. These include things that one knows how to do as opposed to necessarily doing them. For example, one can have a knowledge of teaching because he understands the principles of teaching. That is different from necessarily being able to teach. To assess these special knowledges accurately, individuals must be able to break out of the boxes that they may have put themselves into—namely, identifying themselves in a certain role and, therefore, able to do only that one thing.

By examining each of the issues proposed by the petals of the job flower, a job searcher should have a fairly clear picture of the kind of job preferred. Next, one needs to seek out the job which matches the personal areas which have just been defined.

Interviewing for Information

There is a three-step process of interviewing for information which every job hunter should participate in prior to requesting a position. Not only is the information gained in this process necessary to the job hunt, it also provides excellent practice at interviewing before one must assume the vulnerable role of job applicant.

The first step in this process, after having clarified what is important from the seven items in the job picture, is to practice interviewing. Initially it would be advisable to begin in some area in which the job seeker is fairly sure he or she would not be hired. Doing so would reduce the pressure and anxiety the applicant might otherwise experience. Making an appointment with someone who is in that field will reduce the anxiety felt, for the applicant will be the one interviewing, not vice versa. This exercise places the job seeker in control. Questions one might ask include:

1. How did you become interested in this work?
2. What do you like about it?
3. What do you dislike about it?
4. Will you refer me to three, four, or five other people who share our mutual interest?

If this exercise is performed several times, the job seeker will develop some valuable interviewing skills and will be preparing for the next step: informational interviewing. In the information interviewing step, the needs of a potential employer must be determined. What is he looking for in a potential employee, and what kinds of problems exist in the company that this employee might be expected to resolve? Sometimes the answers to these questions are easy to ascertain—as easy as learning why the last person was fired if that was the case. At other times, extensive research may be required to answer them. But, however long it takes, the applicant must be able to show a familiarity with and interest in the company and demonstrate to the potential employer that he has the skills to meet the employer's needs.

Finally, after having done this research and determining what the employer and job seeker wants, one must identify who in the company has the power to hire. In most cases, the personnel department has little or nothing to do with selection except, perhaps, in the broadest sense of screening. What one needs to determine is who has the most authority or the final word with regard to the position sought. This might necessitate meeting that person face to face to demonstrate skills possessed and inform him that you are indeed the person who can solve his problems.

Conclusion

What is suggested in this chapter is a nontraditional approach to the job hunt. Applicable to both the able-bodied and the disabled, this approach emphasizes the need for two new perspectives in job hunting: that the job seeker can be in control of his job hunt and that the abilities the person has are more important than the disabilities he possesses. Specific techniques for using these new ideas are then described. These techniques increase the individual's knowledge about both himself and employment possibilities. As a result, obtaining a job becomes a creative, self-fulfilling enterprise rather than a mechanical, automatic procedure. In the final analysis, then, the job searcher himself is the person who is most familiar with his needs and requirements for employment. Thus he must do much if not all of his own job hunt or career change. If a vocational counselor assumes total responsibility for this process, the client will have lost his power and abrogated his destiny to another.

References

Bolles, R. *The quick job-hunting map, advanced version.* Berkeley, Calif.: Ten Speed Press, 1979.

Bolles, R. *The three boxes of life and how to get out of them.* Berkeley, Calif.: Ten Speed Press, 1977.

Bolles, R. *What color is your parachute?: A practical manual for job-hunters and career-changers.* Berkeley, Calif.: Ten Speed Press, 1981.

Crystal, J., and R. Bolles. *Where do I go from here with my life?* Berkeley, Calif.: Ten Speed Press, 1974.

Holland, J. L. *Making vocational choices: A theory of careers.* Englewood Cliffs, N.J.: Prentice-Hall, 1973.

17 Independent Living

The Right to Choose

Center for Independent Living

> Independent living is freedom of choice to live where and how one chooses and can afford. It is living within the community in the neighborhood one chooses. It is living alone or with a roommate of one's choice. It is deciding one's own pattern of life—schedule, food, entertainment, vices, virtues, leisure, and friends. It is freedom to take risks and freedom to make mistakes. (Laurie, 1979)

> The dignity of risk is what the independent living movement is all about. Without the possibility of failure, the disabled person is said to lack true independence and the mark of one's humanity—the right to choose for good or evil. (Dejong, 1979)

> Independent living refers to disabled peoples' ability to actively participate in society—to work, to raise a family, and to be able to share in the joys and responsibilities of community life. (CIL, 1979)

A text which examines the second-class citizenship of the disabled and attempts to discuss means of combatting discrimination must, of course, include in its discussion the independent living (IL) movement, probably the brightest spot in the disabled people's struggle to achieve full rights and benefits. Spawned in the early 1970s by small groups of disabled students at the University of Illinois and at the University of California (Berkeley), the idea has caught on and spread throughout the country, beyond student communities. It is now affecting state and national policy, culminating in the passage of the 1978 Amendments to the Rehabilitation Act which authorize funding for "Comprehensive Services for Independent Living."

The IL movement represents the efforts of the disabled to organize, to become political, and to take greater control over their own

Material for this chapter was prepared by Michael Winter, Bruce Curtis, Mary Dudziak, Judy Humann, Belinda Stradley, Jerry Wolf, Frank Folsie, and Barbara Cappa.

lives. The movement is based on the disabled population's desire to lead the fullest lives possible, outside of institutions, integrated into the community, exercising full freedom of choice. The movement began (as is described below) when severely disabled students moved out of their residential hospital settings into the community and organized their own system for delivery of survival services. Since then, not only has the scope and number of such service delivery centers grown, but the philosophy in which they are grounded has spread throughout the rehabilitation world, challenging many of the old attitudes and policies toward treatment of the disabled.

As has been discussed by Dejong (1979), the IL movement has its roots in a number of other significant social movements and ideas coming out of the 1960s and 1970s: civil rights, consumerism, self-help, demedicalization, and deinstitutionalization. Drawing from each of these, the disabled of the IL movement have developed programs which differ significantly from traditional rehabilitation service delivery programs in a number of ways. Cole (1979) points out these differences in the areas of goals, methods of service delivery, and style of program management. With respect to goals, the IL programs insist on "client self-choice rather than incorporation of the client into a set of goals established by program managers, service professionals, or funding mechanisms. . . ." Service delivery is not monopolized by professionals but instead is usually carried out by peer counselors. Personal attendant care is directed by the disabled consumer himself, who hires and manages his own attendant. Finally, the programs are run by the disabled themselves; the managers are not professionals but consumers, as it is assumed that they know best the needs of the disabled.

To introduce the reader to the concept of IL, the editors asked us to describe the philosophy, development, and operation of our program. Since the Center for Independent Living (CIL) has grown quite large and come to offer a sizeable number of services, we have chosen to focus on just one of our services—housing assistance—to show how the IL philosophy is translated into action.

Historical Overview

People with disabilities have a long history of forced dependency. In 1504 Henry VII legally authorized the disabled to beg without fear of punishment. The English Poor Laws of 1601 mandated that the primary responsibility for care of disabled people was with their families. If the family could not or would not provide for adequate care, a disabled person would then go to live in an alms house. In the late 1700s and early 1800s, alms houses became very popular throughout the United States, for both the disabled and the poor. People with a variety of disabilities were incarcerated in these institutions because of their impoverished status and the custodial attitude of society. In most states there are still institutions in which disabled people can live, though they are often segregated by disability type. The dehumanizing conditions prevalant during the last 250 years still exist in many of these modern institutions because of the same societal attitudes and lack of fiscal support.

Sterilization of criminals, the mentally ill, and the poor became popular around 1910. This became the only alternative to life-long sexual segregation of the mentally and physically disabled in custodial institutions. By 1937, approximately 28 states had laws allowing the sterilization of "defective" human beings to reduce the genetic possibility of producing still more disabled people. Some cities passed ordinances, still in effect today, prohibiting the appearance in a public place of any person who is "diseased, maimed, mutilated, or in any way deformed so as to be an unsightly, or disgusting object." The Immigration and Naturalization Service can still deny a permanent visa to an immigrant or member of his family who has a physical defect, disease, or disability. Under old common law, people who were deaf could not be a witness nor make a contract or a will, because of an assumption of incompetency. They still can not serve as jury members in some states and cities.

Throughout these centuries of prejudice and oppression, society has made dependency seemingly inescapable. Many disabled people cannot work except in sheltered workshops, at times for less than one-half the minimum wage. Travel on commercial transportation is impossible for many physically disabled people unless they submit to patronizing or inconveniencing regulations that vary from company to company. Many disabled people cannot live in their own homes because funding and personal care attendants are available only if the disabled are segregated from society in institutions. There have been numerous case reports of disabled parents who have had their children taken from them on grounds that the child would not be raised in a "normal environment." In divorce proceedings between a disabled and an able-bodied parent, custody has traditionally been awarded to the nondisabled parent based on this kind of prejudicial concept of normality. Thus people with severe disabilities have lived under centuries of legalized dependency and ostracism. Many laws have been passed supposedly illustrating the liberalization of society's attitude toward disabled people; yet disabled people have come to realize that the discrimination in the community did not really end with such legal enactments. Discrimination continued because oppressive changes were always being introduced to limit society's obligations to the disabled. The few progressive changes that were introduced into the social system were never supported financially. It has become obvious that institutional prejudice will not be overcome by well-intentioned but uncoordinated and financially unsupported movements.

It is under these conditions that disabled people have existed with little or no services. The few services provided were crippled by the bureaucratic red tape and regulations which kept the vast majority dependent. Not available was a coordination of services that could break through this vicious cycle of dependency. With this in mind, the disabled themselves organized the Center for Independent Living (CIL) in 1972.

Center for Independent Living

CIL: the bold, green letters are visible for blocks away from the former car lot in downtown Berkeley. It was the tumultuous times of the late 1960s and early 1970s that drove the former residents from this protest-ridden area. But it was that same spirit of protest and change which engendered a movement soon to replace the fleet of sports cars on Telegraph Avenue.

It started on campus, as did so much of the activity of that era. The cast of characters was small: half a dozen severely disabled students living in Cowell Hospital at the University of California, Berkeley. Faced with such severely disabled persons as Ed Roberts (now director of the California Department of Rehabilitation), a postpolio quadriplegic who spends much of his time in an iron lung, the university considered residence in the hospital to be the only way these students could receive necessary services.

But the students found the hospital to be a sheltered, custodial environment and began making other plans. Their intent was to establish a program that would meet their needs for supportive services in the community, not in another medical residential facility. The program was to have three guiding principles:

1. Those who know best the needs of disabled people and how to meet those needs are disabled themselves.

2. The needs of the disabled can be met most effectively through comprehensive programs which provide a variety of services.

3. Disabled people should be integrated as fully as possible into their community.

The physically disabled students program (PDSP) was established through U.S. Office of Education seed money, and it began providing community based services in July of 1970. Of its nine staff members, five were severely disabled or blind. Through their efforts, many disabled students were able to move out of the hospital and into the community.

That the program addressed previously unmet needs was apparent through its steadily increasing clientele of students and nonstudents alike. The program's ability to serve disabled students was soon restricted, however, by the demand for services by the nonstudent community. Plans were then developed for a community-based organization founded on the same principle as PDSP but not affiliated with a particular institution. It was to be called the Center for Independent Living.

Seven years since its inception, CIL has grown to a staff of 140 people, over half of them disabled. The range of services has also been expanded greatly. Yet the focus of the program remains the same: The disabled providing services for the disabled with the intent of maximizing the disabled person's control over his or her life.

CIL is, most emphatically, *not* a residential facility. The care services (such as attendant referral, housing assistance, blind services, deaf services, transportation, financial advocacy, job development, peer counseling, and wheelchair repair) are designed to enable clients to live independently in the community.

One of CIL's first clients was Phil Draper. At seventeen Phil had been a typical high school student. His idea of weekend fun was cruising the streets of Vallejo, California and drinking beer. One night, while out driving with friends, his car crossed the center divider. Although he does not remember the events that led up to the accident, its results have changed the direction of his life.

Phil broke his neck, leaving him a quadriplegic. He spent most of the next three years in and out of hospitals. He then moved to Oakland. However, without adequate supportive services, his mobility and activity were limited, and soon he became very, very bored. Phil's health deteriorated, and he found himself back in the hospital with pressure sores. While there he met a disabled person who told him about PDSP. "It was the first time I'd heard of a central resource disabled people could turn to for survival services," he says. He decided to return to school, but along the way got involved in discussions about setting up a similar organization in the community. Phil became one of the original incorporators of CIL. He is now its executive director. The services provided at CIL are very important to him because, like many other staff members, he uses them himself. "It's hard to describe the frustration disabled people can face. [You] worry about whether your attendant will come in. If your attendant doesn't come, will you be stuck in bed all day? Who will feed you? If your chair breaks down you have no mobility, you're cut off. CIL services have relieved me of the twenty-four hour worrying about surviving." Once those basic needs are taken care of, Phil continues, "disabled people can take control of their lives, become involved in decision making, and start pursuing those things everyone else does."

At CIL, independence does not necessarily mean living by yourself or doing things totally by yourself. Rather, it means having as much control as possible over your environment. It means knowing what you need and making decisions about meeting those needs. For example, if you can get out of bed and get dressed by yourself but it takes you three hours, when, with the help of an attendant you can do it in half the time, use of an attendant frees your time and energy to do other things. You do not have to struggle every morning to get yourself out of bed in order to be independent. As long as you have control over your attendant so that you are making decisions about when you get up, what you will wear, what you will eat, and so on, then you are making choices.

Since CIL's inception in 1972, twenty similar programs have been established in other parts of California. All are based on CIL's model of comprehensive services and consumer control. By comparison, there are only eight or ten independent living programs in the rest of the country. It is not by happenstance that programs like CIL have flourished in California as opposed to elsewhere in the country. Since 1958 California has had an in-home supportive service program which provides funding for low-income disabled people in need of assistance in activities of daily living. This allows disabled people to hire attendants to assist in bathing, dressing, cooking, shopping, and other needs. Additionally, California's medical program allows low-income disabled persons to receive necessary equipment, such as wheelchairs, and to keep this equipment maintained.

CIL's policy of consumer control is important for many different reasons. First, since disabled people have designed their own service delivery system, a program which meets their self-defined needs was thus developed. Traditionally, facilities had not been addressing the problems encountered by CIL's severely disabled founders.

Disabled people controlling their own independent living program is, in itself, a model of the purpose of the organization. Disabled people in the CIL administration make decisions about the service program which, in turn, facilitates their clients' ability to make decisions in their daily life. Just as CIL is designed to enable disabled people to take control of their personal lives, it is also a model of control by disabled individuals of the larger institutions which affect their lives. This concept is important because throughout history disabled people have been excluded from the social mainstream, excluded from positions of authority and power, and so they have been unable to participate in the decision-making processes which govern all our lives. The resulting social policies of segregation are just beginning to be fought through such legislation as Title V of the Rehabilitation Act of 1973 which forbids discrimination in federally funded programs on the basis of disability.

Disabled people, however, are in a double-bind. Their struggle to fight discrimination is hampered by the lack of services to meet their needs for daily survival. Without services, civil rights laws are not worth the paper they are written on. If there were no attendant referral services, if there were no money to hire attendants, if assistance in finding accessible housing did not exist, if the disabled did not have wheelchair repair and accessible transportation, there would only be civil rights for people who could not get out of institutions to exercise those rights.

However slowly, gains are being made. Through the 1978 Rehabilitation Act Amendments, Congress authorized federal funding for programs like CIL. While the appropriations levels have been far below the amounts authorized, they will enable the start up of a limited number of programs. As more disabled persons have access to independent living services, their energies can turn from daily survival to a fuller involvement within their communities.

CIL is predicated on the belief that disabled individuals, irrespective of their particular disability, must begin to work together. Although the needs of persons who are blind, deaf, physically disabled, mentally retarded, substance abusers, or have other disabilities are sometimes different, lack of appropriate services results in the same systematic discrimination in the areas of education, employment, transportation, housing, and medical care.

One of the major services provided by an independent living program such as CIL is aid in securing (and retaining) appropriate housing. Although by no means the only service offered by independent living programs (ILPs), nor even the most important, residential provision or registry is offered by 62 percent of the ILPs currently functioning and was rated by the programs themselves as one of the three most important services ILPs provided to the disabled. Indeed, independent living would not be possible without physical housing units in the community available to the disabled consumers. Residential location is also one of the most difficult and troublesome of services to provide, for both rehabilitation settings and independent living centers. Especially in rural areas or areas in which there is a great demand for available rental units, making them both expensive and difficult to obtain, the provision of housing will require much ingenuity and hard work.

Because provision of suitable housing is such a difficult problem and typical of most dealt with by ILPs and traditional rehabilitation centers, we have chosed to discuss it in depth, thereby illustrating how an ILP such as CIL works.

Housing Department of CIL

Background and Purpose

Independent living is not possible without a place to live. Housing is the most critical need of people desiring to live independently. We at CIL believe that it is the right of all persons, regardless of physical condition or age, to adequate, safe, and healthy housing. To create environments that make it possible for physically disabled and elderly persons to live independently in the community, housing must be available that is responsive to the special needs of these populations and is not segregated from the mainstream of society. All people, we feel, should have *choices* of where to live. To offer these choices, there first must be affordable dwelling units for the physically disabled and elderly, most of whom have low or fixed incomes. These dwellings must be rental units, as home-ownership is an enterprise beyond the financial means of most of the disabled and the elderly. Although there is a shortage of rental units in Berkeley (and in many metropolitan areas), especially with the current trend toward condominiums, this availability is vitally necessary to integration of the disabled into the community. These units must also be accessible and suitable to the needs of the disabled.

The appropriate level of support from services of a facility and from the community encourages independence. To determine that appropriate level, consciousness raising and counseling about the home situation are needed. In this way it is determined exactly what is needed by each client, and psychological blocks to independence are alleviated. Technical assistance with modifications may be necessary to make the living unit usable. Barriers to mobility, both in the home and into the larger environment, may need to be removed. Without mobility, participation in the community is denied. In making these changes, services must be designed to allow the disabled person to progress from dependency to his full potential.

Housing necessarily entails more than the physical structure alone. Other aspects of the environment must also be considered, such as recreation, transportation, work, and finances. Government regulations that encourage appropriate housing solutions for the physically disabled and elderly populations need to be created or implemented as some disincentives currently exist in present regulations.

To accomplish the above goals, a comprehensive, programmatic approach to housing was developed at CIL with the following objectives:

1. Provide listings of vacant housing, indicating accessibility.
2. Help with modification design for the home: sketch plans, estimate costs, locate funds, refer contractors.
3. Ensure that the wider environment be accessible to and usable by all people.
4. Counsel people on their housing rights and on problems of adjustment to the environment. Refer people to necessary support services.
5. Develop financial support for renters and homeowners.

History of the Housing Department Services

The Housing Department at CIL was the last of the survival core services to receive funding. This service was provided because of the large number of requests by clients searching for a place to live.

Because CIL had no funds to pay a staff, we began by using an all-volunteer staff. We searched for foundations that would fund services of this type, but at the time there were none (this was pre-1978 legislation authorizing funding for ILPs). In 1976, we submitted an application for a Community Development Block Grant to the City of Berkeley. Our application was approved by the City Council for about one-third of what we requested. However, it was rejected by the Department of Housing and Urban Development (HUD) because it did not comply with the funding requirements of the Community Development Act, the federal law under which cities apply to HUD. Eventually it was approved, and our funding began April 1, 1977.

When we began providing services, we thought that we should take our clients to look at available rentals, but we soon discovered that this service was too time-consuming. Such a procedure severely limits the number of people we can serve, inasmuch as it is sometimes weeks before suitable housing may be located for a particular client.

The vacancy rate in this area (Berkeley, Albany, and North Oakland) is approximately 1%; when accessibility is taken into account, this 1% figure is reduced even further. The severe housing shortage drives up rental prices to a level impossible for someone on SSI or SSDI to afford. Our problem, of course, is to locate housing that is available, affordable, and accessible.

Housing Department Services

A variety of resource materials is used to locate potential housing units for clients. The primary source consists of listings, published Monday through Friday, of houses and apartments that become available. These listings include a brief description of each dwelling, outlining the amount of rent and deposit required, the number of bedrooms, location, and so on. Realty and management agencies are regularly contacted for additional listings. Clients are encouraged to notify the Housing Department if they or their friends move, thereby passing along accessible housing. In addition, local colleges and universities are contacted for listings and also for prospective roommates. Finally, local newspapers and newsletters, neighborhood and grocery store bulletin boards are checked systematically for rentals as they become available.

The available units are then checked against a reference book, compiled by CIL, which lists the area's apartments known to have level or rampable entrances. This book was compiled by taking an exterior visual survey when a building was listed as having a vacancy. There has been no new construction of multiunit housing in Berkeley for a number of years; much of Berkeley's housing stock consists of buildings that have been adapted as apartments, thereby making door-to-door surveys all the more difficult. At one point a University of California architecture class led by Raymond Lifchez undertook such a survey in the area near campus. Because of limited staff and resources, however, the Housing Department has been unable to survey other areas of the city. Only limited knowledge, therefore, is available against which to check listings for accessibility.

In addition to listings of available dwelling units, CIL also keeps an updated listing of people who are willing to share housing for a variety of reasons. It may simply be necessary to keep rent costs down and within a limited budget. Or perhaps a quadriplegic who needs attendant care but cannot quite afford it would like to share the costs and services of a personal care provider with another quadriplegic in like circumstances. Perhaps a blind person would like to share an apartment with a sighted person disabled in some other way. Being open to such arrangements can greatly maximize the possibility of a disabled person's living in the community. CIL also provides information on other alternative living situations such as communes and co-operatives, with both able-bodied and disabled persons.

Because most of our clients must live on a low, fixed income, we attempt to find as many ways as possible to ease the financial burden of the high-cost housing market. In addition to the roommate-referral mentioned above, we also work closely with the housing authorities in Oakland and Berkeley and Alameda County to assist clients in getting Section 8 rent subsidies. (Californians are fortunate to have a program of "aftercare housing assistance" which subsidizes rents for developmentally, mentally, or physically disabled persons who "are capable of living semi-independently or independently" and who are "financially unable to afford decent adequate housing within their own resources" (State SB 49—Federal Section 8.).

In the event that a residence is not accessible or usable by the disabled client, in many cases it can be modified or adapted so that it is habitable. We give technical assistance to people needing to make modifications and help them secure funding for such barrier removal. Funding for a project like this could come from a number of different sources. For example, Medi-cal or other medical plans will pay for much of the equipment and adaptions needed by the disabled person. The Veterans Administration (VA) will do the same, and in the case of service-connected veterans, they will give as much as $25,000 toward the house itself. Special groups or agencies, such as the Multiple Sclerosis (MS) Society or Catholic Family Services, and the local Department of Vocational Rehabilitation may also be potential sources of monies to remove architectural barriers. If private business is involved, for example, if the modification will also make a private business accessible, then that business can claim the modification as a tax deduction. The law states that Family Services, the Easter Seal Society, or the local Department of Vocational Rehabilitation may also be potential sources of monies to remove architectural barriers. The Welfare Department may even be of help, as sometimes there are special circumstantial funds or emergency loans for those who demonstrate the need. Though the law does not require property owners to make changes to their property for disabled renters, clients are not on their own in paying for these modifications!

The Housing Department of CIL will also help the disabled plan and execute these modifications. The housing counselor will first carefully inventory the client's needs and the house's shortcomings, and then assist him in deciding what changes must be made. He will help the client sketch plans for these changes and estimate the costs of these modifications. Finally, the housing counselor will refer the disabled person to a reputable, experienced contractor.

Many of CIL's clients, because this is the first experience with independent living, are ignorant of their rights and responsibilities as tenants. Therefore, our staff provides them information on these subjects and assists them in disputes they may have with their landlords. Clients should be familiar, for example, with the State of California Civil Code regarding discrimination. They should also know something about basic tenant/landlord relations. The staff of the Housing Department will act as advocates for clients whenever they may have problems in such tenant-landlord matters. The staff can advise clients of their rights concerning such things as eviction, security deposits, raising of rent, seeing-eye dogs, and the like. If clients feel that they may have been discriminated against because of disability, they may first be counseled by the Housing Department and then, if necessary, referred to CIL's Disability Law Resource Center for further legal advice.

When a suitable living space has been located, the housing counselor and client will evaluate its accessibility to the wider environment from the dwelling unit. What public transportation will the client use? Will he be able to get to it? Where will he shop? Will he have access to recreational activities and the like? To address these issues other departments of the CIL may be called upon, as the client's concern turns from the housing unit itself to the broader environment. Finally, the Housing Department will assist the disabled person in making arrangements for moving.

All the services that have been described in this chapter are delivered on an individual basis. When a client is referred to the Housing Department, he is assigned to a housing counselor. This counselor works with the client from start to finish—from referral to moving in. Counselors may or may not be disabled (although over one-half of our staff are disabled), but they must be able to counsel clients in all the areas mentioned thus far. They must be familiar with the city and also with rental policies and social service/funding sources available to their clients.

Besides direct service delivery, CIL's Housing Department is dedicated to the larger struggle of making the environment, especially in the area of dwelling units, more responsive to the needs of the disabled and elderly populations. Therefore, the Housing Department staff, especially the Housing Services Manager, works regularly with other agencies, government authorities, and the City of Berkeley, advising them of the housing needs of the disabled and campaigning for increased housing and supportive programs.

Of course, it is not enough merely to help clients obtain adequate living quarters. For many of our clients this would be useless to them without attendant care or transportation arrangements. The Housing Department is part of an integrated service delivery system that is CIL. But examining how the Housing Department works illustrates the basic values and goals of an ILP. Housing counselors are used as consultants; they suggest, refer, offer information and skill, but never make decisions for the client. The client is in control and chooses what living arrangements he desires, rather than the counselor deciding what would be best for him. With this model the client indeed may make mistakes. He may enter an inappropriate living situation and experience negative consequences as a result. He may fail. But as was mentioned earlier, this is one of the definitions of independent living: the right to make mistakes like everyone else. Examination of the operations of the Housing Department also illustrates CIL's close working relationship with the community. Every step of the way, counselor and client are working with neighborhood groups, with individual landlords, and with community organizations.

With the passage of the 1978 Amendments, the independent living movement stands at a crossroads. Previously strictly a grassroots movement struggling to survive through the efforts of dedicated and competent individuals, the movement has in effect become legitimate. Whether this will help or harm it remains to be seen. Whether substantial amounts of monies channelled through state departments of vocational rehabilitation will actually help disabled individuals achieve autonomy and independence is, as yet, an unanswered question. The independent living movement could become another bureaucracy, administered by professionals whose first allegiance will be to funding sources and not to the client. It depends on the determination of the disabled themselves to resist cooptation and remember the meaning of the term "independent living" if the original purpose of the movement is not to be subverted.

References

Center for Independent Living. *An introduction to the Center for Independent Living.* Unpublished manuscript. Berkeley, Calif., 1979.

Cole, H. What's new about independent living? *Archives of Physical Medicine and Rehabilitation,* 1979, *60,* 458–62.

Dejong, G. Independent living: From social movement to analytic paradigm. *Archives of Physical Medicine and Rehabilitation,* 1979, *60*(10), 435–446.

Laurie, G. Independent living programs. *Rehabilitation Gazette/79,* 1979, *22,* 9–11.

18 Consumer Activists

Promoting Equal Access to the Marketplace

Lilly Bruck

At the 1980 Annual Conference of the President's Committee on Employment of the Handicapped, Curtis Brewer was honored as the "Disabled Man of the Year." Mr. Brewer, paralyzed from the neck down by a progressive disease that started in his late twenties, is dependent in all the physical functions of life, including breathing. After years of inactivity, he entered law school and, at age 45, passed the bar. He is now a practicing lawyer specializing in disability rights. Presenting the committee's award to Mr. Brewer, President Carter paid verbal tribute to the honoree and then called on Mrs. Brewer to receive the plaque for her husband.

Sometime later, CBS aired a brief documentary on Mr. Brewer's life and accomplishments. At the program's conclusion, Mr. Brewer made a statement. He related events surrounding the presentation of the plaque and criticized the President, asking, "Why did he call on my wife? It is I who got the award. I am a person. I was there. The President should not have acted as if I was not present."

It took courage to voice this criticism on national television. The President may not have known how to present a plaque to a man who could not use his hands to accept it, but the man of the hour was offended. Perhaps he felt like the paraplegic or blind diner in a restaurant when the waiter addresses the able-bodied companion with the question, "What does he want?"

There is a lesson to be learned from this vignette. Should not all disabled people be encouraged to follow Mr. Brewer's example and say, "Hey, I am here! I am a person. Count me in!" It was perhaps Brewer's ability to do just this that explains in part his successful entry into a world constructed for the able-bodied, an all-too-often hostile environment which allows entrance only to those who can tolerate the pain and have the strength and persistence to ask and, sometimes, demand equal access, rights, and responsibilities.

Purchasing Power of the Largest Minority

Every physically disabled person need not be as outstanding an individual as Mr. Brewer, exhibiting his strength and courage in the fight for equal rights in the community. Fortunately, by working together, the disabled population can utilize already existing social and economic forces to help them gain their rights. A good example of this is found in the following statement announcing the recent opening of a new casino in Atlantic City. It stated:"Twenty-nine slot machines were specially adapted for the handicapped. Some are low, to be accessible for guests in wheelchairs; others have symbols, such as cherries or bells, brailled for identification by the blind."

What could be the cause of such consideration? Are gambling casinos subsidized by federal funds, or was the management afraid it would be accused of discrimination if all one-armed bandits were inacessible? One reason alone probably motivated the casino owners: profit. They simply acknowledge that the money of disabled gamblers is not impaired, at least no more so than anybody else's in this era of the shrinking dollar. Therefore, disabled visitors are made comfortable and given equal access to that elusive pot of gold.

Why has it taken business so long to recognize 36 million handicapped Americans, the country's largest minority, as consumers? Until recently they were largely ignored by the providers of goods and services. The image of unproductive shut-ins, living on handouts from relatives or society, did not project them as profitable customers.

As handicapped citizens are becoming a more visible part of the American scene, business has become aware of the purchasing potential of disabled consumers. It is up to the disabled themselves and those who work with them to learn to use their strongest weapon, their purchasing power. It is up to them to learn how to assert their rights as consumers and demand accommodations from those who want to sell them goods and services. The profit incentive will motivate those making accommodations. Competition will continue the momentum. Merchants will discover that an individual's disability does not mean inability, either to function as a first-class citizen or to be counted as a paying buyer of wares.

A Hostile Environment

Interestingly enough, astronauts can be viewed as handicapped people. Yes, up there in space only the most sophisticated adaptations permit them to function in a hostile environment: adaptations such as pressure suits, oxygen, food squeezed from tubes, chemical waste disposals, and electronic communication devices. If such sophisticated technology were put at the disposal of people with physical impairments, they could become equal consumers in the currently hostile environment of the average marketplace.

The power to obtain this sophisticated technology and the needed changes in business practices can come, in part, from the consumers' movement. The 1960s are generally considered the decade in which consumerism blossomed and developed into the force it has become. In 1962 President Kennedy identified four basic consumer rights:

1. The right to choose—free competition, no price fixing, and the opportunity to compare before buying.
2. The right to safety—flame-retardant fabrics, shatterproof glass, nonharmful food additives, and tested drugs and medical devices.
3. The right to be informed—full disclosure about the products we are about to purchase, content on labels on foods, care labels on clothing, energy consumption of appliances, warranties, and rates and conditions of credit.
4. The right to be heard—legitimate complaints about defective or unsatisfactory goods and services and consumer input to the deliberation of federal agencies when new regulations are proposed and discussed.

Consumers with physical impairments ask themselves if this Consumers' Bill of Rights really applies to them or if it was designed with only the able-bodied in mind. How can it apply to them if the store is inaccessible or when there may not be any federal, state, or local standards for braces, wheelchairs, hearing aids, or optical devices? How does the visually impaired consumer gain access to printed information? How does one make himself heard if he cannot communicate orally?

In 1975 President Ford added a fifth consumer right, the right to consumer education. A *right,* not a privilege. But is consumer education made available to disabled consumers of all ages? Have disabled children received formal consumer education in institutions? Did they gain the consumer practice their peers experienced when they spent their allowances in neighborhood stores?

While President Carter was still a candidate for his office, a suggestion to declare a Disabled Consumers' Bill of Rights was proposed (Bruck, 1978) to include:

The right to accessibility for the mobility impaired
The right to information for the visually impaired
The right to communication for the hearing impaired
The right to consideration for the mentally impaired
The right to consumer education

It is the need for this fifth right, the right to consumer education, on which we focus in this chapter.

Rehabilitation professionals concerned with preparing their clients for gainful employment and independent living should realize that teaching consumer skills must be a part of the preparation for earning money and spending it wisely. Knowledge of the laws that protect them in the marketplace enables consumers to assert their rights as buyers of goods and services. Consumers with disabilities must be assured that they, too, have equal rights and that they should demand accommodations that will eliminate environmental barriers which prohibit them from exercising their full rights as consumers. The profit motive and competition will support their arguments.

Coincidentally, adaptations made to accommodate consumers with disabilities will benefit many other customers as well. The invention of the telephone, for example, resulted from an effort to assist the hearing-impaired and opened communication for the world at large. Although closed captions were developed specifically for the hearing impaired, they also hold potential for those who are learning-disabled, those with reading problems, and those learning English. Ramps designed to accommodate those using wheelchairs also serve other "wheelers," those pushing baby carriages, youngsters with tricycles and bicycles, persons pushing shopping and delivery carts, those using canes, crutches or walkers, and elderly citizens, many of whom prefer gentle inclines to stairs. Disabled citizens are indeed not alone in their need of a benevolent environment.

It's Not Kindness, It's Good Business

The following pages contain accounts of efforts made to gain accommodations and adaptations in private industry. To help clients and colleagues make the community more accessible, these examples can be described to them. They should be encouraged to quote them to local suppliers, hotels, restaurants, and say: "If they could do it, why don't you give it a try? We'll see to it that you get publicity among groups of disabled residents and the local press. Besides, your action will not only create good will, you'll find it reflected in the bottom line—profit. It's not kindness you are practicing; it's good business to help the disabled become first-class citizens."

While clients are on their lobbying visits, they may find it useful to cite some concrete information. For instance, that it costs 1¢ per square foot to design a new building to be accessible, while it costs 13¢ per square foot to clean the floor. Businessmen willing to remove architectural barriers in their existing premises could be reminded that tax deductions of up to $25,000 per year are available to them for their efforts.

The Electronic Billboard

Television, the electronic billboard, is designed to make us all superconsumers. But has television discovered that disabled people exist outside of telethons, where they are displayed as pitiful characters, afflicted, imprisoned in defective bodies, conveying the message: "Send money as a thanks-offering for your own perfection"? Thankfully, yes. Indeed, television programming has begun to discover that many disabled persons live rich lives, as reflected in growing numbers of televised broadcasts and specials.

But have commercials discovered that one out of nine of their intended customers are members of America's largest minority? Does a disabled model ever appear on a television screen selling soap, toothpaste, soft drinks, food, or headache remedies? No, not any more often than black models huckstered in the early 1960s. And even when blacks first began to appear in commercials, they were shown in group scenes, slightly out of focus and never, never touching the merchandise. Only now are commercials more accurately reflecting blacks as a significant part of the consumer population.

A course titled "Consumer Education for and by Disabled Citizens" was conducted in 1977–1978 under the auspices of the American Coalition of Citizens with Disabilities. The 48 visually, hearing, or mobility impaired individuals participating in this course were asked to write letters to executive officers of each of four major advertisers selected: Bristol Myers, Proctor and Gamble, Best Foods, and Revlon. Some of the questions posed by these students to the advertisers included, "Because I am in a wheelchair, don't I brush my teeth?" "Though I am hard of hearing, don't you want to take care of my headaches?" "Don't children in wheelchairs eat Thomas's Muffins?" "Does Miss Wheelchair America not use cosmetics?" All letters received replies, because these conglomerates have good public relations departments and they do care about their public image. Of course, all responses were similarly polite and noncommital. "Everybody is beautiful; we do not differentiate." "We could be accused of exploitation." "Modeling requires highly skilled professionals." Perhaps the worst offender was Best Foods, who, in recognition of the writers' efforts, patronizingly sent coupons for the next purchase of Thomas's Muffins which were, incidentally, returned by the student with the comment, "We disabled want equality, not charity."

Alone, no one can convince the multibillion dollar advertising empire to include the disabled in their advertisements. But people working together can, perhaps, begin to make an impact. If network broadcasting cannot yet be moved to include the disabled in their advertising campaign, where one minute on prime time can cost up to $200,000, local advertisers can be approached.

An activism training program in a rehabilitation facility could begin with organizing disabled clients to contact local merchants. Individually, in pairs, or in groups, they could visit merchants, assuring them that disabled consumers use the same goods as do the able-bodied and pledging their business to those merchants who in their advertising pay them the courtesy of recognizing their existence.

Response is the Key

Corporations, like individuals, appreciate the public's recognition of their special efforts. When I complimented General Motors Corporation on having their 1978 Annual Report produced on tape for visually impaired stockholders, a member of their public relations staff responded: " . . . I have shown your letter to the young lady on my staff who conceived of and carried out this project. Often our individual efforts are lost . . . and your letter served to give proper credit where it was due." At National Airlines, not only the president, to whom the letter was addressed commending them on installation of a telephone for the deaf (TTY), but also the director of their reservations systems and programs responded: "We at National are quite proud of the opportunity to service Miami's deaf community, and the initial response to our limited system has been enthusiastic. In fact, we are already considering expansion of the service to a statewide basis, and who knows what might come next."

Response . . . this is the key to the expansion of services. Not only demands for accommodations by disabled consumers, but approval, in word and deed, when they are offered.

To Market, to Market . . .

In preparation for a pamphlet, *Consumer Rights for Disabled Citizens* (New York City, Department of Consumer Affairs, 1976), questionnaires were sent to airlines, banks, department stores, and food markets. Questions were asked about the width of doors and aisles, the accessibility of dressing rooms and restrooms, how information was disseminated to the visually impaired, the nature of orientation, and available acommodations.

Responses were received from seven of the 10 airlines, two of the 10 banks, five of the 19 department stores, and eight of the 26 food markets. The returned questionnaires were summarized and published together with the name of the responders. An adjoining column listed those not responding.

The enthusiastic reception of this book, locally and nationally, led to four reprinted editions within a few months. With every subsequent edition, the list of responders lengthened, while the list of nonresponders shrank. Undelivered or misplaced questionnaires, misunderstandings by staff, and missed deadlines for returning questionnaires were often used as excuses by those not responding, while management must have rubbed their eyes in wonderment that disabled consumers should actually be recognized and accommodated as customers. The questionnaires were reprinted in the pamphlet, accompanied by the statement: "It will be up to the disabled community to effect changes, to demand accommodations, and to vote with their shopping dollars for those merchants who cooperate, giving consumers with disabilities equal access to their services."

Armchair Shopping

For disabled consumers, shopping by mail or telephone may be the preferred method and the great equalizer. It makes disabled and nondisabled consumers not only equal customers but also equal victims of fraudulent practices. In 1978, $30 billion of merchandise was ordered from catalogs, brochures, and other mail promotions. Eighteen percent of all general merchandise sold in the country was sold by 10,000 mail-order houses, with Sears and Roebuck spending $125 million on printing their catalogs alone.

Unfortunately, the mail-order business also gives rise to some unethical practices. Mail orders are among the most often cited sources of all consumer complaints, even when no fraud is involved.

Moreover, in 1977 an estimated $1.8 billion was lost to mail fraud. The most vicious frauds are perpetrated by quacks offering miracle cures, sure-fire medicines, or beauty aids to gullible victims.

Overselling by high-pressure salespeople can be controlled, provided consumers are knowledgable of the laws that protect their rights as mail-order and direct-selling customers. The Federal Trade Commission will gladly provide consumers with free publications explaining in easy language what the cautious consumer should know.

To help those persons who shop by telephone, the telephone company's classified directory occasionally displays the international symbol of accessibility in some restaurant, store, and theater advertisements. The American Telephone Company suggested this innovation to all salespeople of space in classified telephone directories so that consumers in wheelchairs could identify not only where they were admitted but welcomed as customers. Both the disabled population and business community would be well served if all advertisements carried such designations. It would make it easier for the consumer to identify accessible businesses. It could also increase the trade in stores which are designated as being able to accommodate the disabled consumer.

Check that Checkout

The character in the cartoon may not have chosen the best way to gain accessibility to the food store. Perhaps he did not understand the distinction between aggression and assertion that all disabled shoppers must practice if they want to spend their money wisely and get the best value for their shopping dollar.

Shopping in the food market, being a repetitive chore, ranks among the most frustrating consumer experiences for those with impairments. Here deafness may be the least important inconvenience, since self-service demands little verbal communication with sales help. One recommendation to store owners which can help accommodate the hearing-impaired consumer is to request that those working counter areas that issue numbers, such as a deli or a bakery, flip these numbers as well as call them out; otherwise a deaf customer may patiently wait for 83 to be called, while 85 and 86 are already being served. This is simply one small accommodation, requiring no cash investment by the store, which can be quickly and effectively implemented.

Problems of the visually impaired consumer are more difficult to overcome. Blind customers are not only deprived of money-saving

"I widened your doorway so that it could
accommodate my wheelchair!"

coupons found in newspaper advertisement and store flyers, but also
of the wealth of printed content and use of information found on
packages of merchandise. It would be unrealistic to expect brailled
labels on canned foods, cleaning supplies, or unit-price shelf stickers.
Yet the visually impaired consumer can find ways of sharing the benefits offered the able-bodied consumer. For example, arrangements
can be made with the local branch manager of a supermarket chain to
be assisted by a helper at mid-week off-peak hours. Eunice Fiorito, a
blind activist, found herself poorly treated in her neighborhood food
market. She switched to a nearby competitor where arrangements
were made for a store clerk to help with her weekly shopping. A few
weeks later, she met the manager of the inhospitable store. "I

Cartoons on this page and on following pages are reprinted with permission of
Raymond Cheever (Ed.), *Laugh with Accent*. Bloomington, Ill., Accent Special Publication, 1975.

haven't seen you lately," he commented, "Where have you been?" Eunice replied, "You didn't seem to care for me as a customer so I took my business to another store where it is welcomed and I get the service I need."

Mobility-impaired shoppers encounter their major problem at entry and exit. These difficulties are caused by such barriers as heavy manual doors, often located at the store's entrance, and protruding floor posts at the exit. Such impediments were originally installed to prevent loss of shopping carts but are now illegal as fire hazards. Again, to prevent loss of costly carts, narrow checkout lanes in most inner city stores prevent customers in wheelchairs from passing through the lane and observing the checker ringing-up purchases.

In New York City an incident had far-reaching, positive consequences in correcting this situation. Betty Furness, Consumer Affairs Director for NBC, sent her "Action 4" crew to a downtown food market. Illustrating her shopping problems was a vociferous disabled consumer. She complained that she was unable to watch the checker ringing-up her purchases because the lane was too narrow to accommodate her wheelchair. Arriving at the store on the morning of the television filming, one lane, under a handwritten sign reading "This checkout lane for the handicapped," had been widened. Questioned, the manager replied, "We knew you were coming with the television cameras. My back still hurts from moving the counter this morning." A telephone call to the president of the company elicited the promise that the improvement would remain permanently under a professionally produced symbol of accessibility. Not only would the widened lane remain in place in that particular store, but widened lanes would be installed to accommodate wheelchairs in many other branches of the chain. Soon competition took its course, and now other chains have followed their lead.

This tactic can be used effectively in other locales. Clients can be encouraged to contact a local television crew and repeat this scenario. It would not only make more stores accessible and generate positive publicity for their facility, but it would also enhance the handicapped's self-esteem and sense of control over their environment.

Friendly Skies and Assorted Welcome Mats

The current upswing in travel by handicapped individuals and groups has altered the attitudes and appearance of the hotel and public transportation industries. Highly competitive airline companies have recognized that many disabled travelers can become their passengers. This has caused them to change their previous prohibi-

*"I suppose the hardest part to accept is
the not being able to get around!"*

tive restrictions to actively soliciting disabled consumers with accommodations and services. *Access Travel: Airports* (available from the Consumer Information Center, Pueblo, Colorado 81002) describes design features, facilities, and services at 220 airport terminals in 27 countries that are accessible to the handicapped.

The Washington Metro, San Francisco's BART, Amtrak, and some private bus companies are among several transportation systems striving to construct accessible facilities for disabled travelers. Several offer free passage or considerable discounts for companions of handicapped passengers.

Increasing numbers of hotels and motels are making their lobbies, dining rooms, restrooms, and a percentage of guest rooms architecturally accessible. For example, the Washington Hilton has available accessible public and guest rooms, raised table tops for the comfort of wheelchair guests in the coffee shop, low-mounted public and house phones with sound amplification, brailled menus, and brailled elevator buttons. The Century Plaza Hotel in Los Angeles welcomes blind guests with sets of brailled menus. Raised floor plans of the guest rooms, indicating location of doors, closet, furniture, and telephone are also available to the visually impaired guest.

Although accommodations for deaf guests are not available in even these hospitable inns, their needs could be met by making the following accommodations: provision of room phones that have visual page systems, so that a guest could be notified by the front desk; a portable TTY for the guest's room to call friends and family and another at the front desk or in the assistant manager's office so deaf guests can call for services available to other guests, such as room service or valet; bed vibrators for wake-up calls; and flashing fire alarm warnings to alert deaf guests while alarm bells notify others to vacate the premises.

At Your Service

"I entered so many restaurants through their kitchens," stated Max Cleland, former director of the vast Veterans Administration bureaucracy, "that people thought I was a food inspector." Being ushered into an eatery past garbage cans and clutter while one's dinner companions walk up carpeted steps at the front entrance is not and should not be tolerated as "equal access." In New York City not only do several posh restaurants offer brailled menus but some fast food chains also do. Several McDonald locations have menus brailled in metal on the counters. Accessible tables with fixed chairs removed are indicated by the international accessibility sign overhead.

Equal hospitality is extended to blind guests' guide dogs at these restaurants, which is not the case at all eating places. Although the law states that guide dogs may accompany their masters wherever they go, on public carriers, in airports, post offices, stores, and banks, some restaurants still refuse admittance even to those privileged canines. Blind activists often make it a point to insist, quoting the law. Faced with continued resistance, they ask that the owner of the restaurant call a policeman, not, as some owners hope, to obtain assistance with barring the dog, but rather to enforce the law.

Your Friendly Banker—How Friendly Is He or She?

In the previously quoted responses to accessibility questionnaires distributed by the New York City Department of Consumer Affairs, banks were shown to be the poorest responders—two out of ten. Conceivably this could be interpreted as reflecting little interest by banks in acquiring disabled customers. With all the wooing banks do, offering gifts to new depositors and praising their friendly services, only one bank in New York City makes any provision for their disabled depositors. Chemical Bank prepares statements in braille and furnishes checks with raised lines for blind and visually impaired clients.

If disabled clients are not courted to become depositors, how welcome are they as borrowers? Does a disabled applicant for a loan receive consideration equal to that of his nondisabled neighbor? What is the disabled community's share of the almost $1.2 trillion consumers owe on their homes, $280 billion of installment debt, and $64 billion in charge credit? Is credit, the motor that drives our economy and the key that makes possible full participation in the benefits of our society, denied to physically handicapped citizens? Theoretically, only the ability and willingness to repay a loan or pay for items charged or purchased on installments should determine the applicant's credit-worthiness. Application for loans by lending institutions are evaluated by point scores, with some criteria including place and length of employment, length of residence at the same address, and listing in the telephone directory. According to the Equal Credit Opportunity Act, age, sex, marital status, nation of origin, or receipt of public assistance may not be considered. The law does not prohibit discrimination because of physical handicap. The human factor, however, enters into the granting of a loan in the form of the loan officer's personal judgment. Whether applicants in wheelchairs, walking with canes, or accompanied by guide dogs or sign language interpreters will receive the same objective evaluation must be carefully considered.

It is important for disabled consumers to become aware of their rights in the credit market and the laws that protect them. In case of rejection of a loan application, the Fair Credit Reporting Act requires that the lender state the reasons for the rejection. This act also guarantees the would-be borrower's right to investigate them. Disability is not one of the legitimately acceptable reasons for denial of a loan. All facts of the "Truth in Lending" law are described in clear language and are free for the asking from the Federal Trade Commission's Consumer Protection Bureau.

Be Sure of Your Insurance

In research for Bruck's book *Access* (1978), people who worked in sales and in administration of major insurance companies were interviewed. The results can be summarized thusly: "You won't find any exclusionary clauses in any manuals. But neither will you find an executive of an insurance company who will swear on a stack of bibles that discrimination does not exist."

In the preceding section we have seen that the rejected loan applicant has the right to be informed of the reason for denial. In a recent court case brought by a rejected applicant for life insurance, the defending insurance company's counsel admitted that insurance has been denied because the applicant was gay. "Did actuary tables exist proving that homosexuals had shorter life spans?" asked the plaintiff's attorney. "No," was the response, "but gays have the tendency to hang out in bars where brawls ensue and they can get killed." It is interesting to note that the rejected disabled applicant had to go to court to determine the "scientific" reason for his denial while, if denied credit, the law would have given him the right to demand disclosure. A similar law is now being considered for the insurance industry and should be vigorously supported by consumers. Given the enormous wealth and lobbying power of the insurance industry, such a law will not be passed easily. But, then, the banking industry was not enthusiastic about the Truth in Lending Law, either.

At present, disabled applicants for life insurance have to be their own consumer advocates. Comparison shopping among various companies and careful study of terms must precede the purchase. Again, help is offered in the form of publications written in popular language, many of them produced and distributed free of charge by the government and by insurance companies.

Discrimination is also practiced by those selling automobile insurance. Though disabled drivers have statistically equal or better safe driving records than do the able-bodied, they are frequently assigned to risk categories that carry with them the highest premiums. Here again, assertion, comparison shopping, and assistance from local consumer agencies, legal aid consultants, or human rights offices may help the disabled driver to pay the already high rates for automobile insurance charged to all motorists, without having them additionally inflated by discrimination.

Equality for disabled consumers will not be given freely or easily. It can, however, be achieved if disabled individuals recognize that they possess "consumer power." Like other constituencies, they have the ability to exert pressure and to influence the political and economic decision-making processes that affect them. Equality as citizens can be legislated; equality as consumers must be acquired through the exercise of this consumer power. It is the rehabilitation practitioner's responsibility to teach their disabled clients how to gain access to this untapped reservoir of power in order to obtain their full and equal rights as consumers.

References

Bruck, L. *Access, the guide to a better life for disabled Americans.* New York: Random House, 1978.

Consumers' Union, *Talking book,* RC 12104. Library of Congress, DBPH.

19 Social Crisis and the Future of the Disabled

Elliott A. Krause

There's a chill in the air as I write this, in October of 1979, here in New England. Part of the chill is autumn, of course. Certainly the leaves are putting on their usual spectacular show. But this year the oncoming winter has another dimension—a political one. If there were ever a winter of our discontent—all over the nation—this will be the one. The big squeeze—wages not keeping up with prices, a powerful and utterly shameless energy industry grinding the wheels of inflation (with us between them) and an apparently powerless federal government standing by and wringing its hands—all are leading to a social, society-wide crisis, for all but the independently wealthy. Yet we are not dealing with blind forces of nature here—we are dealing with willful greed by large corporations and a prostrate, unorganized citizenry, with systematically unrepresentative institutions. And if things are getting this bad for most of us, it is clear that the disabled are bound to suffer even more.

I would like to begin by sketching a broad sociological and political-economic overview of the crisis, using a variety of theories developed precisely for this purpose—modern Marxian theory on the role of the state in advanced capitalist societies, especially in times of so-called "fiscal-budgetary crises" in the area of human services. Then I can relate the theoretical insights of this view to three key areas: the production of disabled individuals, the state's official definitions of disability, and the ideologies presently governing the process of rehabilitating, or not rehabilitating, broad classes of our people. I can then conclude by presenting some strategies for action to change the situation.

The Nature of the Social Crisis

When capitalism first appeared on the scene, in the trading cities such as Venice or Florence or in the Hanseatic League on the North Sea, it brought with it much social change and chaos. The hierarchical order of the Middle Ages gave way, and the authority of the church was challenged by a new rising merchant class. In place of the concept of the subject under a king whose divine right to rule was provided by the Pope, we saw instead the rise of individualism and the fall of a moral order. Everyone in his place, the feudal order of caste with mutual protection up and down, was replaced by the new message, everyone for himself (Ullmann, 1966). The brutality and criminality of the first merchant princes of capitalism had another side, of course, for they created the conditions which freed men's minds for science and art, for the Renaissance (Von Martin, 1963). In fact, the great painters were often permanent houseguests in the great houses of merchants such as the Medici, and art flourished at least in part to present a positive public image for the new princes.

As capitalism rose, the feudal order fell, for it was powered with the strong backs of the serf or peasant class. When these people fled to the city or were driven off the land by new laws passed because of capitalistic power, they left the lords of the manor high and dry, with no one to work their land. For these lords no labor force meant declining power and wealth, while power and wealth was at the same time increasing for the new factory-owning class. By the early 1800s in Europe and England and by 1840 in the north of the United States, capitalists were increasingly the political power of the nation. Karl Marx began his work at this time. Two basic observations he made are critical to the approach used in this paper. The first was that history is a succession of class struggles, with in each age a small and well-organized oppressing class exploiting a weak, large, and unorganized class that does not own the productive process and is therefore not in a position to set their wages or working conditions (Marx, 1977). His second observation was that, in the early capitalism of his day, "The state is the executive organ of the bourgeoisie" (Marx, 1963). Or in other words, the capitalist class proposes; the state takes its orders and disposes. But those were simpler times.

Modern Marxian theory, especially as it deals with the role of the state in advanced capitalism, has taken the basic theory and observations of Marx and updated his theory to make it more relevant to today's more complex relationships between the state, capitalist sectors, the working class, and other segments of our society. This updated theory is widely in use today in the West and should not be confused with the dogmatic pronouncements of Lenin and the secular religion known as "Marxism–Leninism" in Eastern Europe (Anderson, 1976). Serious scholars such as Poulantzas (1975, 1978) in France, Miliband (1969) in England, and O'Connor (1973) and

Wright (1978) in the United States are proceeding in an objective and interdisciplinary manner. With historical, political, economic, and sociological data and a knowledge of social systems they are doing pioneering work on the how and why of social crises in the West. They are particularly concerned with the role of the state (defined as all organs of public government at all levels) in advanced capitalism. Within this concern, they are even more interested in the role of the state in times of "fiscal crisis" or budgetary cutbacks, especially as this concerns human services and health protection for the population.

For example, Mandel (1975) has shown that capitalism itself has gone through phases, from early merchant prince or sailing ship capitalism, to early industrial capitalism, to the early monopoly-building robber baron capitalism of the 1880–1910 period, to monopoly capitalism with large near-monopoly or oligopoly sectors (energy for example) with a much less powerful medium to small business sector. Finally, in the post World War II era, in both the United States and Europe, we are approaching a new era, that of *state capitalism,* where the top 1000 corporations work jointly with national chief executives and plan the future economic policy, bank lending rates, degree of unemployment, degree to which government regulations will be supported or relaxed, and most important here, whether the funding for the human services sector will be added to, left alone, or cut back. In his recent analysis Gough (1979) shows this growing interconnection between corporate sectors and the state, with the need to cut back on services if profits in the private side of the arrangement begin to become affected:

> In the real world the final burden of taxation is determined by the ebb and flow of class conflict, and will vary with the economic and political strength of the contending classes. Simultaneously, the scale and direction of state expenditure, including that on the social services, is also largely influenced by the class balance of forces. (Gough, 1979, pp. 126–127)

Gough goes on to note that one outcome of the conflict is inflation and social instability. He notes that the public human service sector is even there at all only because workers and their representatives struggled to place it there. But once there it constitutes a drain on profits. In good times corporate capitalism can afford to fund it, but in bad times cutbacks must occur. But those cutbacks, by their nature, take things away from people who have become used to getting them as a normal part of life, for example, good public schools, health care, rehabilitation services:

The ever-growing level of state impositions and welfare expenditures exacerbates the conflict between capital and labor in the economic, political, and ideological spheres. The combination of upward pressures on welfare spending and problems of financing it result in what O'Connor (1973) refers to as "the fiscal crisis of the state." But this can only be understood as one moment in the present economic crisis, brought about by the very nature of capitalist growth and development. (Gough, 1979, p. 127)

Now we come to the budgetary or fiscal crisis itself. Workers who struggle and who even partly succeed in getting wages pushed up force corporations to economize elsewhere—and they choose their tax burden, especially that part of it that goes for public services and welfare. The cost accountants within the state are then given near-supreme power—cut everything you can.

Economic and employment policy, as well as long-term fiscal and monetary policy, is part of this struggle. Production costs to many sectors, because of labor and energy requirements, push inflation up, and then the technique of choice is to recommend more unemployment and raise interest rates—which take even more money out of the hands of the middle and working class while cutting back on money for services to them and to the poor. The crisis is now reaching the point where the middle class is becoming proletarianized, in Marxian terms, or pushed down into the bare subsistence struggle that has always characterized the life of the industrial working class. This is the social crisis upon us—the crisis is business as usual within an advanced capitalist nation, with the centralization of power in the corporate sectors leading to more pushing, not less. External factors then squeeze the corporations, leading to further increases in the squeeze on us. This war against the middle and working class, in addition to the usual war against the poor and the disabled, is the social dynamic that characterizes the present era. It is heating up with passage of time, not cooling down. And the dynamics of the crisis directly affect three areas directly relevant to the concerns of workers with the disabled: the creation of disability, the official definition of disability, and the rehabilitation process itself. It is to each of these areas that we now turn.

Capitalism, State Controls, and the Production of Disability

In the first place, the *sources* of disability are closely related to the extent of the struggle underway, and the sources have effects that are more marked than usual in times of social crisis. Five areas can be briefly considered: occupational disease of a physical nature, the psychosomatic and mental illnesses related to stress, the incapacitation caused by highway accidents, the disease and handicapping of children, and the chronic illness of those out of work and staying at home. This is by no means an exhaustive list, but it will begin to illustrate the dynamics of the system as it normally functions to produce—to manufacture—disability.

We can begin with OSHA, the Occupational Safety and Health Administration. Though activists working within the labor movement worked for more than 50 years to get protective laws on the books, it was not until 1970 that President Nixon signed the OSHA act into law. Then, with the utmost cynicism and in a series of steps carefully described by Page and O'Brien (1973), he fired half of the already existing occupational health and safety inspectors in the federal government. He used his executive authority to reallocate back to the states (who were almost powerless against large industry in their areas) the regulatory power granted to the federal government by the new law setting OSHA up. He let it be known to all major industries that he had no intention of pushing ahead on the act with any real speed. The Public Health Service estimates that 390,000 new cases of occupational disease appear annually. Ashford (1976) notes that epidemiological analyses of excess mortality among workers in several industries suggest that as many as 100,000 deaths occur each year as a result of occupational disease.

The philosophy of nonenforcement of safety regulations has a clear economic payoff in many industries—that of saving the money the often expensive antipollution equipment would cost, were the state to force them to buy it to protect workers. Labor leaders pushed to get OSHA passed in 1970 and have continually spoken since then about the need to actually implement it. But,

> In the five years since the OSHA Act was passed, the labor movement, spearheaded by the AFL–CIO and its Industrial Union Department (IUD), has become increasingly disillusioned with the implementation of the Act and the government's inadequate commitment to protecting worker health. . . . The IUD has strongly opposed state takeover of occupational health and safety, on-site consultation, and the low funding and manpower provided both OSHA and NIOSH. (Ashford, 1976, p. 27)

What must be understood in terms of our model is that this kind of nonfunctioning of the state regulatory apparatus is business as usual under advanced capitalism. The function of OSHA is as much ideological as real, for it serves to show consumers that the government and the corporations care, whereas in practice they don't. The very first regulatory agency, the ICC (Interstate Commerce Commission), had the same problems; Jay Gould suggested that the federal government set it up so that he could stock it with his own men. Given the functional constraints on the state in advanced capitalism—that is, not to hurt the capitalist class even in a conflict of interest situation with worker health—it should be no surprise to note that performance of OSHA under Ford and Carter has not changed from that under Nixon. Carter's peanut processing plant in Plains, years ago, was not exactly a model of worker health. But even if in the White House he were to get converted, or reborn if you will, to the cause of safety in the workplace, the constraints of "the economy" would prevent him from acting significantly. Califano, incidentally, began to try—and his fate was related in part to his attempt in this area.

In the 1980s the fiscal crisis ideology will provide an excuse for further cutbacks, as will any real turn toward recession. Workers are told, and sadly believe, that the only choices they have are a job with a risk of cancer or no job at all. Meanwhile, the right-wing antiregulation ideology in Washington, emanating from such conservative think tanks as the American Enterprise Institute, offers a "scientific" justification for cutting back on regulation—it is necessary to save American business. It is also necessary, according to this reasoning, for the carnage to continue.

A second area of disability creation lies in the area of pressure to produce. Two classic signs are speedup on the assembly line and pressure for a reduced work force to produce at the same level and speed as the full work force that used to be there. Note that production pressure takes its toll. From the time of Marx's first writings on alienation (1963) concerning the psychic and economic costs paid by those on the line, to the most recent epidemiological work by such workers as Eyer (1977) on the social epidemiology of hypertension, the dynamics are the same. People are not machines. When pushed to behave as such, they break into alcoholism, addiction to tranquilizers, neurotic conflict, wife and child beating, and, according to some studies, psychosis as well (Rosen, Locke, Goldberg, & Babigian, 1970). Again, in the service of profit of those who own and control the workplace, the disability is produced. The social crisis of inflation, recession, and cutback in service will provide these owners with a rationale for cranking up the pressure and a fiscal excuse for refusing to treat the mental and spiritual wreckage the speedup will produce. The excuse will be that there's no more money to help them—given the budgetary crisis and the need to keep profits up.

A third area of disability production lies in the area of automobile safety. Traumatic injury in accidents, leading to many spinal cord injuries as well as other partial and total disabilities, can often be prevented. But to do so would require the passage of new laws, new engineering mechanisms (such as passive restraint systems like the air bag), and new costs to industry. In a time of social crisis and recession, with sales declining, the automobile production sector of the capitalist class says to the state—make us do this and we'll have to raise the price. We won't eat the development and production costs, and raising the price in this market will mean we will sell fewer cars. You must not make us do this, they say, for our economy must be protected along with the jobs of auto workers. The Congress stays its hand; the executive branch counsels patience to consumer activists; the carnage continues on the highways as it does in the factories. And the physical medicine and rehabilitation world gets another set of paralyzed clients to work with. Again, the social crisis provides a convenient ideological justification for total retreat in this area, an area where any progress at all was made only after years of struggle against the power of the auto industry.

Finally, there are the lower visibility areas of disability production relating to the home and the natural environment. Welfare payments stay at near-starvation levels while the cost of food and energy rise through the ceiling. The state—and the corporations working in tandem with it—pleads poverty and cost-effectiveness. The so-called middle class is set politically against the poor, for the middle class are told that they (not the corporations, of course) will pay the money for any additional support for the poor and disabled. The consequence is the chronic and increasing malnutrition of the poor, with its direct toll in chronic respiratory disease and insufficiently fed pregnant mothers and consequent retardation of a new generation of infants. Also here we have the fixed-income retired and elderly, whose choice is now increasingly between insufficient food or insufficient heat. In the winter of 1979, and unless something drastic is done, in all the winters to come, they will pay the price of the social crisis. At the same time, the banks are not going to give away the extra interest dollars they get, nor will the oil industry. Thus for the segments of the population we have been considering, the class struggle is a simple struggle for survival. Unless something is done soon, they will lose it, first through increased incidence of new disability and aggravation of existing chronic disability, and then in upswing in the death rate.

To sum up, the four areas of physical occupational health, mental health, auto safety, and provision for the poor and retired all illustrate in different ways how the social crisis has strong consequences in terms of increased production of disability. But for "disability" to exist officially, to the point where the disabled can get help, their disability must be officially recognized by the state. It is to this aspect of the crisis that we now must turn.

Cutbacks and the Definition of Disability

While an individual's own subjective and psychological definition of disability is critically important in understanding the progress of that individual in the rehabilitation process, others do defining as well. And these other definitions are more fateful, more consequential, for they determine whether there is going to be a rehabilitation process in the first place. Three main types of definitions may be distinguished: the medical, the sociological, and the legal. With each step from the first to the third, the dynamics of the social crisis come increasingly into play and affect the consequences of the definition process. After discussing these definitions and relating them to the social crisis, we can take up the politics of disability definition in the 1973 Rehabilitation Act, the political economy of Workmen's Compensation definitions, and the deinstitutionalization crisis in mental health. Each issue in its own way bears the marks of the present social crisis.

Disability definition can be considered from many points of view. Here we are particularly concerned with what the definition of disability refers to. *Medical definition,* made by physicians or physician extenders, refers to the abstract degree of physical or mental health of the defined individual, with the medical profession doing the defining. Capacity to function is the criterion there. Pure medical definitions are rare, of course. They are usually mixed, in real-world cases, with *sociological role definitions,* in which the capacity to perform a role is the issue. For example, two people with paralysis from the waist down (medical definition of disability) are given two different degrees of role disability for the first is a college professor, who can work and lecture sitting down, while the second is a steel worker who will need an entire new occupation to hold a job. Finally, there are *legal definitions* of disability—the law of a given state or nation, which takes medical definitions, or medical and social role definitions of disability made by experts in medical and vocational rehabilitation, and then says: you *qualify* as disabled in our program, and therefore our state program will provide the funds for your support or your training and placement in a new job.

The progression from medical definitions through social role definitions into legal support definitions is a progression at the same time from science to politics. Social role definitions involve what state a society's labor market is in, whereas legal definitions are the outcome of political struggles to provide or to not provide laws and state programs and funds for the disabled. Thus to the extent a society is in social crisis, the labor market will tighten and throw more of the medically disabled into the social role category of unemployable, given the competition. And the greater the crisis, the less likely it is that the state will even maintain the status quo in terms of allowing official legal definitions of disability to go unchallenged and unchanged. The greater the crisis, the tighter the money for programs and the stronger the pressure on those bureaucrats in a position to make the legal definitions and thus cost the state money.

One primary example of this lies in that area of legal decision making involving the use of medical and social role data that we call Workmen's Compensation decision making. As the cost of living has risen, Workmen's Compensation systems have not risen in their payments for injury, even with the rate of inflation, nor has the nation developed one overall federal system. According to the National Commission on State Workmen's Compensation Laws (1972), the payment system is grossly inadequate; it continues the adversary relationship between employer and employee through quasi-judicial proceedings with lawyers on both sides; and it often denies benefits for arbitrary reasons. Need I note that the corporate sector fights against any major reform of the system, especially increased benefits which might come out of their pocket?

When I last wrote on this issue (Krause, 1976), it already appeared as if the governmental appeals system—the administrative law judges—were getting pressured to quit reversing appeals by workers whose Workmen's Compensation benefits had been denied further down the line. When the ideology of "fiscal crisis" and "bankruptcy of the Social Security system" was spread, and federal policymakers chose to push up the rates and percents of Social Security income, they also chose to lean on the administrative law judges in the Social Security Administration, Bureau of Hearings and Appeals. Howard Grossman, a highly respected administrative law judge who works in this area, wrote the following article which carried the subhead "The Planned Ending of Impartial Disability Adjudication":

> The bankruptcy crisis set the stage for an attack upon the administrative law judges' "reversal rate," i.e., the percentage of state agency denials which are "reversed" by administrative law judges and changed to allowances of benefits. Thus began the attack upon due process of law and

upon fair hearings for the country's most vulnerable citizens, the handicapped and the disabled, the aged and the blind. (Grossman, 1979,
p. 45)

Specifically, the Workmen's Compensation system is jointly
funded in most states between industry and government or, to use
the terminology of modern Marxian theory, between sectors of the
capitalist class and the state apparatus. To protect profit margins by
keeping expenses under control, a limit is set on the total size of the
award an agency such as SSA can award. If expenses rise or demands
increase, the state machinery must stand firm. If political organizations of the working class are too weak, or if the public can be
convinced that cutbacks are necessary to save "the economy" (whose
economy?), then positive cutbacks—going beyond level funding—
can occur. Even Congressional Investigation Committees found that
the pressure on judges within SSA had escalated, from the mid-1970s
on. The judge shows how this worked:

> Differences between the Bureau of Hearings and Appeals . . . and the
> ALJ's escalated beginning in 1975, with the appointment of a new Bu-
> reau Director. "Management techniques" were instituted with the al-
> leged purpose of reducing a "backlog" of cases, and ALJ's were as-
> signed production quotas. A large number of grievances and lawsuits
> were filed by ALJ's against the Bureau Director and other management
> officials, based on various allegations of mismanagement and capricious
> exercise of authority. Class actions were filed by claimants alleging
> denial of due process of law because of managerial interference in the
> decisional process. (Grossman, 1979, p. 45)

The Bureau of Hearings and Appeals responded to the protest of the
judges by trying to fire them en masse. In addition:

> The medical advisory staff was drastically reduced in size, and the
> "managers" were assigned the task of making medical judgments. BHA
> contracted with a former BHA management official to study the entire
> problem: his report was highly critical of the new "management initia-
> tives" and bureau reorganization. (Grossman, 1979, p. 45)

The judges won the short-run battle. But Grossman goes on to note
that new legislation is being proposed that will let nonjudicial
agency employees screen all appeals before they get to the administrative law judges. This legislation is being proposed not just in
Workmen's Compensation cases but also for cases of welfare cut-off
and other areas as well. This is precisely the mechanism that I sug-

gest characterizes the functioning of the state in this area in advanced capitalism, especially in a recession period. If one technique for denial of service doesn't work, change the mechanism to make it possible. New legislation is always being written and sometimes even passed to counter these trends, such as Ross (1979) notes on building rehabilitation processes into the compensation process. But the problem is more basic—the size of the pie, the amount of gold in the pot. Capitalism determines this, not the disabled or the health workers—at least, not yet.

One other area shows the same dynamics at work on a different population—the deinstitutionalization of the severely disabled mentally ill. The Joint Commission's report in the early 1960s (Joint Commission of Mental Illness and Health, 1962) was titled *Action for Mental Health.* It recommended against long-term institutionalization and recommended for expensive, thorough, well-staffed community mental health centers. National and state fiscal policies and the downturn in mental health service funding after Nixon's election (after correction for the inflation rate) led to a mass discharge phenomenon, the emptying out of the institutions as a cost-saving matter. While the goal of discharge is a progressive one, we are dealing here with something else, according to the latest reports of President Carter's Commission on Mental Health (1978). We are now dealing with false definitions of cure or capacity to function, by state hospitals unable to care for patients, which then as a "solution" shoves them into the community. Becker and Schulberg (1976) show that this has led to an upswing in rehospitalization rates and to community turmoil. But it is cheaper than feeding all of them within the walls and paying for all that staff or building expensive new community mental health centers. The same general political-economic forces we have described work here to deny a haven and service to the chronic mental patient.

In general, we are simply making the point that the social crisis has direct implications for who is defined as officially needing help, and as the crisis escalates, fewer and fewer people will be defined as needing it, while their true human need will rise, not fall. The present dynamics also indicate less and less support, even for those who qualify officially.

Ideology and the Rehabilitation Process

Rehabilitation costs money. This basic fact gets us immediately into the level-funding and cutback phenomena that characterize the fiscal crisis of today. The first ideological aspect of the cutback lies in the presentation of the literature as a *fait accompli*. Given the crisis, say the spokesmen, we must tighten our belt and not ask for the things we need. One typical message was that by Joe Califano (1977) concerning the Rehabilitation Extension Act of 1976, Public Law 94-230:

> The human predicaments you face, the handicaps and human tragedies you work to overcome, have been made even more challenging by other difficulties: constricted federal budgets; a troubled economy; a depressed job market; and the danger that, as we reorganize state and Federal agencies, programs for handicapped citizens may lose their organizational identity. (1977, p. 31)

I'm on your side, says Califano, but the budget *will* be constricted, and you might get reorganized with less power and control over your budget.

Another example of the gap between stated ideals and reality in the area of law-making lies in the earlier legislation—the 1973 Act with its stress on the rehabilitation of the *severely* disabled. Three years later, at the same time as Califano's speech above, LaVor and Duncan (1976) observed:

1. The "severely handicapped" population has not been clearly identified.
2. The law does not appear to be definitive regarding what is required for "severely handicapped" people.
3. REA's targets or quotas are putting great pressure on states to produce new numbers in order to comply with a confusing directive created by the 1973 Act.
4. It is being alleged that little is being done to implement the requirements of the law regarding this population. (p. 56)

In the 1960s (Krause, 1965) I noted that state vocational rehabilitation counselors were pressured to produce "numbers" to maximize the number of "closed, rehabilitated in employment" cases for each state, in order to justify further federal spending on the rehabilitation program. The social crisis of the past decade has, if anything, increased this pressure, producing dynamic forcing agencies to serve the least disabled first, that is, those most quickly and cheaply rehabilitated in large numbers. Then they can turn to the severely disabled with the scraps that are left. Of course, special demonstration projects are developed from place to place and time to time, but that is never the point. The cost accountants' ascendancy in power at HEW (especially under Nixon, Ford, and Carter) bodes ill for any upswing in spending here, as long as the broader context is not acted upon and the ideology of "belt-tightening" is not challenged. By contrast, I don't see the Defense Department tightening its belt, nor too many within the government or the corporate world preaching to it that it should.

In general, what seems to be happening is the growing acceptance by rehabilitation professionals, and the disabled themselves, of a cost-accounting terminology and ideology that they can only suffer by. Accept the premise and the battle is over—you have lost. Note this, from a recent issue of the *Journal of Rehabilitation*, in an article on zero-based budgeting:

> In the increasingly stiff competition for limited dollars for human ser-
> vice programs, those who are able to make the best case for both the
> values of their programs' results and the maximization of available re-
> sources, will be the ones who flourish in a new era of accountability. . . .
> (Journal of Rehabilitation, 1977)

Who made the competition stiff? Who limited the dollars? What about a group of the retarded who have only an *average* value program? Who decides who is accountable to whom, and what are the criteria of success? We are dealing here with a war of world views, which do battle in lieu of the more basic conflict. We now have a government organizing its fiscal and human services policy toward minimum costs for corporate capitalism, through the processes outlined above. In such times, the economist becomes king within such places as HEW's Health Care Financing Administration. Not that costs shouldn't be a concern, but the degree to which they outrun all else is the phenomenon of concern here.

What Can Be Done?

In a recent analysis of the American health care system, I had to search for a title. I came up with *Power and Illness* (Krause, 1977). The facts demanded a political sociological analysis of service systems, including who gets what and how. Rehabilitation is just one aspect of the picture. But the picture will not change, in general or in the field of rehabilitation, unless people act to make it change. Action in dealing with this crisis must be, in my opinion, both short-run and long-run.

In the short run, action should be taken against the present trends in each area of analysis considered above. In the area of *pro-*

duction of disability, those active in work in the rehabilitation field can and should join forces with those fighting for occupational, environmental, and transportation safety. You may often be a key ally to these groups in their fight to prevent many of the problems of disabilities with which you deal. Concerning the *definition of disability,* the workers in rehabilitation must be as political in their counterattack against the attempt to narrow categories and tighten definitions which exclude classes of the disabled as their opponents are political in instituting these processes. Legal action is recommended. Popkin (1977) notes that even in nonadversary proceedings in three programs (Federal Employees Compensation Act, Social Security, and Veterans Disability Program) the programs awarded benefits more frequently when the client had a legal representative present than when he didn't. Challenges, including class-action suits, are a good way of stopping, if not reversing, certain trends. In addition, Varela (1979) recommends working with self-help action organizations run by the disabled themselves, in the disability rights movement. And in the area of funding for state vocational rehabilitation programs, far greater action is needed to demand full funding of the new legislation on the books. At the same time, we must make sure that new profit-making rehabilitation organizations do not do to this program what the Medicaid mills did to that program.

But these are short-range goals. In the long run, we must question whether capitalism may be allowed to exist in its present form in the United States, given the costs we must pay to keep it healthy. It will not do to argue blithely with the far right that capitalism provides the milieu necessary for freedom of speech. Capitalism has flourished in Nazi Germany and in Franco's Spain. Nor will it do to automatically discount a more socialized economy as leading to bureaucracy—for we have that already.

We must ask, then, whether in the last analysis the social crisis is nothing but a particularly intense example of business as usual under advanced capitalism, business that is certainly not impeded when the people are as weak and disorganized as they presently are. Greater political organization, and the drastic diminution of the power of the American corporations, if not their abolition in their present form, is a goal of many new, nondoctrinaire organizations such as the Committee for Economic Democracy. They are working toward a changed economy while preserving our present political freedoms. If my analysis of the context of the disabled is correct, and if this social context affects their chances as I think it does, the radical solution may in fact be the only practical one. After the winter, but only if we act, comes the spring.

References and Bibliography

Anderson, P. *Considerations on western Marxism*. London: New Left Books, 1976.

Ashford, N. A. *Crisis in the workplace: Occupational disease and injury. A report to the Ford Foundation*. Cambridge, Mass.: M.I.T. Press, 1976.

Becker, A., & Schulberg, H. C. Phasing out state hospitals: A psychiatric dilemma. *New England Journal of Medicine*, 1976, *294*, 255–261.

Califano, J. Address to National Rehabilitation Association National Conference. *Journal of Rehabilitation*, 1977, *43*(4), 31.

Eyer, J. Hypertension as a disease of modern society. *International Journal of Health Services*, 1977, *7*(1), 31–38.

Gough, I. *The political economy of the welfare state*. London: Macmillan, 1979.

Grossman, H. I. A new concept of disability. *Journal of Rehabilitation*, 1979, *45*(3), 41–49.

Joint Commission of Mental Illness and Health. *Action for Mental Health*. New York: Wiley, 1962.

Journal of Rehabilitation. *Editorial*. 1977, *43*(1), 19.

Krause, E. A. Structured strain in the role of the rehabilitation counselor. *Journal of Health and Human Behavior*, 1965, *6*(5), 55–62.

Krause, E. A. The political sociology of rehabilitation. In G. S. Albrecht (Ed.), *The sociology and social psychology of rehabilitation*. Pittsburgh: University of Pittsburgh Press, 1976.

Krause, E. A. *Power and illness: The political sociology of health and medical care*. New York: Elsevier, 1977.

LaVor, M., & Duncan, J. G. Vocational rehabilitation: The new law and its implications for the future. *Journal of Rehabilitation*, 1976, *42*(4), 22–23.

Mandel, E. *Late capitalism*. London: New Left Books, 1975.

Marx, K. *The eighteenth brumaire of Louis Bonaparte*. New York: International Publishing Co., 1963.

Marx, K. *Economic and philosophical manuscripts of 1844* (M. M. Iligan trans.). New York: International Publishing Co., 1964.

Marx, K. *Capital: A critique of political economy*. (B. Fowkes trans.). New York: Random House, 1977.

Miliband, R. *The state in capitalist society*. New York: Basic Books, 1969.

National Commission on State Workmen's Compensation Laws. *The report of the National Commission on State Workmen's Compensation Laws*. Washington, D.C.: U.S. Government Printing Office, 1972.

O'Connor, J. *The fiscal crisis of the state*. New York: St. Martin's Press, 1973.

Page, J., & O'Brien, M. *Bitter wages*. New York: Grossman, 1973.

Popkin, D. The effect of representation in nonadversary proceedings: A study of three disability programs. *Cornell Law Review*, 1977, *62*(6), 989–1048.

Poulantzas, N. *Classes in contemporary capitalism*. London: New Left Books, 1975.

Poulantzas, N. *State, power, socialism*. London: New Left Books, 1978.

President's Commission on Mental Health. *Report of the President's Commission on Mental Health*. Washington, D.C.: U.S. Government Printing Office, 1978.

Rosen, B. M., Locke, B. G., Goldberg, I. D., & Babigian, H. M. Identifying emotional disturbance in persons seen in industrial dispensaries. *Mental Hygiene*, 1970, *54*(2), 271–279.

Ross, E. M. Legislative trends in workers' compensation rehabilitation. *Journal of Rehabilitation*, 1979, *45*(3), 20–23.

Ullmann, W. *Individual and society in the Middle Ages*. Baltimore, Md.: Johns Hopkins University Press, 1966.

Varela, R. A. *Role of self-help organization in VR with severely disabled individuals*. Washington, D.C.: American Coalition of Citizens with Disabilities, 1979.

Von Martin, A. *Sociology of the Renaissance*. New York: Harper & Row, 1963.

Wright, E. O. *Class, crisis and the state*. London: New Left Books, 1978.

Appendix

Disabled Peoples' Bill of Rights

Preamble

We believe that all people should enjoy certain rights. Because people with disabilities have consistently been denied the right to fully participate in society as free and equal members, it is important to state and affirm these rights. All people should be able to enjoy these rights, regardless of race, creed, color, sex, religion, or disability.

1. The right to live independent, active, and full lives.
2. The right to the equipment, assistance, and support services necessary for full productivity, provided in a way that promotes dignity and independence.
3. The right to an adequate income or wage, substantial enough to provide food, clothing, shelter, and other necessities of life.
4. The right to accessible, integrated, convenient, and affordable housing.
5. The right to quality physical and mental health care.
6. The right to training and employment without prejudice or stereotype.
7. The right to accessible transportation and freedom of movement.
8. The right to bear or adopt and raise children and have a family.
9. The right to a free and appropriate public education.
10. The right to participate in and benefit from entertainment and recreation.
11. The right of equal access to and use of all businesses, facilities, and activities in the community.
12. The right to communicate freely with all fellow citizens and those who provide services.

Reprinted by permission of the American Coalition of Citizens with Disabilities, 1200 15th Street, N.W., Washington, D.C. 20005.

13. The right to a barrier free environment.
14. The right to legal representation and to full protection of all legal rights.
15. The right to determine one's own future and make one's own life choices.
16. The right of full access to all voting processes.

Author Index

Abram, H., 146
Allen, B., 44
Allport, G., 22, 23
Anderson, E., 225
Anderson, P., 277
Annand, D., 49
Anthony, W., 10
Ashford, N., 280
Austin, G., 4

Babigion, H., 281
Bakal, D., 176
Baker, W., 8
Bandura, A., 174, 180, 183, 186, 188, 189, 190
Barger, S., 141
Barker, R., 182
Baxter, D., 49
Becker, A., 286
Becker, E., 59
Becker, H., 6
Bell, N., 49
Beller, E., 181
Berkman, A., 73
Blackwell, B., 188
Block, J., 10
Bolles, R., 236, 237, 241, 243
Brady, O., 199
Brennan, D., 156
Brodner, R., 225
Brown, C., 146
Bruck, L., 113, 117, 263, 274
Brunner, J., 4

Cahnman, W. J., 43, 44
Caldwell, A., 222, 223
Califano, J., 287
Carley, E., 123
Carling, E., 11
Chase, C., 222, 223

Chilgren, R., 73
Chipouras, D., 71
Chyatte, S., 144, 145, 181
Cogswell, B., 158
Cole, S., 73
Cole, T., 73
Cornelius, D., 71
Couch, G., 49
Cruickshank, W., 173
Crystal, J., 241
Cummings, C., 225
Czaczkes, J., 144, 146

Daniels, S., 71
David, R., 44
Davidson, P., 199
Davidson, S., 199
Davis, D., 156
Davis, F., 9
DeBeneditti, M., 225
Dembo, T., 188
DeNour, A., 144, 146
Devaul, R., 227
Deyoe, F., 157
Dickson, S., 10
Dornbuster, S., 181
Drotar, D., 146
Duncan, J., 287
Durkheim, E., 218

Eisenberg, M., 11, 72
El Ghatit, A., 125, 157
Ellison, R., 53
English, R., 181
Erikson, K., 8
Evanski, P. M., 225
Eyer, J., 281

Faillace, L., 227
Farberow, N., 218, 220
Ferguson, J., 199

Subject Index